READING RULES FOR RUSSIAN

A Systematic Approach to Russian Spelling and Pronunciation
With Notes on Dialectal and Stylistic Variation

Bruce L. Derwing   Tom M. S. Priestly

Department of
Linguistics

Department of
Slavic Languages

The University of Alberta

1980

Slavica Publishers, Inc.

For a list of some other Slavica books, see the last three pages of this book. For a complete catalog with prices and ordering information, write to: Slavica Publishers, Inc.
P.O. Box 14388
Columbus, Ohio 43214

ISBN: 0-89357-066-4

Printed in the United States of America.

CONTENTS

ACKNOWLEDGEMENTS

Responsibility for the contents of this book may be apportioned as follows. The idea was Derwing's in the first place, and he first used it in Russian Phonetics and Phonology classes in 1968-70. Priestly took it over for the same classes, making his own adaptations and adding the sections on stylistic variation, the lexicon of specified words, and the exercises. Chapter V was developed entirely by Priestly.

Our thanks to Dr. Bohdan Medwidsky, who used the text in a Russian Phonetics course and made some valuable comments; and to Mrs. Doreen Hawryshko for her really excellent typing of the manuscript.

Even after ten years' use in the classroom, perfection is not claimed for this text. The authors will be very glad to receive suggestions and criticisms.

iv

ABBREVIATIONS

The page references are to the first occurrence of each abbreviation.

CSR — Contemporary Standard Russian (p. 5).

CW — Component Word (p. 32).

IW — Independent Word (p. 32).

OM — The "Old Moscow" style (p. 9).

PO — Phoneticized Orthography (p. 28).

PP — Phonological Phrase (p. 32).

PT — Phonetic Transcription (p. 130).

RLP — Avanesov (1972) (p. 5).

RLPU — Avanesov & Ožegov (1960) (p. 6).

RO — Regularized Orthography (p. 13).

RR — Rapid Russian (p. 158).

SO — Standard Orthography (p. 11).

VR — Vowel Reduction (p. 102).

YG — The "Younger Generation" style (p. 125).

MAJOR TABLES AND DIAGRAMS

TO THE STUDENT

This is essentially a detailed handbook on Russian pronunciation. More accurately, it is a book which will teach you how to write or "transcribe" Russian words, phrases or sentences in a way that is consistent with the manner in which they are pronounced, at least in the "officially approved" or "standard" dialect variant described in Chapter I. In other words, this book will enable you to supply for any Russian expression a satisfactory *phonetic transcription*. It will not, of course, teach you how to "make the sounds" which are represented in such a transcription; no book alone can do that (although some good phonetics texts, such as Jones & Ward (1969), can be very helpful in this endeavor). Unless you have already received a good deal of training in articulatory phonetics, your oral mastery of most foreign speech sounds will inevitably require considerable and intensive practice with a native model, either live or recorded, in order to "sound right." But this book will enable you to negotiate the first and often most difficult step: to overcome the "classic fallacy" (Lyons, 1968:9) of confusing the *sound* (or phonetics) of the Russian language with its *spelling* (or orthography) and to develop, in as systematic and painless a way as we have found possible, a consistent notation system for the former which can be derived from your already available knowledge of the latter. In other words, the "reading rules" which you will find in this book will tell you how, in principle, any given Russian spelling should be "read aloud." Thus, by using the rules provided, you can begin with the traditional spelling of any Russian expression of interest to you (supplemented, as required, by the various diacritical or "accent" marks provided in any standard dictionary) and readily convert this into a notation which *is* phonetic and which *does* tell you, to a quite satisfactory level of detail, how that word ought to be pronounced.

In the process of learning to use these rules you will also learn a great deal more than this. For one thing, you will learn many general principles of the sound system (or "phonology") of the Russian language, and the most important of these will become virtually automatic for you, in time, through practice. It may seem tedious indeed at first to work through a long series of rules (many of which simply

1

fail to apply in the case at hand) and associated "rewrites" or "levels of representation" in order to derive a phonetic transcription for some particular simple Russian word or phrase. But it is the general principles which are reflected in these rules which are really the important things in the long run, for these can be useful in making predictions about the pronunciation of *any* Russian expression, not just the particular one which you happen to be working with at the moment. You will eventually discover a practical utility, as well, for each major level of representation that you are required to work through as you use the rules (see pp. 7 - 8 below). And you will also be exposed to many common notational devices which are utilized in formal linguistic analysis, an added benefit should you ever decide to go beyond this course into general linguistics *per se*. There are many other advantages which will come your way, too, if you are serious enough in your efforts to follow the instructions provided and to be diligent in doing the practice exercises. These advantages, however, and to a great extent even the ones already described, can only be understood and appreciated once you have acquired the basic background which this book can provide for you. On the basis of many years experience with large numbers of students in the past, we can say with confidence that most of you will find your initially painstaking investment in time and effort to have been well worth the cost.

Bruce L. Derwing
Tom M.S. Priestly

CHAPTER ONE

INTRODUCTION

1.0 BACKGROUND FOR THE BOOK

This book arose out of the practical need to
find an effective and efficient way to teach students
to transcribe Russian phonetically and, conversely,
to enable them to identify Russian utterances already
written in a phonetic transcription. Both of these
skills are central concerns for any course in Russian
phonetics *per se*, while a phonetic transcription can
also serve as a very useful visual aid in any purely
practical program in Russian pronunciation, as well.
In our case, however, the problem arose in conjunction with a general introductory course in The
Structure of Russian taught in the Department of
Slavic Languages at The University of Alberta from
1968-70. It was difficult enough to attempt to teach
the basic concepts of Russian phonemics and morpho-
nology to students with little or no prior linguistic
training, but the added burden of requiring these
students to manipulate unfamiliar phonetic data whose
source and purpose were obscure proved overwhelming
in many cases. Obviously, Russian phonetics was
basic to the entire enterprise and some means had to
be devised to teach this material thoroughly, yet
also quickly enough that sufficient time was left
over to cover the other, more central topics.

It was obvious at the outset that the required
level of efficiency could not possibly be achieved by
means of the traditional "sunburn" approach to the
problem: to expose the student to a large, but
largely random, corpus of forms in phonetic transcription in the vague hope that he would eventually
"get the idea." What the student usually got instead
was an extremely spotty and piecemeal command of the
material, at best, usually combined with a large dose
of uncertainty, if not total confusion. The phonetics of any language is simply far too complex a
matter to be entrusted to so haphazard and helter-
skelter a methodology. Some much more systematic
approach was urgently required, and the approach
which we eventually adopted is the one reflected in
this book, which begins with the standard orthography
or spelling for each word in the language.

3

1.1. ON PREDICTING THE PRONUNCIATION FROM THE SPELLING

Since the acquisition of speech is ontogenetically prior to the acquisition of skill at reading - and because all known human languages are or were spoken, but only a relatively few ever represented in written form - there was a time when many linguists and linguistically sophisticated language teachers dismissed spelling as a topic of only marginal concern or interest - or even castigated orthographies as handicaps which the serious student of language had to "unlearn," if possible.

We regard this attitude as both extreme and counterproductive (cf. Swan 1975). Orthographies are here to stay and, whether good, bad or indifferent, will for many inexorable practical reasons probably continue to change only very slowly and in relatively minor ways, being much less subservient to the whims of ideological preference among linguists than to the more relevant pragmatic forces of everyday social life. Rather than bemoan the occasional complication which this situation brings to the linguist or language teacher, it seems to us much more expedient to reap whatever benefits we can from it. For the hard fact is that every literate person (by definition) has learned the standard orthography of some language, and, as a practical matter, students of all of the most commonly studied foreign languages, Russian included, do most of their visual learning in standard orthographic terms, as well. Furthermore, virtually all standard dictionaries, reference grammars and other pedagogical aids are also presented in this form. In short, with few exceptions, the standard orthographic representation of a language is by a wide margin the most familiar and readily accessible form which the typical student is likely to encounter and to learn, and it is only sensible to take maximum advantage of this fact.

One potential disadvantage of a spelling-oriented approach to proper pronunciation, of course, is that it must be, at least to some extent, remedial in character: some kind of pronunciation will be acquired willy-nilly by the student even while he is learning enough of the standard spelling to enable him to make use of a book such as this one. Furthermore, since the normal effect of the spelling on pronunciation can be properly described as detrimental, at least to some degree, the student is likely to possess a number of bad pronunciation habits by the time he even reaches this volume for the first

time. But one very important pedagogical advantage
more than compensates for this, in our view: the
student is at least in a position to proceed from
what is relatively simple and already known to him
(the spelling) to what is more complex and largely
unknown - or misknown (the pronunciation). In fact,
even the *non*-student of Russian can make use of our
rules in order to gain access to phonetic forms in
the language (for purposes of linguistic analysis,
for instance), merely by transforming the entries
which are readily available in any standard dictionary.   For what we call "reading rules" are simply
rules of pronunciation[1] which operate on the standard
orthography as input,[2] i.e., rules which serve to
derive from the traditional spelling of any Russian
form a transcription which is indicative of how that
form is properly pronounced. The particular phonetic
prescriptions adhered to in this volume are essentially those sanctioned by Avanesov (1972; henceforth
referred to as RLP) and which collectively describe
that somewhat artificial dialectal and stylistic
variant commonly referred to as "Contemporary Standard Russian," or *CSR*.

1.2. SOME UNIQUE FACTORS OF THE BOOK

This kind of utilitarian approach to the problem
is not, of course, by any means original. Most previous attempts to teach foreign language material, in
fact, have been largely oriented towards the standard
orthography (though many have failed to recognize the
significance of the sound-spelling distinction and
have thus often proved misleading, if not downright
wrong, in many of the things they say). Nor is the
idea of writing spelling-based "rules of pronunciation" particularly novel, either (cf. Wijk 1966, for
example). What does distinguish this book from previous attempts along these same general lines are the
following three considerations, which have captured
the bulk of our attention in the production of this
volume:
(1) First, we have endeavored to formulate a
reasonably concise and non-redundant set of general,
ordered rules which are sufficient to account for all
spelling-sound correspondences in the Russian language, up to some practical limit of phonetic detail.
This kind of *systematicity* and *homogeneity* of approach has been lacking in past works of this kind
which have come to our attention. The initial inspi-
ration for this book, for example, was a short,
unpublished summary of "Russian Reading Rules" which

was circulated by the Department of Slavic Languages
and Literatures at Indiana University some years ago
and which exemplifies the usual approach to this type
of problem. This paper was organized on a letter-by-
letter basis and attempted to illustrate the various
ways in which each letter of the Russian alphabet
could be pronounced.[3] Though many examples were also
included, it was not at all clear from the exposition
what the specific conditions were which determined
which of the various alternatives was to be selected
in any given case. Moreover, in order to interpret
any particular new work or expression by means of
these "rules," the student was forced to jump back
and forth from one section of the paper to another.
This paper also failed to note a large number of patterned or otherwise important exceptions to the
broad, general principles which were illustrated,
thereby presenting a greatly oversimplified picture
of the situation as it actually obtains and severely
limiting the general usefulness of the rules.

Much the same letter-by-letter approach is typical of Soviet pedagogical practice, as well, as
illustrated, for example, in Avanesov & Ožegov (1960;
henceforward, *RLPU* and in Avanesov (*RLP*). These
studies are generally very good as regards detail,
but, once again, extremely difficult to use without
committing the entire exposition to memory. For just
as with the Indiana outline, the notion of list pre-
dominates: long lists of letter-sound correspondences are given, supplemented by even longer lists
of patterned or quite idiosyncratic exceptions, with
only a relatively few "helpful hints" provided which
are of more general applicability. Presented in this
form, the amount of material to be mastered by the
student in order to gain even a semblance of secure
control of the complexities of Russian phonetics is
simply too immense and unwieldly to handle. Furthermore, considerable redundancy is also introduced into
these studies, making the problems sometimes seem
much more complicated than they really are. We have
attempted to reduce this great mass of information to
manageable proportions and, in doing so, have even
found room to incorporate additional findings from a
number of smaller research papers widely scattered
throughout the literature.

(2) Second, we have also tried to achieve a
level of *comprehensiveness of coverage* and *attention
to detail* which is lacking in previous works on the
subject. Our goal is no less than to provide the
student with sufficient information in one place and

in convenient enough form to allow him to derive or
predict the pronunciation of *any* word or utterance
that he is likely to come in contact with in his
study of the modern Russian language, and an extensive, coded LEXICON OF SPECIFIED WORDS is included
which lists all of those items which have come to our
attention which are in any way exceptional to any of
our rules or which otherwise require special treatment. (For detailed instructions on how to use the
lexicon, see p. 180 below). We have even included detailed information regarding some of the
most important and widespread types of stylistic and
dialectal variation. After ten years of classroom
use and considerable revision and expansion, we now
believe that our material is sufficiently complete
and accurate to be of general use.

    (3) Finally, because of the somewhat unique
framework in which our material is presented, we have
been able to incorporate a good deal of *supplementary
information* about Russian grammar which goes well
beyond the details of Russian phonetics *per se* and
which lays the groundwork for a deeper study of the
linguistic structure of the language. In the first
place, the reading rules themselves provide a great
deal of essential information related to the regular
phonological processes of the language, both phono-
tactic and morphonemic. By the time a student has
derived merely a handful of phonetic transcriptions
using these rules, he will inadvertently have become
familiar with a number of the more general of these
processes, such as voicing assimilation (rule-block
3E), palatalization assimilation (rule-block 3P) and
vowel reduction (rule-blocks 3T-3X). We have found
this background to be extremely beneficial for students who intend to continue their study of the
language or to move into more general courses in formal descriptive linguistics.

    In addition, the reading rules are ordered into
blocks and chapters on a principled basis, which is
also designed to have certain important pedagogical
advantages.[4] The rules which appear in Chapter II
of this book, for example, are especially designed to
yield as output a unique kind of intermediate level
of representation - the "regularized orthography" -
which comes very close to satisfying the fundamental
orthographic or lexical principle that each meaningful unit (morpheme) in a language should have a
single, invariant written representation. Instructors will find that the basic principles of Russian
morphology will be much clearer and easier to teach

at this level of representation than at any other, and students familiar only with the standard orthography will likely find that this "regularized" spelling reveals to them a good deal more pattern and structure in Russian word-formation and inflection than they ever realized was there before (cf. Swan 1975).

By the same token, the ordered blocks of rules which make up Chapter III yield as output a special "phoneticized orthography," which is a level of representation in standard Cyrillic characters which comes closest to indicating how Russian forms are actually pronounced. This level is thus the optimum one for the phonetic interpretation of the orthography of *CSR*. The conversion to a more detailed phonetic transcription (in familiar Latin characters) is then achieved by the set of rules which appear in Chapter IV. (Alternative phonetic symbols, including those of the International Phonetic Alphabet and common Cyrillic systems, are also provided in a conversion table which appears on pp. 148-52.) For students who are unfamiliar with phonetic notation and its interpretation, the examples provided may serve as the basis for a training program in Russian pronunciation, with the help of a trained instructor or native model. For this purpose, however, a supplementary phonetics text is strongly recommended, such as Jones & Ward (1969), which will provide many other examples for each phonetic symbol, as well as complete articulatory descriptions for each speech sound symbolized.

Chapter V, finally, presents a partial set of rules for "Rapid Russian," that is, for the more "casual" or "allegro" style of speech which is rather poorly described and understood, yet is actually much more typical of ordinary Russian conversational usage than is *CSR*. Since the rules of this chapter are far from complete, however, and present only a few helpful hints as to the main characteristics of this rapid style of speech, many instructors and students may prefer to omit it altogether.[5]

One final class of supplementary information provided in this book appears in the sections headed STYLISTIC VARIATIONS. These sections provide a great deal of general information on both stylistic and dialectal variation in Russian which has not been previously available in any one source, and virtually unavailable in English at all. Students who wish to learn the system of pronunciation of *CSR* as prescribed by Avanesov may prefer to ignore this material, but those interested in how the actual pronunciation of Russian by Russians departs from Avanesov's norms on either a social or geographical basis will find here convenient summaries of the most important facts, as well as references to all of the original sources. It must be emphasized, however, that although we have made every effort to achieve a comprehensive and detailed thoroughness insofar as Avanesov's standard for *CSR* is concerned, the remarks on variations from that standard are intended only as introductory summaries and have pretensions neither to complete accuracy nor exhaustiveness.

We have based our description of these variations from *CSR* on the premise that such variations occur along four axes: in TIME (historically), in SPACE (dialectally), in REGISTER[6] (socially), and in TEMPO (i.e., from allegro to lento speech).[7] *CSR*, following Avanesov's prescriptions, may be described with reference to each of these axes in turn as follows: it is the speech of Russians *born since 1925* who are *Muscovites* using the *normal literary style* (*RLP* 16-23) at a *moderate tempo*. For simplicity, when referring to another variety, we move from *CSR*, as thus defined along one axis; so, for example, the "Old Moscow norm" (*OM*) refers only to a change along the historical axis from the coordinate just described. Avanesov's *CSR* has the merits of being both an accepted norm and an occurrent one, and is therefore strongly recommended.

The reader will notice, especially in Chapter III, that although in many cases the characteristic differences between different styles of pronunciation rest on rather fine phonetic distinctions, there are a number of these differences which should be recognized by the foreign learner of Russian. These features place the speaker who pronounces them firmly in a certain stylistic (social?) group. If, therefore, students of Russian adopt features which are characteristic of mixed styles, their pronunciation will sound awkward or incongruous; they will negate some of the advances they have made in learning how to pronounce the language, and aggravate the effects of whatever foreign "accent" they still have.[8]

Students are therefore advised to keep one consistent aim in mind. They may, for example, aim at the pronunciation of *CSR* which Avanesov prescribes and on which the rules of this book are based. Alternatively, they may choose a more "up-to-date" style of pronunciation. In any case, features which are clearly "bookish" or which obviously belong to the *OM* style should be avoided.

Since much of the supplementary material

provided in this volume will be of interest chiefly
to specialists in Slavic linguistics and largely
superfluous to the average student who is using the
book for the main purpose described, we have consequently resorted to a double system of footnoting.
Tangential remarks which we feel are of some likely
interest to the general reader are denoted by aster-
isks and appear at the bottom of the page in question,
whereas the numbered footnotes (such as the ones already indicated for this chapter) contain material of
less general interest and so are arranged on a chap-
ter-by-chapter basis at the end of the book.[9]

1.3. GENERAL INSTRUCTIONS FOR USING THE BOOK

It has been our experience that most students
quickly find it an extremely routine and mechanical
process to make use of the reading rules provided in
this book. All the student is required to do is to
write down the particular word, phrase or sentence of
interest in its standard orthographic form (verifying
the spelling and accentuation with the help of a
standard dictionary, if necessary) and then to rewrite it successively according to the instructions
provided for each set or "block" of rules, skipping
those rules which happen not to apply to the particular string in question. The final output will
always be (assuming that our rules are properly formulated and all exceptions accounted for) an acceptable phonetic transcription for the string. Our
experience has indicated that some initial period of
instruction and practice is necessary before the
average student can use the rules effectively, and
for this purpose a list of EXERCISES is provided on
pp. 199-202. It has not proved necessary that students commit any of the rules to memory, however;
once the initial instruction period is completed, in
fact, the concise summary of the rules provided
at the end should prove adequate for most tasks. In
actual practice, though, it frequently happens that
students do learn most of the more important rules
which are provided, simply out of repeated practice
and familiarity with them.

CHAPTER TWO

FROM STANDARD ORTHOGRAPHY
TO REGULARIZED ORTHOGRAPHY

2.0. THE STANDARD ORTHOGRAPHY OF RUSSIAN

The standard orthography (*SO*) of Russian refers
to the way in which the language is ordinarily represented in written form, as in books, magazines,
newspapers, etc. In other words, it is the familiar
and traditional spelling system of the language, incorporating all of the major spelling reforms of
1917-18. The standard spelling of most Russian words
in general use can be found in any good Russian-
English dictionary (such as Smirnitsky, 1959, or
Wheeler, 1972) or dictionary of the Russian language
(such as Ožegov, 1963, or Ušakov, 1934-40). A useful
supplementary work is a good orthographic and pronouncing dictionary such as Avanesov and Ožegov
(1960), which not only provides the standard spelling
of an extremely wide range of words, but also notes
irregularities in the spelling of inflected forms of
many words and provides additional hints as to idiosyncracies of pronunciation.

There is one important difference which should
be noted between the spellings provided in all of
these standard reference works and the spelling found
in ordinary reading material intended for native
speakers of the language. This is that the reference
works ordinarily indicate the position of maximum
stress (and, in compound words, secondary stress, as
well), and also make the distinction between e and ё
(by means of the dieresis), contrary to normal practice elsewhere. This is, of course, a great convenience for reference purposes (to native and non-
native speakers of the language alike), but a luxury
hardly required in ordinary reading material (cf. the
parallel situation in English, where stress is always
indicated in dictionaries, but almost never anywhere
else). Since information about Russian stress and
the dieresis is readily accessible to all students in
the standard reference works, we shall construe the
term "standard orthography" here to refer to the
standard spelling with both stress and the dieresis
supplied. (Remember that ё will always receive
either primary or secondary stress.)[1]

It is also important to make a clear distinction

11

at the outset between the standard orthography or
spelling of a word (i.e., the *letters* which are traditionally used to represent a given Russian word in
writing) and a phonetic transcription (i.e., symbolic
representation of the sequence of speech sounds--or
phones--which are articulated by a speaker when a
word or utterance is actually pronounced, whether
spontaneously or in reading aloud). It should first
of all be recognized that (even in the case of "reading aloud") the letters of the standard orthography
are not actually "pronounced" (at least not by most
speakers). There can be no doubt that any alphabetic
writing system (such as the Cyrillic, which is used
for Russian) exerts a considerable influence on the
actual pronunciation of words over a period of time;
nonetheless, the typical acquisition sequence remains
one in which the native speaker learns to pronounce
most of the words of his language (and especially the
most common words) some time before he ever learns
how they are spelled. Furthermore, variations in
pronunciation, whether stylistic or dialectal, are,
for obvious reasons, much more readily tolerated than
are variations in spelling. Consequently, we can
expect that the writing system of any language will
only provide a rather crude and imperfect indication
of how words are actually pronounced, even under the
best of circumstances. In other words, no spelling
system is absolutely "phonetic"--or is intended to be.

Nevertheless, in all languages which employ alphabetic writing, a fairly close relationship ordinarily exists between the spelling of a word and its
pronunciation, although this relationship is often
rather abstract and indirect, and usually manifests a
good deal of inconsistency and irregularity, as well.
Still, it is generally possible to determine the pronunciation of a word whose (alphabetic) written form
is known (though often not the reverse--and even in
the former case one must often resort to long lists
of "irregularities" in order to make the prediction
complete). If this were not so, a set of "reading
rules" of the kind developed and presented here
would, of course, be impossible. Our purpose here,
therefore, is to take advantage of those systematic
correspondences which do exist between the spelling
and pronunciation of Russian words in order to provide a convenient and practical approach to the study
of Russian phonetics and morphophonemics.

To distinguish the standard orthography (*SO*)
from all other levels of representation employed in
this book, the *SO* will be supplied throughout in

BOLDFACE TYPE. The regularized orthography (*RO*) is discussed in 2.4. below.

2.1. A PRELIMINARY CLASSIFICATION OF THE LETTERS OF THE RUSSIAN ALPHABET

In this section the letters of the Russian alphabet are grouped into classes to which repeated reference will be made on the pages to follow. For convenience, the terms used to name these classes are all borrowed from articulatory or acoustic phonetics, but the reader should not be confused on this point: we are talking here about groups of alphabetic *letters*, not sounds, and the class labels used relate to letter-sound correspondences which hold only approximately. The reader should familiarize himself with all of the cover symbols introduced below and with the classes of letters which they represent, as future reference to these classes will generally be given only in terms of these labels.

2.1.1. THE CONSONANT LETTERS (c)

There are 21 consonant letters in the Russian alphabet. The term "consonant letters" is used as an appropriate mnemonic here on the ground that each of these letters is ordinarily used to represent a class of consonant sounds.[2]

2.1.1.1. THE PAIRED CONSONANT LETTERS (c$_p$)

Of the 21 consonant letters, 15 are "paired" in the sense that they may represent classes of sounds which are pronounced either "hard" (i.e., non-palatalized) or "soft" (palatalized). For example, the first sound in the word ПОЛЕ 'field' is hard, while the first sound of the word ПЁК '(he) baked' is soft, but the spelling of both of these words begins with the same letter. These paired consonant letters may be conveniently subcategorized into those which ordinarily represent obstruent sounds (stops or fricatives) or resonant sounds (nasals or liquids). These subcategorizations are as follows:

(a) Obstruent Letters
    (1) Stop Letters: п, б, т, д, к, г
    (2) Fricative Letters: ф, в, с, з, х

(b) Resonant Letters
    (1) Nasal Letters: м, н
    (2) Liquid Letters: л, р

Any future reference to the cover symbol C_p therefore, is to be construed as a reference to any or all of the 15 characters listed above, while a reference to the "stop letters" (or, for convenience, simply "the stops") will refer only to the particular subclass in question, etc.

2.1.1.2. THE UNPAIRED "HARD" CONSONANT LETTERS (H)

Three consonant letters are ordinarily not used to represent "soft" consonant sounds at all, and so can be thought of as representing classes of sounds which are inherently "hard".[3] These letters are ш, ж and ц.

2.1.1.3. THE UNPAIRED "SOFT" CONSONANT LETTERS (S)

Three other consonant letters are ordinarily not used to represent "hard" consonant sounds at all, and they can conveniently be thought of as representing classes of sounds which are inherently "soft".[3] These letters are ч, щ and й.

2.1.2. THE VOWEL LETTERS

There are 10 vowel letters in the Russian alphabet (if е and ё are treated as distinct), and each of these letters is used to represent a class of vowel sounds. Seven of these letters are "basic" in the sense that they are required to indicate various phonological distinctions in Russian. The remaining three vowel letters are, however, redundant, since the phonological information which they convey can be equally well indicated by means of other orthographic devices already available for the language. The main purpose of the rules which appear in this chapter, therefore, is to produce a revised or "regularized" orthography for Russian from which such fully redundant letters are eliminated (cf. 2.2. below for further discussion).

2.1.2.1. THE "BASIC" VOWEL LETTERS (V)

The seven vowel letters which are to be retained in the regularized orthography are the letters а, у, о, ы, э, и and е. Since these are the only vowel letters to which reference need be made in subsequent chapters of this book, the cover symbol "V" will be used to refer to this set of symbols only.

2.1.2.2. THE "SOFT" OR "FRONT" VOWEL LETTERS

Because of their unique status in relation to
the phenomenon of palatalization in Russian, two of
the basic vowel letters can be usefully regarded as a
separate subclass. These are the letters и and е.
Because this subclass contains only these two symbols,
it does not seem worthwhile to devise a new cover
symbol for it. As in the case of the "stop" and
other subclasses of the Paired Consonant letters discussed in 2.1.1.1. above, however, it will prove convenient to have a cover term available for ease of
reference to this important pair of vowel letters.
The label "soft" is suggested by the role these vowel
letters play in subsequent palatalization rules,
while the label "front" is appropriate from the stand-
point of the articulatory class of vowel sounds which
these letters are ordinarily used to represent,
particularly in stressed syllables. Either of these
cover terms may therefore be used in later chapters
to refer to these two vowel letters.

2.1.2.3. THE REDUNDANT VOWEL LETTERS

The three vowel letters which are fully redundant in the standard orthography of Russian are the
letters я, ё and ю. Since these letters will be
eliminated in the development of the regularized orthography, no cover symbol is required for them, and
no reference will be made to these vowel letters in
any subsequent chapter.

2.1.3. THE HARD AND SOFT SIGNS

Two letters of the Russian alphabet do not represent separate sound segments at all, but rather
indicate something about the nature of the consonant
sound, as represented by the consonant letter which
immediately precedes them. These letters are the
"soft sign" ь (so called because one of its functions
is to indicate softness or palatalization in a preceding consonant) and the "hard sign" or "separation
sign" ъ (whose chief function in the modern Russian
alphabet is to indicate the presence of an intrusive
palatal fricative or glide element).

2.2. SOME INCONSISTENCIES IN THE STANDARD ORTHO-
GRAPHY OF RUSSIAN

The three redundant vowel letters are all superfluous artifacts of an old Slavic spelling system

from which the modern Russian orthography has evolved.
As the situation exists today, the Russian spelling
system employs ten distinct vowel letters to represent no more than five or six contrastive vowel
sound-types (or phonemes).[4]   The redundant vowel letters are employed to supply information about pre-
vocalic consonants, but this information can be
indicated more systematically by means of other orthographic devices which are also available in the
standard orthography.

Consider, for example, the words TÓK 'current'
and TËK 'flowed'. If one pronounces these two words
aloud, one finds that the vowel sound of the first is
not appreciably different from the vowel sound of the
second; nonetheless, different vowel letters are used
in the traditional spellings of these two words. The
important difference in *sound* between these two words
is a difference in the articulation of the initial
consonants: the initial consonant of TÓK is pronounced "hard", whereas the initial consonant of TËK
is pronounced "soft"; otherwise, the sounds of the
two words are nearly identical. In most situations
like this, therefore, the softness of a pre-vocalic
consonant is indicated in the standard orthography by
means of a different symbol for the *vowel* sound which
immediately follows it.

At the end of a Russian word, however, as in the
word БРÁТЬ 'to take', the softness of a consonant is
indicated by means of the "soft sign", ь (cf. the
word БРÁТ 'brother' in which the final consonant is
hard). This means that the spelling system of modern
Russian is not completely consistent in the way softness (palatalization) in consonants is indicated:
sometimes the letter ь is used for this purpose,
while at other times a different vowel letter is used
instead. A more consistent and less redundant orthographic system would emerge, therefore, if a transcription could be devised in which palatalization
were always represented by the single symbol ь and
each vowel phoneme by the same vowel letter. Such a
transcription would represent the words TÓK and TËK
as тóк and тьóк, respectively. The interpretation
rules for the redundant vowel letters which are presented in 2.3. below are designed in part to accom-
plish this.

There is one further inconsistency in the standard orthography of Russian which can be conveniently
eliminated at this early stage. Notice that the
Russian jod (phonetically, a palatal fricative or
glide element, [j]) is sometimes represented by the
letter й in the standard spelling, but not always.

At the beginning of a word, for example, the redundant vowel letters once again enter the picture in representing this segment, as well. Clearly, the word Я 'I' could just as well be spelled йа; and ЁЛКА 'fir tree' could be йблка. The fact that these words are not spelled in this way is simply a measure of the outdatedness of the modern Russian orthography. The same is true when the [j]-sound appears between two vowels (as in МОЯ́ 'my (fem.)', which would be more sensibly spelled мойá), or after another consonant sound (as indicated by a hard or soft sign; thus ПЬЯ́Н 'drunk' might be spelled пьйáн, СЬЁЛ 'ate up' as сйéл, and ОБЬЁМ 'volume' as обйóм).[5] All of these inconsistencies can be simply and systematically removed from the standard orthography of Russian by the application of the two sets of interpretation rules which follow, one for the redundant vowel letters and one for the hard and soft signs. (For clarity of exposition, these first few rules will be broken down into their constituent parts so that attention can be directed to the notational conventions in terms of which these and subsequent rules will be expressed.)

2.3. INTERPRETATION RULES FOR THE REDUNDANT VOWEL LETTERS

Rule for я:

$$
я \rightarrow \begin{cases} ьа \ / \ C \ \text{———} \\ йа \ / \ elsewhere \end{cases}
$$

The symbol → (arrow) in this rule may be read "is rewritten as", and the oblique stroke / as "in the environment". The ——— indicates the position or environment in which the symbol or string to the left of the arrow must appear in the input if the rule in question is to apply to it, i.e., in order for the rewrite instruction to be permissible. The braces to the right of the arrow indicate an *ordered choice*: first rewrite a я which occurs in the environment indicated on the first line within the braces (i.e., a я which occurs immediately after a consonant letter); then rewrite any remaining я's in the input string according to the instruction on the second line. In prose form, therefore, this rule says the following: "The letter я is rewritten as the sequence ьа if it follows immediately after a consonant letter (i.e., *within the same orthographic word*); in all other positions ("elsewhere") я is rewritten as the sequence йа (i.e., after a *vowel letter*, after a *hard or soft sign*, or after a *space*, which is to say at the beginning of an orthographic word)." Notice that one important effect of this rule is to eliminate the letter я from all orthographic representations.

Examples: ДЫ́НЯ   СА́ДЬ   *BUT*   МОЯ́   ПЬЯН   Я́СНО
     →ды́н̬ьа   сьа́дь   мойа́   пьйа́н   йа́сно

Rule for ё:

$$ ё \rightarrow \begin{cases} ьó \ / \ с \text{———} \\ йó \ / \ \text{elsewhere} \end{cases} $$

This rule states that the soft vowel letter ё is rewritten as the sequence ьо whenever it appears immediately after a consonant letter, and as the sequence йо everywhere else.

Examples: НЁС   *BUT*   ЁЛКА   РУЖЬЁ
     →ньо́с   йо́лка   ружьйо́

Rule for ю:

$$ ю \rightarrow \begin{cases} ьу \ / \ с \text{———} \\ йу \ / \ \text{elsewhere} \end{cases} $$

This rule states that the letter ю is rewritten as ьу directly after a consonant letter, but as йу elsewhere.

Examples: СЮДА́   *BUT*   ЗНА́Ю   ПЬЮ
     →сьуда́   зна́йу   пьйу́

The reader may have noticed that the three rules just provided, share many similarities; (1) they all apply to redundant vowel letters; (2) they all rewrite these letters as the sequence ь plus the corresponding "hard" vowel letter in the environment immediately after a consonant letter; and (3) they all rewrite these letters as the sequence й plus the corresponding "hard" vowel letter in all other environments. On the basis of these similarities, we may now introduce the convention of the square brackets to conflate these three sub-rules into a single rule-schema for all three of the redundant vowel letters:

$$\text{(2A1)} \quad \begin{bmatrix} я \\ е \\ ю \end{bmatrix} \rightarrow \left\{ \begin{matrix} \begin{bmatrix} ьа \\ ьо \\ ьу \end{bmatrix} & / \ \text{C} \ \underline{\quad} \\[2mm] \begin{bmatrix} йа \\ йо \\ йу \end{bmatrix} & / \ \text{elsewhere} \end{matrix} \right\}$$

The reader will observe that this rule-schema is equivalent to the three individual rules introduced earlier, provided the general interpretation principle for the square brackets is followed: symbols which appear within square brackets on the left-hand side of a rule are to be paired off on a line-by-line basis with symbols within square brackets on the right-hand side. The braces indicate an ordered choice, just as in the previous examples. In this conflated form, our rule is now concise enough to have a permanent number assigned to it for reference purposes; this number is "2A1", as indicated above, and is to be interpreted as follows, reading from left to right: Chapter 2, Rule-block A, Rule 1. Using this system, the student can quickly locate any rule in the book.

The rule for the two "front" or "soft" vowel letters can most conveniently be written as a very general rule plus a restriction indicating a specific environment where the general rule does *not* apply:

$$\text{(2A2)} \quad \begin{aligned} \begin{bmatrix} е \\ и \end{bmatrix} &\rightarrow \begin{bmatrix} йе \\ йе \end{bmatrix} \\[2mm] &\text{restriction} \\[2mm] \begin{bmatrix} е \\ и \end{bmatrix} &\nrightarrow \begin{bmatrix} йе \\ йи \end{bmatrix} \quad / \ \text{C} \ \underline{\quad} \end{aligned}$$

The symbol $\nrightarrow$ used in the restriction portion of Rule 2A2 is to be read IS *NOT* REWRITTEN AS. Thus Rule 2A2 says that the two vowel letters е and и are rewritten with a preceding й in all environments *unless* they are immediately preceded by a consonant letter in the input string. In this latter situation the vowel letters in question are left unchanged.*

Examples: ÉСТЬ   СЪÉЛ   *BUT*   ДО́МЕ̲   ДÉНЬ

→йе́сть съйе́л   n/c** n/c

МОЙ   ИДУ́   ЧЬЙ   *BUT*   КНИ́ГИ̲

→мойй̲   йиду́   чьйй̲   n/c

2.3. INTERPRETATION RULES FOR THE HARD AND SOFT SIGNS

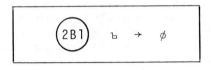

Rule 2B1 introduces the new symbol ∅ (null). The appearance of this symbol to the right of an arrow is used to indicate that the symbol or string to the left of the arrow is to be deleted. Since no environmental restriction is associated with Rule 2B1, this rule states that the hard sign may now be deleted wherever it occurs. Rule 2B2 below, then, states that the soft sign is also dropped, but only in the particular environment indicated, i.e., only after an H consonant *or* after an S consonant (cf. 2.1.1.2. and 2.1.1.3. above).

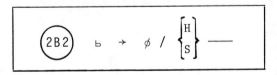

*In the standard dialect the sequence йи is misleading in word-initial position, as well. Rather than further complicate Rule 2A2 to reflect this fact, we deal with this problem instead in the following chapter (see Rule 3I on p. 58).

**The symbol n/c means NO CHANGE (see pp. 24-27 below for a general discussion of the conventions for rules).

Examples: СЪЕ́Л   ИЗЪЯ́ТЬ   ОБЪЁМ   ОТЪЕ́ХАТЬ

  съйе́л   изъйа́ть   объйо́м   отъйе́хать

→сйе́л   изйа́ть   обйо́м   отйе́хать

  МЫ́ШЬ   РУЖЬЁ   ЧЬЙ   ВЕ́ЩЬ   *BUT*   БРА́ТЬ

  мы́шь   ружьйо́   чьйй   вье́щь   бра́ть

→мы́ш   ружйо́   чйй   вье́щ   n/c

It should be emphasized at this point that all rule-blocks in this book are *ordered* with respect to one another. In the examples above, therefore, all the rules in Rule-block 2A (viz., Rules 2A1 and 2A2) must be applied before any of the rules in Rule-block 2B (Rules 2B1 or 2B2). Thus while the input to the Interpretation Rules for the Redundant Vowel Letters is the *SO*, the input to the Interpretation Rules for the Hard and Soft Signs is the *output* of the Interpretation Rules for the Redundant Vowel Letters. This ordering convention must be maintained throughout the book if the proper results are to ensue. Unless otherwise indicated, no ordering is required of rules *within* a given rule-block, but the reader may, if he chooses, treat *all* rules as if they were ordered and no harm will come of it. (Thus Rules 2A1 and 2A2 may be applied sequentially or, alternatively, simultaneously to the same input string, since both procedures will yield the same results; but Rule 2A1 must be applied *before* Rule 2B1; etc.).

2.4. CHARACTERISTICS OF THE REGULARIZED ORTHOGRAPHY

The result of the ordered application of the rules in blocks 2A and 2B above to the standard orthography of Russian is a *regularized orthography* (*RO*) which has a number of advantageous characteristics. The three most important of these are as follows:

(1) Contrastive softening (palatalization) of consonants is consistently represented in the *RO* by means of the soft sign ь, regardless of environment. In the examples below, the underlined letters all represent contrastively palatalized consonant sounds, but only in the column marked *RO* are these letters consistently followed by a soft sign to indicate this:

SO	RO
БРА́ТЬ	бра́ть
СА́ДЬ	сьа́дь
ДЫ́НЯ	ды́ньа
ПЁК	пьо́к
СЮДА́	сьуда́

(2)   The palatal fricative or glide segment [j] is consistently represented in the *RO* by means of the letter й, but not in the *SO*, as shown below:

SO	RO	
БО́Й	бо́й	(pronounced [bo_j_])
ПЬЯ́Н	пьйа́н	(= [p'_jan_])
ЁЛКА	йо́лка	(= [_j_ólkə])
ЗНА́Ю	зна́йу	(= [zná_j_u])
Е́СТЬ	йе́сть	(= [_j_ést'])
ЧЬЙ	чйй	(= [č_j_i])

(3)   Finally, as a direct consequence of (1) and (2) above, we find the morphemic structure of Russian words is much more clearly and consistently indicated in the *RO* than in the *SO* (or at any other level of representation to be developed in this book). By the "morphemic structure" of words we refer to the sequence of minimal *meaningful* or *grammatically functional* sequences of symbols--the so-called "morphemes" of the language--out of which these words may be constructed. For example, the pronoun О́Н is spelled with two letters (and is articulated as a sequence of two distinct sounds) which make up a single meaningful unit, namely, the morpheme meaning something like 'pronoun, third person, nominative case' (and also 'masculine' and 'singular' by default, hence 'he'). The word ОНА́, however, contains two meaningful sequences: the morpheme он, once again, plus the (suffix) morpheme а, meaning 'feminine' and 'singular'. Similarly, the word ОНО́ consists of the morpheme он plus the suffix о meaning 'neuter' and 'singular'. Finally, the word ОНИ́ is made up of он plus the suffix и, meaning 'plural' (undifferentiated for gender). In this particular example both the *SO* and the *RO* reveal morphemic structure equally well. In other examples, however, as in words whose standard spellings involve the use of the redundant vowel letters, the *SO* is somewhat misleading from this

point of view. Consider, for instance, the case of
the possessive pronoun forms МО́Й, МОЯ́, МОЁ and МОЙ.
In the *SO* only the sequence мо is common throughout
this list and a completely new set of "endings" are
seemingly attached to this. But in the *RO* these
words are represented instead as мо́й, мойа́, мойо́ and
мойи́. Now we can plainly see that the stem morpheme
meaning 'my' which all of these forms share in common is actually the sequence мой, to which the same
three gender-number suffixes can be added as in the
previous example. Compare also the partial noun
paradigms below and note that only in the *RO* representation do all the stem and suffix forms indicated
appear with a constant shape for a constant meaning:

	SO	*RO*
N. Sg.	КНИ́ГА	кни́га
A. Sg.	КНИ́ГУ	кни́гу
G. Pl.	КНИ́Г	кни́г
L. Pl.	КНИ́ГАХ	кни́гах
N. Sg.	НЕДЕ́ЛЯ	неде́льа
A. Sg.	НЕДЕ́ЛЮ	неде́льу
G. Pl.	НЕДЕ́ЛЬ	неде́ль
L. Pl.	НЕДЕ́ЛЯХ	неде́льах
N. Sg.	А́РМИЯ	а́рмийа
A. Sg.	А́РМИЮ	а́рмийу
G. Pl.	А́РМИЙ	а́рмий
L. Pl.	А́РМИЯХ	а́рмийах

Because of these desirable characteristics, the
RO can be recommended to instructors of courses on
the structure of Russian as the best available orthographic representation for the study of Russian morphology and morphophonemics. Indeed, the *RO* is an
almost ideal morphophonemic representation (in
Jakobsonian terms, at any rate),[6] though a few inconsistencies do remain. In particular, the *SO* of some
Russian words indicates detailed phonetic information
which is not suited to a strictly morphophonemic or
lexical representation, and naturally such spelling
idiosyncracies will carry over to our *RO*, as well.
For example, in the words ИЗДАВА́ТЬ, ИСХОДИ́ТЬ and
ИЗОЙТИ́, the prefix is spelled in three different ways
both in the standard and regularized orthographies,

just as the stem is spelled differently in the words
ИГРА́ТЬ and СЫ̲Г̲РА́ТЬ. Such inconsistencies could be
removed from our *RO* only at the expense of a large
number of *ad hoc* rules, whose inclusion would introduce much complexity at very little gain. We think
it best that students simply be made aware of such
irregularities in spelling when they occur and remain
alert to the fact that the *RO* will not be *completely*
regular and consistent although it does represent a
considerable improvement over the *SO* from the stand-
point of making more transparent the morphological
structure of the language.[7]

2.5. SOME GENERAL CONVENTIONS ON RULE INTERPRETATION

It will be helpful at this point to specify a
number of general conventions on rules and their interpretation, over and above the purely notational
devices already introduced (arrow, environment bar,
braces, brackets, etc.), which are vital to a proper
understanding and the correct application of all of
the rules in this book. These conventions are as
follows:

1. In general, all rules which appear in this
book should be applied in the following fashion:
first, identify and mark all letters or sequences of
letters in the input string which are subject to the
rule; second, rewrite each marked letter or sequence
according to the instructions provided by the rule;
finally, copy the remaining, unchanged portion of the
string. This new, revised string may now serve as
input to the next rule. If there are no letters in
an input string to which a given rule applies, of
course, simply skip the rule and move on to the next
one. This procedure is illustrated below using the
word ДОБАВЛЯЮ as a simple input string and Rule 2A1
as an illustrative rule:

Step 1: Identify and mark all relevant letters
ДОБАВЛЯ̲Ю̲

Step 2: Rewrite the marked letters as indicated
by the rule
ьа́йу

Step 3: Copy the remainder of the input string
добавльа́йу

Step 4: Repeat these steps for the next rule

(In this example, neither Rule 2B1 nor
Rule 2B2 will apply to the string in
question.)

The only exceptions to this general procedure are those few rules which are explicitly labeled as ITER-ATIVE and which are intended to be applied repeatedly, in a cyclical fashion. (See 3.5. below for the first example of such an ITERATIVE rule, together with a discussion of how such rules are to be applied.)

2.   All *rule-blocks*, each of which is identified with a number and a letter (such as 2A, 2B, etc.), are *strictly ordered*. That is to say, the rules in rule-block 2A are all to be applied (as required) before any of the rules in rule-block 2B, those in 2B are to be applied before those in 2C, and so on throughout the book. Although not all of these or-derings are crucial, incorrect results will often be obtained unless this ordering convention is strin-gently maintained. Even in this present chapter, for example, if Rule 2B1 were applied to a word like ОБЪЁМ before Rule 2A1, the result would be the string обьо́м, which would eventually lead to the incorrect pronunciation *[ʌbʼóm], rather than [ʌbjóm].

3.   The individual rules *within* a particular rule-block (such as 3C1 and 3C2 below, for example) need *not* be applied in any particular order (with the sole exception of the rules in rule-block 3A, as in-dicated below). Any numbers or letters provided to the right of the rule-block identification are thus supplied only for purposes of identification and cross-reference. Since the results will be the same whatever order is chosen for such rules, the reader may find it just as convenient to apply *all* rules in the strict order in which they are presented. Within rule-blocks, however, this approach is obligatory *only* in the case of rule-block 3A.

4.   Some rules (such as 3B1, 3B3, 3E1) can be applied in *more than one different environment*. In such cases, each separate environment is identified with a lower case letter in parentheses, which, for reference purposes, is placed immediately to the right of the rule identification number (e.g., 3E1(a), 3E1(b), etc.). These labels, too, are sup-plied for identification purposes only and do *not* imply any necessary ordering.

5.   The term *LIST* (which is first used in 3B1(b) is to be understood as an abbreviation for the phrase *IN A LIST OF SPECIFIED WORDS ONLY*. Simi-larly, the abbreviation *EXC. LIST* means *EXCEPT IN A LIST OF SPECIFIED WORDS*. Examples of words in a pertinent list are provided in the DISCUSSION section following the rule; a complete list of *all* specified

words is provided in the LEXICON (Chapter Six), with cross-references to the particular rules for which each such word is specified.* Before carrying any derivation beyond the rules of Chapter 2, the reader should check the LEXICON to see if any of the words in his initial (*SO*) string are listed and, if so, then proceed to follow the instructions on the use of the LEXICON which are provided on page 180.

6. Each rule-block is followed by a number of EXAMPLES, which are intended to illustrate the application of each rule and sub-rule in that block. These EXAMPLES are all presented in the same format. For ease of reference, *the SO is given first, in bold face*. Immediately below this, the example is re-written in the form it would take upon the application of all rules *up to and including the immediately previous rule-block*. Finally, the example is re-written on a third line in the form derived by application of the particular rule or rules under discussion; this last line of a derivation is also marked with the arrow →. Thus, for example:

РУЖЬЁ (= *SO*)

ружь̲йо́ (by the rules through rule-block 2A)

→ружйо́ (by rule 2B2)

If it should happen that more than one rule in a set of *ordered* rules is to be exemplified, then each relevant sub-stage of a derivation is also presented in order to show the effect of each individual rule or rule iteration involved (see p. 34).

7. For ease of identification, the relevant letter or string of letters affected by a rule are *underlined* in the EXAMPLES, either on the next-to-last line (in the case of a deletion, as in the example just above) or, more normally, on the last line of a derivation, showing the letter or other symbol produced as the *result* of applying a rule. In

---

*When a rule or exception pertains only to a very small number of words (usually just one or two), these words are not listed in the LEXICON but are rather dealt with by one or more of the "ad hoc rules" in rule-block 3Z. In this way a proliferation of minor rules and minor exceptions is avoided. However, cross-references to and from the relevant rule-blocks are still provided.

the case of examples illustrating *exceptions* to a rule, that letter is underlined which *would have been affected* by the rule had the form in question not been exceptional. All of these conventions are illustrated by one or more of the EXAMPLES on p. 38.

8. Each section may also contain one or more paragraphs under the heading STYLISTIC VARIATIONS. Generally speaking, these remarks relate to a variety of *alternative pronunciations* for certain words or classes of words which vary somewhat from the norms prescribed by Avanesov, but which are nonetheless rather widespread and popular. The alternative styles most frequently considered in these sections are the Old Moscow (*OM*) and the Conversational *CSR* (see pp. 8 - 9 above for a more detailed discussion of the whole question of stylistic variation in Russian).

CHAPTER THREE

FROM REGULARIZED ORTHOGRAPHY
TO PHONETICIZED ORTHOGRAPHY

3.0   INTRODUCTION

In this chapter we present 25 blocks of rules to derive a Phoneticized Orthography (*PO*) from the Regularized Orthography (*RO*) derived in Chapter Two. These rule-blocks are set out under fourteen different headings, the titles of which serve to emphasize the fact that only a limited number of discrete processes are actually involved. For example, nine different rules are collected into the three rule-blocks 3P through 3R, and these are all presented under the general heading *Palatalization Assimilation* (section 3.11.); and indeed in this instance, as in most, though the details may be rather complex and may require many rules to describe fully, there is but a single phenomenon to be treated.

Before attempting to use any of the rules presented in this chapter, the reader may find it helpful to review first the general remarks and conventions for rules which were presented on pp. 24-27 above.

3.1.   A SECOND CLASSIFICATION OF THE RUSSIAN LETTERS

In this section, the letters are grouped in three classes. As in section 2.1. phonetic terms are used as labels for the classes; but once again, it must be remembered that the terms are not to be understood as phonetically precise.

The classification made here cuts across the one made in 2.1.1.; for example, the consonants here grouped in the class of VOICELESS OBSTRUENTS include letters which in 2.1.1. were labelled C_p (Paired), H (Unpaired Hard), and S (Unpaired Soft). This means that consonant letters may henceforward belong simultaneously to two different classes. In 3.7. below the matter is further complicated, when five more classificatory labels are assigned. In that section (p. 60) the reader will find a reference-chart which may help him become more familiar with these classificatory labels.

Two new consonant letters are introduced here:

ґ and ў. The first of these* is required for our Phoneticized Orthography (*PO*), and will be carried over
into Chapter Four, where it will be rewritten as two
distinct phonetic symbols.[1] The second letter, ў, on
the other hand, is to be regarded as a convenient,
temporary device which is used in 3.5. to simplify
the formulation of the rules in blocks 3D, 3E and 3F.[2]

   Three letter-combinations (*digraphs*) are also
referred to here: дз, дж and жж.[3] These are to be
treated as single units.

   Our classification is, firstly, into RESONANT
LETTERS and OBSTRUENT LETTERS. The resonant letters
normally represent sounds which are voiced, rather
than voiceless; the new letter ў is included in this
class.

(R) Resonant letters: м н л р й ў

   The twenty other consonant letters and digraphs, on the other hand, normally represent sounds
which have both voiceless and voiced counterparts;
these counterparts are shown in vertical columns in
the display below.

(C_{v1}) Voiceless Obstruent
        Letters: п т к ф с х ц ч   ш   щ

(C_{vd}) Voiced Obstruent
        Letters: б д г в з ґ дз дж ж жж
   Since the new letters and digraphs have not
been classified according to the groupings set out in
2.1., the following remarks must be borne in mind:

   ґ, like its voiceless counterpart х, is a Paired
Consonant Letter (C_p), and is a fricative.

   дз, like its voiceless counterpart ц, is an
Unpaired Hard Consonant Letter (H).

   дж, like its voiceless counterpart ч, is an
Unpaired Soft Consonant Letter (S).

   жж, UNLIKE its voiceless counterpart щ, is an
Unpaired Hard Consonant Letter (H); see *Stylistic
Variations* below.

*Note that we use ґ to represent a fricative, in dis-
tinction to г, which represents a stop. This is the
reverse of the usage of the former *SO* of Ukrainian
(and the present *SO* of émigré Ukrainians); readers
whose first Slavic language is Ukrainian must if
necessary make this mental switch.

Stylistic Variations

We here specify the digraph ЖЖ as an Unpaired Hard Consonant (H); but in the *OM* style (and given equal status in *CSR* by Avanesov: *RLP* 139-40) the sound it represents when it occurs *within stems* and when derived by rule 3H4 below from ЗЖ, is "soft" (examples: ЕЗЖУ, БРЫ̄ЗЖЕШЬ). Also typical of *OM* speech is a "soft" pronunciation of the sound represented by ЖЖ in other circumstances (examples: МОЖЖЕВЕ́ЛЬНИК, ЖУЖЖА́ТЬ).[4] For further discussion, see pp. 56, 59, 61, 63-65, 136.

A Note On Digraphs

Two of the digraphs introduced above may cause some confusion, especially when the preposition- and prefix-boundary / (introduced in 3.2. below) is involved. The following notes are therefore given for future reference:

When not bisected by a boundary symbol such as /, the combinations дз and дж are to be treated as *single units*.

When bisected by a boundary symbol, the letters д and з in, e.g., д/з, and the letters д and ж in, e.g., д/ж, are to be treated as *separate units*.

The digraph дз, therefore, is always to be regarded as an Unpaired Hard Consonant (H); however, the з in д/з (being a separate letter) is a Paired Consonant Letter (C_p); and the sequence д/зь is therefore possible (and indeed is derived in 3K below).

The digraph дж, similarly, is always to be regarded as an Unpaired Soft Consonant (S); but the ж in д/ж (being a separate letter) is an Unpaired Hard Consonant (H).

3.2. SYNTACTIC UNITS AND BOUNDARIES

We now present rules for inserting three different BOUNDARY SYMBOLS into the strings of letters as they appear in the *RO*. Using these symbols, we are able to greatly simplify the rules in this chapter; without them, the rules would be in many cases extremely complex and difficult to use.

It is an unfortunate fact of life that, for a description of the processes which operate in the pronunciation of Russian, frequent reference must be made to their *scope of operation*. To take a simple example: one process may operate on prepositions, while another may not. We may mention this fact either informally ("Rule X applies to prepositions...")

or formally, i.e., by incorporating it into the rules, as here ("Rule X operates across the / boundary").

In writing rules for the derivation of Russian pronunciation, it is possible to distinguish at least five[5] different sorts of boundaries in this way. Some of these, however, only appear once or twice in the whole set of rules; in cases of this nature, we have chosen to make the rule slightly more verbose[6] and thus to avoid creating a plethora of special boundary symbols with only very limited utility. Where, on the other hand, a boundary-symbol can be used time and again, it is clearly advantageous to make use of the economy which this device offers. Our pragmatic choice, then, is to use three symbols, as follows:

##	Phrase-Boundary[7]
#	Word-Boundary
/	Preposition- and Prefix-Boundary

Before presenting the rules for the insertion of these symbols, it is necessary to define three types of sentence-constituent, as follows:

PP	(Phonological Phrase) -- a sentence-constituent, occurring between actual or "potential" pauses; normally, in the *SO* or the *RO* occurring between punctuation marks (excluding hyphens).
IW	(Independent Word) -- any orthographic word except an unstressed noun or preposition.
CW	(Component Word) -- each stressed component of an orthographic word which supports two or more stresses.

Discussion

PP's: for the application of the Reading Rules, it will normally be sufficient to use the punctuation of the *SO* (unchanged in the *RO*) as a guideline. Thus, whenever a period/full stop, comma, colon, semi-colon

or dash (but NOT a hyphen)[8] occurs in the *SO*, this
mark may normally be considered to signal an "actual
or 'potential' pause" (usually, an actual pause), and
hence to signal the end of one and the beginning of
another *PP*.

However, "potential" pauses may occur in a text
(and a person reading a text may make pauses) at
places where there is no punctuation device to mark
their occurrence. For example, the sentence ВА̋Ш БРА̋Т
ПРИЕ̋ХАЛ? may be uttered with no pauses (except those
before ВА̋Ш and after БРА̋Т), and with the primary sentence-stress (shown here with the symbol ") falling
on the verb: ВА̋Ш БРА̋Т ПРИЕ̋ХАЛ? If, however, the
primary sentence-stress falls on the first word,
thus: ВА̋Ш БРА̋Т ПРИЕ̋ХАЛ, then there MAY be a pause
after this first word.[9] We have here an instance of
a "potential" pause after the word ВА̋Ш; this sentence
is now to be considered as consisting of two *PP's*:
ВА̋Ш and БРА̋Т ПРИЕ̋ХАЛ. (As is shown in 3.5. the word
ВАШ is pronounced differently in the two instances.)

Normally, however, circumstances may not indicate the presence of these "potential" pauses; hence
our suggested general rule, namely that the punctuation of the *SO* be taken as a guide.

If disconnected words or phrases are being considered (as in the exercises provided), they should
be dealt with as separate *PP's*.

IW's: the only problem which may arise with
respect to *Independent Words* concerns prepositional
phrases. This problem will prove slight if it is
remembered that the definition of the *IW* involves a
reference to *stress*; here, the normal word-stress is
meant. If, in a prepositional phrase, *both* the preposition and its object are stressed (e.g., СКВО̋ЗЬ
ОКНО̋) then both words are *IW's*. If (the normal case)
the preposition is unstressed and the object stressed
(e.g., ОТ МОСКВЫ̋), or if the preposition is stressed
and the object unstressed (e.g., И̋З ЛЕСУ), then the
WHOLE PREPOSITIONAL PHRASE (preposition and object)
is to be considered as ONE SINGLE *IW*.

All other orthographic words are considered as
IW's. Although it may seem strange to call unstressed words (other than prepositions and nouns)
"independent", especially particles such as БЫ, ВЕДЬ,
НИ, etc., and most especially the two "words" ЛЬ and
Б, there is no advantage gained in distinguishing
between words like these and fully-stressed[10] words
as far as the Reading Rules are concerned.

CW's: Any orthographic word which bears two or
more stresses is normally termed a compound word.
For our purposes, every compound word must be

considered as consisting of two (or more) *Component Words*. Thus the compound word СЀВЕРОВОСТО́ЧНЫЙ con-sists of the two *CW's* СЀВЕРО and ВОСТО́ЧНЫЙ; and the compound word ГЛА̀ВТО́РГ consists of the *CW's* ГЛА̀В and ТО́РГ.

It may be added here that there is some dis-agreement in the literature as to whether all com-pound words behave in the same way as far as pronun-ciation is concerned. According to some authorities, a number of Soviet "acronyms" (or "stump-compounds") should be treated as a separate category, with (per-haps) a special boundary-symbol inserted between their component elements to indicate that the phono-logical processes operate idiosyncratically. There is not enough evidence to warrant our following this suggestion.[11]

We are now in a position to present our BOUND-ARY-INSERTION RULES.

(3A)

Delete Punctuation Marks and Insert Only One Boundary-Symbol in Each Space, According to the Following *Ordered* Rules:

1. Insert ## before and after every *PP*.

Next,

2. Insert # { (a) between all *IW's* }
              { (b) between all *CW's* }

Finally,

3. Insert / { (a) in all other spaces }
             { (b) after all prefixes }

Discussion and Examples

Note firstly that ONLY ONE BOUNDARY-SYMBOL is to be inserted in each space. Since the rules are OR-DERED, this means that the strongest of the relevant symbols will be inserted in any given space; if, for example, there is a choice between the symbols / and #, only the latter will be inserted.[12] See the example on p. 34.

This example is set out in detail so that each step of the boundary-insertion rules may be observed. Normally, of course, the student will write out the text in the *RO*, omitting the punctuation; and then insert all the boundary symbols in the same, or the next, line.

Example for Rule-Block 3A

SO   Я НЕ ПОНИМÁЮ, ТОВÁРИЩ ЗÁВМÁГ, ЧЕГÓ ВЫ ОТ МЕНЯ́ ХОТИ́ТЕ?

RO   йä не понимáйу, товáриш зäвмáг, чегó вы от меньä хотúте?

3A1   ##йä не понимáйу ##товáриш зäвмáг ##чегó вы от меньä хотúте##

3A2(a) ##йä#не#понимáйу ##товáриш#зäвмáг ##чегó#вы#от меньä#хотúте##

3A2(b) ##йä#не#понимáйу ##товáриш#зäвмáг##чегó#вы#от меньä#хотúте##

3A3(a) ##йä#не#понимáйу ##товáриш#зäвмáг##чегó#вы#от/меньä#хотúте##

3A3(b) ##йä#не#по/нимáйу##товáриш#зäвмáг##чегó#вы#от/меньä#хотúте##

3A1:   ## is inserted instead of the commas, and at
            the beginning and end of the whole sentence.

3A2(a):   # is inserted between all *IW's*. Note that
            the phrase от меньá carries only one stress
            and is therefore a single *IW*.

3A2(b):   # is inserted between the two *CW's* зàв and
            мáг.

3A3(a):   / is inserted in the one remaining space,
            between от and меньá.

3A3(b):   / is inserted after the prefix по-.

Prefixes

        This last step warrants further discussion. It
is to be noted that there is a range of word-con-
stituents occurring in initial position in the word--
from those which are obvious prefixes to those which
can only be thus classed according to dubious criteria; from those which every Russian-speaker (who
understood the term) would agree to be prefixes, to
those which very few would think of in this light.
At the former end of the scale are, e.g., the initial
constituents of the four words ПРИХÓД, ОТХÓД, УХÓД
and ВЫХОД; it would surely not be disputed that here
we have the four prefixes ПРИ-, ОТ-, У- and ВЫ-. At
the other end of the scale are the initial consonants
of such words as ССÓРА and СЧÁСТЬЕ. On the one hand,
C- is a prefix in a large number of Russian words and
we may be tempted to think of it as a prefix in these
instances also. On the other hand, neither -СÓРА nor
-ЧÁСТЬЕ appears to have any separate, distinct "meaning" of its own if this "prefix" is removed.[13]
        An example of a word with a possible prefix, oc-
curring somewhere in the middle reaches of the scale,
is РАССТАНÓВКА. It would probably surprise many
speakers of *CSR* to have pointed out to them that the
element -СТАН has something in common with similar-
sounding elements in the words СТÁНУ and УСТАНОВÍТЬ;
and yet many others would "feel" the connection immediately. For the latter speakers, it would be
better to class the element РАС- as a prefix; for the
former, perhaps it should not be so classified.[14]
        As a general rule, we suggest that if a prefix
is TRANSPARENT (i.e., if it is obviously a prefix),
then the symbol / should certainly be inserted; and
that if a prefix is OPAQUE (i.e., if its standing as
a prefix is in some doubt) that the symbol / is best
not inserted. Clearly, some arbitrary decisions will

have to be made in the absence of definitive evidence.
However, it is probably true to say--insofar as decisions such as these will result in the derivation of
different strings, and hence eventually of different
phonetic transcriptions--that where there is doubt in
the mind of the student trying to make these decisions, there will also be considerable vacillation in
the way in which Russians actually pronounce the
words in question.

On Interpreting the Boundary-Symbols

Before proceeding with the Reading Rules, two
further points must be made with regard to the boundary-symbols.
Firstly, since *only one* boundary-symbol may occur in any one space, the symbols are to be considered as *mutually exclusive*. If, therefore, a rule is
presented as being operative in an environment which
includes one of the boundary-symbols but excludes
another, it is to be understood that the rule operates with respect to the one and does *not* operate
with respect to the other. For example, 3J1(b) is
stated as operating in the environment $C_h \begin{Bmatrix} \# \\ / \end{Bmatrix} \underline{\quad}$ i.e.,
"when preceded by a C_h and either a word-boundary or
a prefix/preposition-boundary". Here, the phrase-
boundary ## is excluded; the rule does not operate
"after a C_h and a phrase-boundary". When a rule
operates with reference both to a phrase-boundary and
a word-boundary, both symbols are shown in the rule
(examples: 3I, 3N, 3S, 3V, 3X).
On the other hand, most of the rules operate
equally well whether the / boundary is present or not
(for exceptional instances, see 3B, 3G, 3N). Rather
than repeat this statement in all the rules concerned,
and rather than formalize it in each rule (which
would be done by inserting the / boundary in the "optional" parentheses, viz.: "(/)"), we here and now
make a general statement:

NOTE: All Rules Henceforth Operate
Across the / Boundary Unless
Otherwise Stated

In cases of possible confusion, readers are reminded
of this general note in the DISCUSSIONS following the
rules, with appropriate examples.

3.3. CONSONANT DELETIONS

These rules ensure the derivation of the correct *PO* for a number of specific CONSONANT CLUSTERS of the *RO*, one letter of which does not represent any sound that is pronounced.[15] Note that many of these rules apply to specified words or word-stems only (as shown by the notation LIST), and that others apply to *all* words with a few specified *exceptions* (as shown by the notation EXC. LIST).

N.B.   These Rules do <u>not</u> Apply
Across the / Boundary

(3B) 1. $\left\{\begin{matrix}т\\д\end{matrix}\right\} \to \emptyset /$

(a)   с — $\left\{\begin{matrix}ч\\ц\\щ\end{matrix}\right\}$

(b) $\left\{\begin{matrix}с\\н\\м\end{matrix}\right\}$ — ск   (list)

(c)   н — к   (list)

(d)   с — (ь) б

(e)   с — л   (exc. list)

(f) $\left\{\begin{matrix}с\\з\end{matrix}\right\}$ — н   (exc. list)

2. $\left\{\begin{matrix}к\\г\end{matrix}\right\} \to \emptyset /$ с — ск   (list)

3.   в $\to \emptyset /$ — ств   (list)

Discussion and Examples

Note that this is one of the three rule-blocks (cf. p. 36) where we specify that the rules DO NOT OPERATE ACROSS THE / BOUNDARY. In fact, most of the consonant clusters concerned do not occur with some letters on one side and some on the other of a / boundary; but when they do thus occur, the rules are inoperative--see 3B1(a) and 3B1(f) for examples. Since no rules operate across the ## boundary, and since the # boundary is not mentioned, we may sum-marize by saying that the two rules operate across NO BOUNDARIES.

3B1: The letter т, д are deleted if they occur in the following six environments:

(a)   after any consonant and before ч, ц or щ (*RLP* 150-51), e.g.:*

СЕ́РДЦЕ	ХВОСТЦА́	ГОЛЛА́НДЦЫ	СЕРДЧИ́ШКО	ГРОМО́ЗДЧЕ
се́р<u>д</u>це	хвос<u>т</u>ца́	голла́<u>н</u>дцы	сер<u>д</u>чи́шко	громо́з<u>д</u>че
→серце	хвосца́	голла́нцы	серчи́шко	громо́зче

ЖЁСТЧЕ	ПРОЦЕ́НТЩИК	ЭМИГРА́НТЩИНА	УЗДЦЫ́	ИСТЦО́ВАЯ
жёс<u>т</u>че	проце́н<u>т</u>щик	эмигра́н<u>т</u>щина	уз<u>д</u>цы́	ис<u>т</u>цо́вайа
→жёсче	проце́нщик	эмигра́нщина	узцы́	исцо́вайа

BUT not across the / boundary, e.g.:

ЧЕРЕЗ ТЩЕСЛА́ВИЕ   ИЗ ТЩЕТЫ́

через/<u>тщ</u>есла́вийе из/<u>тщ</u>еты́

n/c   n/c

(b)   after the consonants с, н or м, and before the string ск, in specified words only (*RLP* 149-50). Consonant clusters involved are:

стск, which ALWAYS → сск, e.g.:   МАРКСИ́СТСКИЙ

маркси́с<u>т</u>ский

→маркси́сский

ндск, which ALWAYS → нск, e.g.:   ГОЛЛА́НДСКИЙ

голла́<u>нд</u>ский

→голла́нский

нтск, which → нск in TWO WORDS ONLY:

ГИГА́НТСКИЙ	ПАРЛА́МЕНТСКИЙ
гига́н<u>т</u>ский	парла́мен<u>т</u>ский
→гига́нский	парла́менский

---

*See 3Z for deletion of д in the three words МУНД-ШТУ́К, ЛАНДША́ФТ, and ФЕ́ЛЬДШЕР. This environment is very similar to that given in 3B1(a); but we have excluded it from the rule because there are so many counterexamples, e.g., words ending in -нтша (РЕ́ГЕНТША, ФАБРИКА́НТША, etc.).

but not in, e.g.:* КОМЕНДА́НТСКИЙ ДОКТО́РАНТСКИЙ
комендáн̲т̲ский доктор́áн̲т̲ский
n/c n/c

and мтск[16] which → мск in the word: ПОЧТА́МТСКИЙ
почтáм̲т̲ский
→почтáмский

(c) the clusters нтк, ндк are simplified to нк in two words, only (*RLP* 151), viz.,

ГУВЕРНА́НТКА ГОЛЛА́НДКА *BUT*, e.g., ШОТЛА́НДКА
гувернáн̲т̲ка голлáн̲д̲ка шотлáн̲д̲ка
→гувернáнка голлáнка n/c

(d) т is deleted from the clusters стб and стьб, in all words, e.g.,

ПАСТЬБА́ ПА́СТБИЩЕ РО́СТБИФ
пас̲т̲ьбá пá̲с̲т̲бище ро̲́с̲т̲биф
→пасьбá пáсбище ро́сбиф

(e) The cluster стл is simplified to сл in ALL stems *except* СТЛА- and КОСТЛЯ́-. For one stem, ХВАСТЛИ́В, the rule is optional (i.e., the т may be deleted or left in, as desired). (*RLP* 149). E.g.:

ЗАВИ́СТЛИВАЯ ХВАСТЛИ́ВАЯ КОСТЛЯ́ВАЯ
зави́с̲т̲ливайа хваст̲ли́вайа костльá́вайа
→зави́сливайа хвасли́вайа or n/c n/c

(f) The clusters стн, здн are simplified to сн, зн in all stems except БЕЗДН-, БЕЗМЕЗДН-, and БЕЗ-ВОЗМЕЗДН- (*RLP* 148), thus:

МЕ́СТНОЕ ПО́ЗДНО *BUT* БЕЗДНУ́
мé̲с̲т̲нойе пó̲з̲д̲но безд̲ну́
→мéснойе пóзно n/c

*See 3G2 for the fate of words such as these where нтск is not affected by 3B1(b) and for further discussion of нтск and ндск.

Note: not across the / boundary, e.g.:   ЧЕРЕЗ ДНЕ́ПР

через/дне́пр

n/c

3B2: к and г are deleted in the clusters скск and ргск in a number of specified words,[17] e.g.:

БА́СКСКИЙ   ПЕТЕРБУ́РГСКИЙ   ВЫ́БОРГСКИЙ

ба́скский   петербу́ргский   вы́боргский

→ба́сский   петербу́рский   вы́борский

3B3: в is deleted when it is the first element of the cluster вств, in the three stems ЧУ́ВСТВ-, -МО́ЛВСТВ-, and ЗДРА́ВСТВ- (*RLP* 151):

ЧУ́ВСТВО БЕЗМО́ЛВСТВОВАЛ ЗДРА́ВСТВУЙ *BUT* БЛАГОВСТВО́

чу́вство без/мо́лвствовал здра́вствуй   благовство́

→чу́ство без/мо́лствовал здра́ствуй   n/c

Stylistic Variations (3B1, 3B2, 3B3)

Other Soviet authorities differ in a number of details concerning these consonantal deletions, and especially 3B1 (deletion of т, д). In non-orthoepic, faster, colloquial speech (cf. 5.4.1.), consonants are deleted much more often in these environments and in others like them; the problem is, how many such deletions are to be granted official sanction in *CSR*?

Panov, for example, cites only *four* roots[18] as having the т or д deleted in environment (f), whereas Avanesov, as we have seen, prescribes deletion in *all* words except three extremely "bookish" ones. *RLPU*, however, lists no fewer than *36* words with deletion in this environment! *RLPU* also disagrees slightly about the specified words for 3B1(b), 3B1(f), and 3B3.[19]

Another example: Panov cites two items (ЖЁСТК- and ПОЕ́ЗДКА) as losing the т, д in the clusters стк, здк; yet this environment is not mentioned in our rules, since Avanesov (*RLP* 149) insists that this deletion should occur in *no* words at all![20]

3B1 may be extended to the environment ж-л, thus ДОЖДЛИ́ВЫЙ→дожд̲ли́вый→дожли́вый (but only in the speech of those Russians who do not pronounce, e.g., дождя́ as дожжьа, cf. p. 56 (Panov 1967:99; optional variant in *RLPU*)).

In colloquial *CSR*, 3B3 (deletion of в) must be extended to the environment тст_ова; but note that the sequence ТСТВ occurring in other environments is not affected (*RLP* 141):

СООТВÉТСТВОВАЛИ	СООТВÉТСТВУЕШЬ	ЛЮБОПЫ́ТСТВО
со/от/вéтст<u>в</u>овали	со/от/вéтст<u>в</u>уйеш	льубопы́тст<u>в</u>о
→со/от/вéтстовали	n/c	n/c

    Not only are consonant deletions more common in faster speech and less common in more careful styles, there are at least two other factors to be consid-ered.[21] Firstly, the younger generations seem to delete fewer consonants than do their parents and grandparents, i.e., they tend to pronounce the clus-ters much more as they are spelled. Secondly, it appears that deletion is more common in everyday items of vocabulary, and less common in "bookish" words (which, being unfamiliar, are more likely to evoke a "spelling-pronunciation").

    These factors may, obviously, conflict with one another, and it is therefore difficult to make a general recommendation. However, it will probably nearly always be acceptable, if clusters such as these are pronounced AS THEY ARE SPELLED--with, as exceptions, a few very common words such as ЗДРÁВ-СТВУЙ(ТЕ), СÉРДЦЕ, ПÓЗДНО, etc.

3.4. IDIOSYNCRATIC RULES

    We now clear up a few odd points which (1) do not come under any of the general headings used else-where and (2) are limited to a few particular words and one particular ending.*

(3C)

1. ГО → ВО / in genitive singulars
                and their derivatives
2. Г → Г´ / list
3. МЬ → М / in compound numerals
                containing СЕМЬ (list)

Discussion and Examples

3C1: In genitive singular forms, and in words de-rived from them,[22] the letters ГО are rewritten ВО

---

*Rules which effect ONE OR TWO WORDS ONLY are listed in 3Z.

(*RLP* 156), e.g.:

БОЛЬШО́ГО	КРЕ́ПКОГО	НА́ШЕГО	СЕГО́ДНЯ	ИТОГО́
большо́го	кре́пкого	на́шего	сего́дньа	йитого́
→большо́во	кре́пково	на́шево	сево́дньа	йитово́

3C2: г is rewritten г̓ in a list of specified words
(*RLP* 81-82, 167, 183), e.g.:

ГО́СПОДИ	СЛА́ВА БО́ГУ	БОГ	ГА́БИТУС	ОГО́	ГО́ПЛЯ
го́споди	сла́ва#бо́гу	бог	га́битус	ого́	го́пльа
→г̓о́споди	сла́ва#бо́г̓у	бо́г̓	г̓а́битус	ог̓о́	г̓о́пльа

Note that in 4.3. the letter г̓ is replaced by one of
two different phonetic symbols, depending on the
lexical item in question.

Stylistic Variations (3C2)

In all except the "interjectional" words (such
as ОГО́, ГО́ПЛЯ) this rule must be regarded as optional,
although still very common; it was much more characteristic of the *OM* style, where it was extended to
the г in the prefix БЛАГО- and in the word БОГА́ТЫЙ.[23]

3C3: мь is rewritten м in two words only (*RLP* 102-
103):

СЕМЬСО́Т	ВОСЕМЬСО́Т
семьсо́т	восемьсо́т
→семсо́т	восемсо́т

Stylistic Variations (3C3)

This rule may, for conversational *CSR*, be extended to the word ВО́СЕМЬ (→ во́сем), which Avanesov
finds acceptable; and further to the word СЕМЬ
(→ сем) which Avanesov condemns; and similarly, to
other labial consonants in final and preconsonantal
position, e.g., ПРИГОТО́ВЬ (→ при/гото́в), ПРИГОТО́ВЬТЕ
(→ при/гото́вте). This type of pronunciation is apparently very widespread, especially in Leningrad;
Avanesov agrees to these facts, but condemns all such
pronunciations except the "hardening" of мь in СЕМЬ-
СО́Т, ВОСЕМЬСО́Т, and ВО́СЕМЬ.[24]

3.5. VOICING ASSIMILATION

In *CSR*, obstruents (that is, non-resonant consonants) assimilate with regard to voice; voiceless
ones are voiced before voiced ones, and vice versa.
Further, voiced obstruents are devoiced when they
precede certain boundaries, and also when they precede certain boundaries followed by non-obstruents
(*RLP* 94-100).[25]

The matter is further complicated by the behav-
iour of в (and, in some respects, by that of the
whole resonant group: see Stylistic Variations below).

3.5.1. SPECIFICATION OF ў

As far as voicing assimilation is concerned, we
may say that в acts like a resonant before resonants
and vowels, and like an obstruent before obstruents.
The DUAL NATURE of в has a historical explanation: it
was once phonetically a resonant in all positions;
and although now phonetically a fricative, it is not
as strident as its counterpart in, e.g., English.[26]
However, in *CSR* it does behave like a fricative (and
thus like an obstruent) when it occurs before another
obstruent.[27]

Our first rule specifies в as a resonant (shown
by the new letter ў) in the necessary environments.
It is to be understood that в in other environments
is still an obstruent.

$$\text{(3D)} \quad \text{в} \rightarrow \text{ў} \ / \ \underline{\quad} \ \left\{ \begin{matrix} V \\ R \end{matrix} \right\} \quad \text{(iterative)}$$

Discussion and Examples

Note, in the following examples, that (1) this
rule operates across the / boundary, since there is
no statement to the contrary; (2) the soft sign ь is
treated as an integral part of the consonant which
precedes it; hence вь → ўь when occurring before vowels and resonants; and (3) the rule may, if circumstances require, operate *more than once*--an example
of what we shall call the ITERATIVE application of a
rule.

ВА́Ш	ВЕ́ДЬ	ВЫ́	ВМЕ́СТЕ	ВНЯ́ТЬ	ВЛЕ́ЧЬ	ВЪЕ́ЗД
ва́ш	ве́дь	вы́	в/ме́сте	в/ньа́ть	в/ле́ч	в/йезд
→ў́аш	ў́едь	ў́ы́	ў́/ме́сте	ў́/ньа́ть	ў́/ле́ч	ў́/йезд

ВСЁ	ВЗИРА́ТЬ	ЧУ́ВСТВОВАВ	ВЯ́НУВШИЙ	ВЁЛ	ВВЁЛ
всьо́	в/зира́ть	чу́ствовав	вьа́нувший	вьо́л	в/вьо́л
→ n/c	n/c	чу́стўоўав	ў́ьанувший	ў́ьо́л	в/ў́ьо́л
					ў́/ў́ьол

In the last example, rule 3C applies twice; in
the first place, the second вь is rewritten ў́ь, since
it occurs before a vowel:

$$в/вьо́л$$
$$→\underline{в}/ў́ьо́л$$

Then the first (and now the only remaining) в is rewritten ў́, since it now occurs before the resonant
ў́ь:

$$в/ў́ьо́л$$
$$→\underline{ў́}/ў́ьо́л$$

When a rule is ITERATIVE, then, we may say that
it applies repeatedly, throughout any string of relevant letters (here, throughout any cluster of в's);
and that this repeated application is to be carried
out FROM RIGHT TO LEFT (since this rule, and other
iterative rules, are all examples of REGRESSIVE AS-
SIMILATION).[28]

3.5.2. DEVOICING RULES

The application of this rule-block requires
careful attention to BOUNDARIES.

$$\boxed{(3E1) \quad C_{vd} \rightarrow C_{vl} \ / \ \begin{cases} (a) \quad \text{---} \ \#\# \\ (b) \quad \text{---} \ \# \begin{Bmatrix} V \\ R \end{Bmatrix} \\ (c) \quad \text{---}(\#)C_{vl} \end{cases} \quad (iterative)}$$

Discussion and Examples

We may now return to and exemplify our general remarks about boundaries. In 3E1(a) devoicing is specified before the phrase-boundary, i.e., in pre-pausal position. In, e.g., the sentence НÓЖ ЗАБЫ́ЛИ?, when the primary sentence-stress is on the verb ("Have you *forgotten* the knife?"), there is no "actual or potential" pause after the noun; hence there is no phrase-boundary and the ж is not devoiced. The same sentence, however, with логическое ударение[29] (i.e., with primary sentence-stress) on the noun ("Is it the *knife* that you have forgotten?") has a "potential" pause after the noun; here a phrase boundary occurs and the ж will normally be devoiced; thus,

НÓЖ ЗАБЫ́ЛИ?	НÓЖ ЗАБЫ́ЛИ?
##нóж#забы́ли##	##нóж##забы́ли##
n/c	→##нóш##забы́ли##

Other examples of 3E1(a):

Э́ТО ПЛÓЩАДЬ	ЛЮБÓВЬ
##э́то##плóщадь##	##льубóвь##
→##э́то##плóщать##	##льубóфь##

As far as 3E1(a) is concerned, we need not include any remarks about the / boundary, since this may never co-occur with ##. Similarly, no special remark need be made in 3E1(b); again, / may not co-occur with #; and the # boundary is a *necessary* part of the rule--devoicing does not occur before vowels or resonants unless this boundary is present.

Examples:

СÁД ВÁШ	СÁД НÁШ	СÁД ÁННЫ
сáд#ў́аш	сáд#нáш	сáд#áнны
→сáт#ў́аш	сáт#нáш	сáт#áнны

ВЀДЬ ÓН	ВЀДЬ ВИ́КТОР	ВЀДЬ ВМЕ́СТЕ
ў̀едь#óн	ў̀едь#ў́иктор	ў̀едь#ў/ме́сте
→ў̀еть#óн	ў̀еть#ў́иктор	ў̀еть#ў/ме́сте

BUT cf.:

СА́Д БРА́ТА	СА́Д ВДОВЫ́	ВЀДЬ БОРИ́С	ВЀДЬ ВДОВА́
са́д#бра́та	са́д#вдоўы́	ўѐдь#бори́с	ўѐдь#вдоўа́
→ n/c	n/c	n/c	n/c

(In these examples, the rule does not apply because the following consonant is an OBSTRUENT) and cf.:

БЕЗ ВА́С	БЕЗ НА́С	БЕЗ А́ННЫ	РАЗЛУ́КА	ВОЗВРАТИ́ТЬ
без/ўа́с	без/на́с	без/а́нны	раз/лу́ка	ўоз/ўрати́ть
→ n/c	n/c	n/c	n/c	n/c

(In these examples, the rule does not apply because the boundary is / rather than #.) Other examples:

ЖЁГ ЛИ́СТЬЯ	ЖЁГ ЛИ?	ÓН ВЫ́ВЕЗ ВРАЧА́
жóг#ли́стьйа	жóг#ли	óн#ўы́/ўез#ўрача́
→жóк#ли́стьйа	жóк#ли	óн#ўы́/ўес#ўрача́

ЧЀРЕЗ ВѐНГРИЮ	ЧЕРЕЗ ВѐНГРИЮ	МЀЖОБЛАСТНÓЙ
чѐрез#ўѐнгрийу	через/ўѐнгрийу	мѐж#обласнóй
→чѐрес#ўѐнгрийу	n/c	мѐш#обласнóй

In 3E1(c) the boundary symbol # is in parentheses, which means that devoicing occurs before the stated consonants (viz., voiceless obstruents) *whether or not* the # boundary is present. We now recall the general statement (p. 36); rules operate across the / boundary unless otherwise stated. If the # boundary is absent, the / boundary may be present; in either case, devoicing will take place. To summarize: devoicing of voiced obstruents occurs before voiceless obstruents (i) if there is no boundary, (ii) if there is a / boundary and (iii) if there is a # boundary. Examples:

ПРÓБКА	РÉДЬКА	СОВХÓЗЫ	ГРОМÓЗДЧЕ	
прóбка	рéдька	совхóзы	громóзче	(no boundary)
→прóпка	рéтька	софхóзы	громóсче	

В ПА́РКЕ	ВПИ́СЫВАТЬ	ИЗ ЧА́ЙНИКА	
в/па́рке	в/пи́сыўать	из/ча́йника	(/ boundary)
→ф/па́рке	ф/пи́сыўать	ис/ча́йника	

ГО́Д ПРОШЁЛ	КЛЮ́В ПТИ́ЦЫ	ГЛА̀ВТО́РГА	
го́д#про/шо́л	кльу́в#пти́цы	гла̀в#то́рга	(# boundary)
→го́т̲#про/шо́л	кльу́ф̲#пти́цы	гла̀ф̲#то́рга	

Iterative Application

This rule, like 3D, is to be applied iteratively, that is, repeatedly from right to left throughout consonant clusters. Example:

ГВО́ЗДЬ	(*SO*)
гво́здь	(*RO*)
→гўво́здь	(by 3C)
→гўво́зт̲ь	(by 3D(a))
→гўво́с̲т̲ь	(by 3D(c))

3.5.3. VOICING RULE

$$\boxed{\text{(3E2)} \quad C_{vl} \rightarrow C_{vd} \ / \ \text{—} \ (\#) \ C_{vd} \ \text{(iterative)}}$$

Discussion and Examples

It will have been noticed that this rule is the mirror image of 3E1(c). The remarks made about that rule will apply here; 3E2, like 3E1(c), operates across the # boundary, across the / boundary, and when there is no boundary. Examples:

ВОКЗА́Л	ФУТБО́Л	ПРО́СЬБА	
вокза́л	футбо́л	про́сьба	(no boundary)
→вог̲за́л	фуд̲бо́л	про́з̲ьба	

С ЖЕНО́Й	СДВИ́ГАТЬ	К ДА́МЕ	К ВЗЛЁТУ	
с/жено́й	с/дви́гать	к/да́ме	к/вз/льо́ту	(/ boundary)
→з̲/жено́й	з̲/дви́гать	г̲/да́ме	г̲/вз/льо́ту	

БРА́Т ДАВИ́ДА	БРА́Т ВДОВЫ́	МО̀СБА́НК	
бра́т#давўйда	бра́т#вдоўы́	мо̀с#ба́нк	(# boundary)
→бра́д̲#давўйда	бра́д̲#вдоўы́	мо̀з̲#ба́нк	

ПА̀РТБИЛЕ́Т   КО́Т БЫ́Л   КО́Т БЫ   МЯ́Ч БЫ

пàрт#билéт   кóт#бы́л   кóт#бы   мьáч#бы   (# boundary)

→пàрд#билéт   кóд#бы́л   кóд#бы   мьáдж#бы

ОТЕ́Ц БЫ   ТОВА́РИЩ БЫ   МО́Х БЫ

отéц#бы   товáрищ#бы   мóх#бы   (# boundary)

→отéдз#бы   товáрижж#бы   мóг·#бы

BUT cf.:

БРА́Т ВО́ВЫ   КО́Т МЫ́Л   КО́Т ВЫ́Л   К ВЛА́СТИ   КЛА́СТЬ

брáт#ўбўы   кóт#мы́л   кóт#ўы́л   к/ўлáсти   клáсть

→   n/c   n/c   n/c   n/c   n/c

(here, the rule does not apply because the following
consonants are not obstruents, but resonants).

Iterative Application

Again, this rule must be applied iteratively
where necessary.

Example:

ГО́СТЬ БЫ́Л ТА́М   (*SO*)

гóсть#бы́л#тáм   (*RO*)

→гóсдь#бы́л#тáм   (by 3D2)

→гóздь#бы́л#тáм   (by 3D2 again)

Stylistic Variations (3E)

One stylistic variation with regard to these
rules must be mentioned. According to some authorities,[30] Soviet "acronyms" and/or "stump-compounds"
are not always pronounced according to the voicing-
assimilation rules; in other words, they require a
special boundary symbol or other formal device for
their exclusion from these rules. Thus, e.g., it is
reported that МО́СБА́НК may be pronounced without
voicing of the с; and that, conversely, ГЛА́ВТО́РГ may
be pronounced without devoicing of the в. As noted
in 3.2. above (p. 33), there is insufficient evidence
of these pronunciations.

3.5.4. DESPECIFICATION OF ў

The letter ў can now be dispensed with. None of
the remaining rules require a distinction between the

two "natures" of в, and by rewriting every ў as в again at this stage, we can emphasize the limited importance of this distinction for the language.[31]

> **(3F)** ў → в (iterative)

EXAMPLES (showing all steps in derivation after 3C):

ВА́Ш	ЧУ́ВСТВОВАВ	ВВЁЛ	БРА́Т ВДОВЫ́	(*SO*)
ва́ш	чу́ствовав	в/вьо́л	бра́т#вдовы́	(by 3C)
→ў́а́ш	чу́стў̲оў̲ав	ў̲/ў̲ьо́л	бра́т#вдоў̲ы́	(by 3D twice)
→ў́а́ш	чу́стў̲оў̲аф̲	ў̲/ў̲ьо́л	бра́т#вдоў̲ы́	(by 3E1)
→ў́а́ш	чу́стў̲оў̲аф	ў̲/ў̲ьо́л	бра́д̲#вдоў̲ы́	(by 3E2)
→в̲а́ш	чу́ств̲ов̲аф	в̲/в̲ьо́л	бра́д#вдов̲ы́	(by 3F)

3.5.5. A NOTE ON THE RESONANT CONSONANTS

The letters р, л, м, н, and й, which we classify as resonants, may behave like obstruents in certain environments, viz.,

(a) C_{v1} — ## : here, р,л,м,н are usually devoiced (as obstruents in 3E1(a)).

(b) $\left\{ \begin{matrix} \# \\ C \end{matrix} \right\}$ — C_{v1}: here, р,л are sometimes devoiced (as obstruents in 3E1(c)), and also fricativized.

(c) V — $\left\{ \begin{matrix} \#\# \\ C_{v1} \end{matrix} \right\}$: here, р,й are sometimes (at least partly) devoiced (as obstruents in 3E1(a), (c)).

See section 4.7. for the major phonetic details.[32]

These data show that it might be possible to treat the letters р, л, м, н, й, and в in a separate group. They could all be classified as obstruents in the first instance, and then rewritten as resonants in certain environments (in the way that we rewrite в as ў in 3D). Or, they could be all classified as resonants in the first instance, and then changed to obstruents in certain positions, viz., before obstruents and pauses. In our Rules, we deal only with в at this point, and leave the other resonants alone; because firstly, the pronunciations listed above are optional for *CSR*; secondly, not all six consonants behave alike; and thirdly, because the rules would introduce unnecessary complications into the *PO* (see

4.7. for a full discussion of the phonetic details).

Note that in *OM*, not only р, й but also л, м, н were devoiced in the environment V — ##; in other words, they *all* once behaved like obstruents in this position. Further, any preceding obstruent was also devoiced; hence a Reading Rule for *OM* would have to specify the change КАЗНЬ → каснь (with a voiceless нь).[33]

Note finally that here, as elsewhere, the ## boundary, and to a more limited extent the # boundary, could well be treated as if they were OBSTRUENTS. From a phonetic point of view, a pause has very much in common with a voiceless stop; it should therefore not be surprising that certain boundaries should behave like obstruents in the Reading Rules.[34]

3.5.6. VOICING ASSIMILATION AND BOUNDARIES: REFERENCE-TABLE

The following table may clarify the rules of this section; it shows the *possible occurrent consonants* according to voicing for each type of environment and each boundary:[35]

boundary	none	/	#	##
environment — $\left\{\begin{matrix}V\\R\end{matrix}\right\}$	C_{vl}, C_{vd}	C_{vl}, C_{vd}	C_{vl}	C_{vl}
— C_{vd}	C_{vd}	C_{vd}	C_{vd}	C_{vl}
— C_{vl}	C_{vl}	C_{vl}	C_{vl}	C_{vl}

3.6. SEQUENCE ADJUSTMENT RULES

In this section we bring together three rather heterogeneous rule-blocks. In 3I we rid our transcription of the letter й in certain environments (for the deletion of й in other environments, see 3Y). In 3H and 3G we treat a number of minor assimilations; the difference between 3H and 3G is that in 3G the rules do not operate across the / boundary, while in 3H they apply without this restriction.

3.6.1. THREE RULES OF LIMITED APPLICATION

N.B.   These Rules do not Operate Across the / Boundary

1.   к → х / — $\left\{\begin{matrix} к \\ ч \end{matrix}\right\}$

(3G)   2.   т → ч / — щ

3.   тс → ц   exc. in reflexives

Discussion and Examples

Note again the restriction on the field of operation of these three rules. For each we give examples below where the rule does not apply because of the / boundary; however, we should point out that this restriction is mentioned in *RLP* only with regard to 3G1 and 3G3; in the other case, we feel that this interpretation is implicit in Avanesov's remarks.[36]

3G1: к is replaced by х, if the following letter is either к or ч (*RLP* 145-46):*

мя́гкий   ле́гче

мья́ккий   ле́кче

→мья́х̲кий   ле́х̲че

BUT not across the / boundary, e.g.:

к кому́   к чему́

к/кому́   к/чему́

n/c   n/c

Stylistic Variations (3G1)

In *OM*, this rule was extended in three respects: firstly, it also applied to the voiced stop г; secondly, it also applied in the position before dental

---

*3G1 does not apply to the one word ТЯГЧАЙШИЙ, for which see 3Z, p. 116.

stops, т and д; and thirdly, it applied even across
the / boundary. Thus, for *OM*:[37]

К ГО́РОДУ	КТО́	ТОГДА́	ДЁГТЯ	НО́ГТИ	К КОМУ́
г/го́роду	ктб	тогда́	дьо́ктьа	но́кти	к/кому́
→г̣/го́роду	х̱тб	тог̣да́	дьо́х̱тьа	но́х̱ти	х̱/кому́

  in this style   in this style   in this style

In conversational *CSR* according to one report,[38]
this rule does not apply *at all*; hence,

МЯ́ГКИЙ	ЛЕ́ГЧЕ
мьа́к̱кий	ле́к̱че
n/c	n/c

    in this style   in this style

3G2: Although this rule concerns only the one cluster тщ, it is expedient to widen our discussion to
include the clusters тш and дж as well. In all three
cases, the first letter of the cluster represents a
stop, but the pronunciation of an affricate instead
of a stop has been remarked in one or another style
of Russian. In *RLP*, Avanesov sanctions this sort of
pronunciation only for the cluster mentioned in 3G2;
we exemplify this first, and return to the other
clusters in the *Stylistic Variations* below.
　　According to 3G2, the cluster тщ is rewritten as
чщ (*RLP* 83), e.g.:

ТЩЕ́ТНАЯ	ТЩА́ТЕЛЬНО
тще́тнайа	тща́тельно
→чще́тнайа	чща́тельно

BUT not across the / boundary, e.g.:*

ОТ ЩУКИ	НАД ЩЕКОЙ
от̱/щуки	нат̱/щекой
n/c	n/c

*The т in such forms will eventually be palatalized
by rule 3P3, leading to a distinction between чщ and
тьщ which Avanesov prescribes, but which is open to
question. See 4.3. for discussion.

Stylistic Variations (3G2)

We may now mention the other clusters listed above, and allow for the following extra rules in certain styles of speech:

$$т → ч \; / — ш \quad (or: \quad тш → чш)$$

$$д → дж \; / — ж \quad (or: \quad дж → джж)$$

In very careful, "elevated" *CSR*, speakers may as it were ignore all of these changes, and pronounce тщ, тш and дж as they are spelled. In normal *CSR*, as we have seen, тщ is pronounced чщ according to 3G2. In faster speech styles, the changes тш → чш and дж → джж* also take effect even across the / boundary (*RLP* 146-47),[39] e.g.:

МЛА́ДШИЙ ОБВЕТША́ЛЫЙ	О́ТЖИЛ	ПОДЖА́РЫЙ	ПОДШУ́БОЙ
мла́тший об/ветша́лый	бд/жил	под/жа́рый	пот/шу́бой
→мла́чший об/вечша́лый	бдж/жил	подж/жа́рый	поч/шу́бой
in this style	in this style		in this style

We should however point out that when a certain speed of enunciation is reached, the phonetic distinctions between the realizations of тщ, тш and дж on the one hand, and чщ, чш and джж respectively on the other, are virtually imperceptible.

For a similar instance of assimilation, see 3G3 below.

Finally, mention must be made of the stem -ЛУЧШ- occurring in, e.g., ЛУ́ЧШЕ and УЛУЧШИ́ТЬ. Avanesov (*RLP* 147) prescribes that this be pronounced as it is spelled (see p. 141 for details), but mentions that in conversational *CSR* it is often pronounced with -чч-, thus, лу́чче, улуччи́ть.[40]

3G3: The cluster тс is rewritten ц (*RLP* 140-41), e.g.:

ДЕ́ТСТВО	НАСЛЕ́ДСТВО
де́тство	на/слѐтство
→де́цтво	на/слѐцтво

Note especially words spelled with -НТСК- and -НДСК-;

---

*Note that джж is to be regarded as a combination of дж + ж and *NOT* a combination of д + жж!

where rule 3B1(b) is inoperative, rule 3G3 will now apply:

ДОКТОРА́НТСКИЙ		*BUT* ГИГА́Н<u>Т</u>СКИЙ	ШОТЛА́Н<u>Д</u>СКИЙ
n/c	(3B1(b))	гига́<u>нс</u>кий	шотла́<u>нс</u>кий
доктора́<u>нц</u>кий	(3G3)	n/c	n/c

N.B.: 3G3 does *NOT* apply across the / boundary,
e.g.:

ПОД СТЕНО́Й	ОТСЫ́ПАЛ	ОТСЮ́ДА*
по<u>т/с</u>тено́й	о<u>т/с</u>ы́пал	о<u>т/с</u>ьу́да
n/c	n/c	n/c

N.B.: 3G3 does *NOT* apply to reflexive verbal forms,
e.g.:

ОТМЕ́ТИТСЯ	УДА́СТСЯ
от/ме́ти<u>тс</u>ьа	у/да́<u>стс</u>ьа
n/c	n/c

(see 3L for the special rule dealing with reflexives).

Stylistic Variations (3G3)

In precise, "elevated" *CSR* the cluster тс may be pronounced цс (*RLP* 140-41);[41] and in conversational *CSR*, the same cluster occurring at the / boundary may be pronounced in this way also, i.e., т/с → ц/с, e.g.:

ОТСЫ́ПАЛ

от/сы́пал

→оц/сы́пал in this style

What we have said about тс applies equally to дз in one instance. The *digraph* дз (cf. 3.1.) represents a single affricate sound, i.e., the voiced counterpart of ц; and we do not therefore have to rewrite дз under normal conditions. At the / boundary, however, in conversational *CSR*, we find a parallel change to the one just given for т/с; namely, д/з**→ дз/з (*RLP* 146), e.g.:

*See 3Z, STYLISTIC VARIATIONS, for the pronunciation of this word in Conversational *CSR*.

**See note on page 30 re the sequence д/з in normal *CSR*.

НАДЗИРА́ТЕЛЬ

над/зира́тель

→надз/зира́тель   in this style

In practice, we doubt whether the fine distinctions between тс, цс and ц, and between дз and дзз,
are very noticeable in anything but very slow speech.
We also suggest that perhaps not many speakers make a
rigorous distinction in pronunciation between words
like ГИГА́НТСКИЙ, ШОТЛА́НДСКИЙ on the one hand and
ДОКТОРА́НТСКИЙ on the other.

3.6.2. "HUSHING" ASSIMILATIONS

Under this heading, we treat a number of rules which
involve the letters ш, ж, щ and жж; the first three
are complete assimilations, while the fourth is only
a partial assimilation.

Discussion and Examples

3H1: The cluster сш is rewritten шш (*RLP* 138), e.g.:

НЁСШИЙ   СШИ́ТЬ   ИЗ ШЁЛКА

ньо́сший   с/ши́ть   ис/шо́лка

→ньо́шший   ш/ши́ть   иш/шо́лка

3H2: All three clusters шч, сч, сщ are written щ
(*RLP* 138-39), [42] e.g.:

МУЖЧИ́НА   ПЕРЕБЕ́ЖЧИК   ИЗВО́ЗЧИК   ЖЁСТЧЕ

мужчи́на   пере/бе́шчик   из/во́счик   жо́сче

→мущи́на   пере/бе́щик   из/во́щик   жо́ще

Note that any intervening / boundary will have to be deleted:

<table>
<tr><td>ИЗ ЧА́Я</td><td>ИЗ ЩУ́КИ</td><td>РАСЩЕПИ́ТЬ</td></tr>
<tr><td>ис/ча́йа</td><td>ис/щу́ки</td><td>рас/щепи́ть</td></tr>
<tr><td>→ищ̅а́йа</td><td>ищ̅у́ки</td><td>ращ̅епи́ть</td></tr>
</table>

Stylistic Variations (3H2)

See 4.3. for different pronunciations of the letter щ.

The word ДО́ЖДЬ (→ до́шть by rule 3E1) was also treated according to rule 3H2 in the *OM* style, viz., → до́щ̅ (*RLP* 95).

In conversational *CSR*, 3H2 is frequently suspended, and the clusters are pronounced more or less *orthographically*, viz., some are pronounced just as they are spelled (e.g., РАСЩЕПИ́ТЬ); others have voicing-assimilations and/or consonant-deletions as in rules 3E, 3B (e.g., МУЖЧИ́НА → мушчи́на; ИЗВО́ЗЧИК → из/во́счик; ЖЁ́СТЧЕ → жо́сче); but the application of 3H2 is suspended. This is particularly noticeable when the / boundary is present.[43]

3H3: The cluster зж is rewritten as жж (*RLP* 139-40). (See 3.1. for further remarks about this digraph), e.g.:

<table>
<tr><td>БРЕ́ЗЖУЩИЙ</td><td>СЖЁГ</td><td>С ЖА́РУ</td></tr>
<tr><td>бре́зжущий</td><td>з/жёк</td><td>з/жа́ру</td></tr>
<tr><td>→бре́ж̲ж̲ущий</td><td>ж̲/жёк</td><td>ж̲/жа́ру</td></tr>
</table>

Stylistic Variations (3H3)

See 4.3. for details of variant pronunciations of жж.

The stem ДОЖД-, when followed by a vowel (and thus not devoiced, cf. ДОЖДЬ above), was also treated according to 3H3 in the *OM* style (*RLP* 140), thus,

ДОЖДА́

дождьба́

→дож̲ж̲ьба́ in this style; note "soft" жжь.

3H4: Both щ and ч are rewritten as ш, in a list of specified words, when occurring before н or т. Three occurring clusters are involved:

щн, e.g. (the only two words specified by Avanesov (*RLP* 83-4)),

ВСЕ́НОЩНЯЯ	ПО́МОЩНИК	*BUT*	ИЗЪЯ́ЩНЫЙ
фсе́нощньайа	по́/мощник		из/йа́щный
→фсе́ношньайа	по́/мошник		n/c

чн, e.g. (the list of specified words is a
lengthy one (*RLP* 142-45)),

КОНЕ́ЧНО	ЯИ́ЧНИЦА	*BUT*	ТО́ЧНО	НОЧНО́Й
коне́чно	йаийчница		то́чно	ночно́й
→коне́шно	йаийшница		n/c	n/c

чт, e.g.:

ЧТО́	ЧТО́-НИБУДЬ	*BUT*	НЕ́ЧТО
что́	что́/нибуть		не́/что
→што́	што́/нибуть		n/c

Note: (НЕ́ЧТО is the only exception to this rule; for
НИЧТО́, the rule is optional (*RLP* 145)).

Stylistic Variations (3H4)

Avanesov specifies long lists of words where чн
is obligatorily replaced by шн, where it may optionally be so replaced, and where it may never be so
replaced. Other authorities disagree as to a number
of details.[44]

Avanesov also allows for (but does not pre-
scribe) щн → шьн in a list of words, e.g., БУ́ДУЩНОСТЬ
→ бу́душьность. This must be regarded as an optional
variant for normal *CSR*, and shows the otherwise very
unusual combination шь (representing the for *CSR* unusual sound, "soft š"); this may also be considered
an example of degemination (cf. 3N(d)).

Other authorities extend the rule щн → шн to a
list of words longer than Avanesov's two.[45]

Note also that in some varieties of colloquial
Russian, ч → шь in *other* environments. This style
has even been noted in the speech of "representatives
of the Moscow intelligentsia",[46] in such words as
ТО́ЧКА, МА́ЛЬЧИК, ВЧЕРА́, КЛЮЧ, ЧЁРНЫЙ, О́ЧЕНЬ, ПЕЧА́ТЬ,
ПРО́ЧЕГО, ИЗУЧА́ЛИ, which become то́шька, ма́льшьик,
фшьера́, etc.

3.6.3. THE LETTER й

In rule 2A we rewrote all the "soft" vowels of
the *SO* so that the phonetic glide element would be
consistently represented in the *RO* by the letter й
(cf. p. 19). In doing this, we achieved a regularity

in the *RO*, but at a slight cost; for in fact the
"soft" vowel и does not always represent the sequence
йи. Where the й is superfluous, it must be removed.
This is done in two stages; firstly, in 3I, here; and
then in rule 3Y below (section 3.13.).

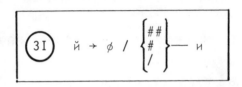

Discussion and Examples

й is deleted in initial position before и, *whatever* boundary precedes it; thus,

ЍВА	КÓТ И ПÓВАР	С ИГЛÓЙ
##йива##	кóт#йи#пóвар	с/йиглóй
→##йива##	кóт#и#пóвар	с/иглóй

Stylistic Variations (3I)

In the *OM* style, this rule did NOT apply to the
initial й in the pronominal forms ИМ, ИМИ, ИХ; these
words were pronounced WITH the glide element.[47]

ИМ

##йим##

n/c   in this style

3.7.   A THIRD CLASSIFICATION OF THE RUSSIAN LETTERS

We now assign some more labels to the Russian
consonant-letters, according to further schemes of
classification. Again, as in 2.1. and 3.1., phonetic
terms are used; and again, they are not necessarily
precise.

Our first scheme of classification uses three
broad articulatory phonetic terms for PLACES OF AR-
TICULATION. As labels, we use capital Latin letters
corresponding to the voiceless stops articulated at
each of these three places in the mouth.

The label P is used to designate the 10 letters,
and combinations of letter plus soft sign, which represent bilabial or labiodental consonants:

LABIALS (P):   п пь б бь ф фь в вь м мь

The label T is restricted to the 14 *paired*

consonant letters and letter-combinations which represent sounds produced at the dental and alveolar
regions of the mouth.*

PAIRED DENTALS (T):   т ть д дь с сь з зь н нь л ль
р рь

The eight letters and letter-combinations representing consonants articulated in the velar region
are labelled K:

VELARS (K):   к кь г гь х хь г' г'ь

Our second classification is into "Soft" and
"Hard" Consonants. It will be recalled that in 2.11.
the 21 consonant letters** are divided into three
groups: Paired (C_p), Unpaired Hard (H), and Unpaired
Soft (S). We now subdivide the Paired (C_p) consonant
letters into two groups according to whether the soft
sign follows them or not (thus: пь versus п, сь
versus с, рь versus р, and so on), and match one
group with the Unpaired Hard, and the other with the
Unpaired Soft, as follows:

HARD CONSONANTS (C_h) -- all C_p and H, viz.:

п б ф в м т д с з н л р
к г х г' *and* ц ш дз ж жж

SOFT CONSONANTS (C_s) -- all $C_{pь}$ and S, viz.:

пь бь фь вь мь ть дь сь зь нь ль рь
кь гь хь г'ь *and* ч щ дж й

Note that in those styles and circumstances
where жж must be considered as an *Unpaired Soft* Let-
ter-Combination (S) (cf. pp.30, 61) it will also have
to be classified as a Soft Consonant (C_s).

We have now assigned eleven classificatory labels. The following table, on which all the consonant-letters used in the Rules and all the labels are
displayed, may be useful for reference-purposes:

*For PAIRED CONSONANTS, see 2.111.

**Now numbering 25, with the addition of the letter г'
and the digraphs дз, дж, and жж.

	C							
	C_p						H	S
	P		T		K			
C_{vl}	п ф	пь фь	т с	ть сь	к х	кь хь	ц ш	ч щ
C_{vd}	б в	бь вь	д з	дь зь	г г'	гь г'ь	дз жж ж	дж
R	м	мь	н л р	нь ль рь				й
	C_h	C_s	C_h	C_s	C_h	C_s	C_h	C_s
	C_p						H	S

3.8. CONSONANT PLUS FRONT VOWEL SEQUENCES

In 2.1.2. we gave the preliminary and rather vague descriptive label of "front vowel letters" to е and и; and we also mentioned the alternative label "soft" for these letters, which is the traditional (although misleading) terminology. In the two rule-blocks in the present section we ensure that the terms are, at least, a little less vague and a little less misleading.

In 3K we insert the soft sign ь before the so-called "soft" vowels, since the chief significance of this traditional term lies in the fact that it is the preceding consonants which are "soft". We only insert ь after Paired Consonants (C_p), since it would be superfluous for the Unpaired Soft Consonants (S).

First, however, we have to ensure that those "soft" vowels which appear in the *SO* and *RO*, and before which consonants are NOT "soft", are replaced by the corresponding non-"soft" vowels. This is done in 3J.

3.8.1.　DISPOSITION OF FRONT VOWEL LETTERS

$$\boxed{3J}\quad \begin{array}{l} 1.\quad \text{и} \to \text{ы} \ / \left[\begin{array}{l} \text{(a)}\ \ \text{H} \ \text{———} \\[4pt] \text{(b)}\ \ C_h \left\{\begin{array}{l}\#\\/\end{array}\right\}\text{———} \end{array}\right] \\[30pt] 2.\quad \text{е} \to \text{э} \ / \left[\begin{array}{l} \text{(a)}\ \ \text{H} \ \text{———} \\[4pt] \text{(b)}\ \ C_p \ \text{———}\ \text{within stems of} \\ \qquad\qquad\qquad \text{loanwords (list)} \end{array}\right] \end{array}$$

Discussion and Examples

3J1(a):　The letter и is rewritten ы after Unpaired Hard Consonants (*RLP* 48-50),[48] e.g.:

ЖИ́ТЬ	ЦИ́РК	ВЗЯ́ВШИЙ	СШИ́ТЬ	БЕЗ ЖИ́РА	ВО́ЖЖИ
жи́ть	ци́рк	взьа́фший	ш/ши́ть	беж/жи́ра	во́жжи
→жы́ть	цы́рк	взьа́фшый	ш/шы́ть	беж/жы́ра	во́жжы

БРЕ́ЗЖИТ	and across the	МЕЖИРРИГАЦИО́ННЫЙ
бре́жжит	/ boundary:	меж/ирригацио́нный
→бре́жжыт		→меж/ырригацыо́нный

Stylistic Variations (3J1(a))

In some speech-styles (3.1.), жж is "soft" in specified instances--namely, when derived from зж (except at the / boundary). For this style and in these instances, 3J1(a) will not apply. Thus, as in normal *CSR*,

БЕЗ ЖИ́РА	ВО́ЖЖИ
беж/жи́ра	во́жжи
→беж/жы́ра	во́жжы

However, with "soft" жж: БРЕ́ЗЖИТ

бре́жжит

n/c　　in this style

In the *OM* style, and in the style spoken on the stage today, the adjectival ending -ий and verbal affix -ива- are replaced by -ый and -ыва- AFTER VELAR CONSONANTS also (*RLP* 23, 137, 155);[49] thus,

РУ́ССКИЙ	ТИ́ХИЙ	ОТСКА́КИВАТЬ	РАЗДЁРГИВАЛ
ру́сский	ти́хий	от/ска́кивать	раз/дьо́ргивал
→ру́сскый	ти́хый	от/ска́кывать	раз/дьо́ргывал
in this style		in this style	in this style

See 3T for the further fate of these particular strings in *OM*.

3J1(b): The letter и is rewritten ы when the preceding word ends in a "Hard" Consonant (C_h), (*RLP* 107-108). This applies equally well whether the boundary be the word-boundary # or the preposition-boundary /; for example, with #:

ДО́М И СА́Д	ЛУ́К ИЛИ ЧЕСНО́К	ГО́СИЗДА́Т
до́м#и#са́т	лу́к#или#чесно́к	го́с#изда́т
→до́м#ы#са́т	лу́к#ыли#чесно́к	го́с#ызда́т

БО̀РТИНЖЕНЕ́Р	СПО̀РТИНВЕНТА́РЬ
бо̀рт#инжене́р	спо̀рт#инвента́рь
→бо̀рт#ынжене́р	спо̀рт#ынвента́рь

and with /:

С ИГЛО́Й	К ИВА́НУ	ОТ ИГРЫ́
с/игло́й	к/ива́ну	от/игры́
→с/ыгло́й	к/ыва́ну	от/ыгры́

Of course, if the Phrase-Boundary ## intervenes, there will be no change, e.g.:

ОНА́ УШЛА́; ИВА́Н ГО́РЬКО ЗАПЛА́КАЛ.

##она́#у/шла́##ива́н#го́рько#за/пла́кал##

n/c

The *SO* normally shows the effects of this rule, so to speak, at the *prefix*-boundary; compare

SO ИГРА́ТЬ	СЫГРА́ТЬ	ОТЫ́ГРИВАТЬ
→ игра́ть	с/ыгра́ть	от/ы́гривать

However, there are some words which require application of the rule after the symbol / when this signifies the presence of a less common or foreign prefix, e.g.:

СВЕРХИЗЫ́СКАННЫЕ   ПАНИСЛАМИ́ЗМ

сверх/изы́сканныйе   пан/ислами́зм

→сверх/ы̲зы́сканныйе   пан/ы̲слами́зм

Stylistic Variations (3J1(b))

A widespread style of pronunciation (*RLP* 107) shows the non-application of this rule, especially when:
either (i) the preceding consonant is a velar, e.g.:

ЛУ́К Й́ЛИ ЧЕСНО́К?

лу́к#й́ли#чесно́к

n/c   in this style

or (ii) the preposition-boundary intervenes, e.g.:

ОТ ИВА́НА

от/и̲ва́на

n/c   in this style

and, most frequently, when both conditions are fulfilled simultaneously, as in, e.g.:

К ИВА́НУ

к/и̲ва́ну

n/c   in this style

3J2(a): The letter е is rewritten э after Hard Unpaired Consonants (*RLP* 57-58),[50] e.g.:

ЖЕНА́ ШЕ́СТЬ ЦЕ́НТР ПО́ЗЖЕ МОЖЖЕВЕ́ЛЬНИК ПОДЖЕ́ЧЬ

жена́ ше́сть це́нтр по́жже можжеве́льник под/же́ч

→жэна́ шэ̲сть цэ̲нтр по́жжэ̲ можжэве́льник под/жэ̲ч*

Stylistic Variations (3J2(a))

In those styles where жж is sometimes "soft" (see 3J1(a) above), this rule will not apply in these instances, hence

*Cf. page 30 on the distinction between дж and д/ж.

БЕЗ ЖЕНЫ́ *BUT* ПО́ЗЖЕ

беж/жены́   по́жже̲

→беж/ж<u>э</u>ны́   n/c   in this style

3J2(b): The letter е is rewritten э after Paired
Consonants (C$_p$) within the stems of specified loanwords (*RLP* 168-75), e.g.:

ШОССЕ́   ТЕ́ННИС   НА ДЕ́ЛЬТЕ

шоссе́   те́ннис   на/де́льте̲

→шосс<u>э</u>́   т<u>э</u>́ннис   на/д<u>э</u>́льте

Note the last example, на/де́льте, where the е IN THE
STEM is rewritten э but the е IN THE ENDING is left
unchanged.[51]
     Although it is true to say that ONLY LOANWORDS
show this change (i.e., do not show the palatalization
of consonants before е), it is difficult to be specific as to *which* loanwords are to be included on the
list.[52] Avanesov devotes more than six pages to the
problem (*RLP* 168-75); normally, look-up in a dictionary is to be recommended. See section 3.15. for a
general discussion of loanwords.
     One rule of thumb may be useful; according to
Avanesov, VELAR consonants are always "Russified",
that is, palatalized before е in loanwords; hence,
we may state that 3J2(b) never applies to velar consonants in loanwords, e.g.:

КЕ́МПИНГ   СХЕ́МА

ке́мпинк   схе́ма

n/c   n/c

Stylistic Variations (3J2(b))

     There is considerable variation with regard to
the list of words affected by this rule. From one
recent report[53] it can be seen that, in loanwords,
labials are more likely to be "softened" before е
than dentals; fricatives, more likely than stops; and
voiceless consonants, more likely than voiced ones.
This report shows that--contrary to *RLP*--velars in
loanwords are not *always* softened before е; see 3K
below.

3.8.2. PALATALIZATION BEFORE и AND е

$$\boxed{\left(\text{3K}\right) \quad C_p \to C_p\text{ь} \ / \ \rule{1cm}{0.4pt}\left\{\begin{matrix}\text{и}\\\text{е}\end{matrix}\right\}}$$

Discussion and Examples

The soft sign ь is inserted between every Paired Consonant and и or е, e.g.:

БИ́ТЬ   ГИ́БНУТЬ   ГДЕ́   ТЕА́ТР   КЕ́М   СОСЕ́ДИ
би́ть   ги́бнуть   где́   теа́тр   ке́м   сосе́ди
→бь̲и́ть   гь̲и́бнуть   гдь̲е́   ть̲еа́тр   кь̲е́м   сось̲е́дь̲и

ДЕ́ЛЬТЕ   КЕ́МПИНГ   СХЕ́МАМИ   ТЕ́ННИС   БРЕ́ЗЖИТ
дэ́льте   ке́мпинк   схе́мами   тэ́ннис   бре́жжыт
→дэ́льть̲е   кь̲е́мпь̲инк   схь̲е́мамь̲и   тэ́ннь̲ис   брь̲е́жжыт

ПАНИСЛАМИ́ЗМ   МОЖЖЕВЕ́ЛЬНИКИ   НАДЗИРА́ТЕЛЬ
пан/ысламм́зм   можжэвэ́льники   над/зира́тель
→пан/ысламь̲и́зм можжэвь̲е́льнь̲икь̲и над/зь̲ира́ть̲ель*

Stylistic Variations (3K)

1. Where, in certain styles (see p. 63 above) 3J1(b) is not applied, in defiance of the "norm", then 3K will of course apply: hence,

ОТ ИВА́НА   К ИВА́НУ
от/ива́на   к/ива́ну
→оть̲/ива́на in this style   кь̲/ива́ну in this style

2. In those styles where жж is "soft" under certain circumstances (see 3J1(a)), there may be some argument for considering жж as a Paired Consonant (C_p) rather than an Unpaired Consonant. In these styles there might therefore be grounds for inserting ь after жж in these particular instances, thus

БРЕ́ЗЖИТ → бре́жжь̲ит and ПО́ЗЖЕ → по́жжь̲е in this style

*Cf. discussion of дз and д/з on p. 30.

3.9. SPECIAL RULES FOR REFLEXIVES

There is considerable variation with regard to the pronunciation of the reflexive particle СЯ in *CSR* (and also, outside the "norm", of the other particle Сь). Broadly, speaking, the norm for СЯ can be covered by the two rules below. Note that they are in separate blocks (i.e., they are ordered) and that they apply ONLY to reflexive particles (and not to other instances of the string СЯ).

(3L)   in reflexives
т(ь)сьа → цца

(3M)   in reflexives
сьа → са / C_h —— except in participles

Discussion and Examples (*RLP* 162-65)

3L: The two strings тьсьа and тсьа are both rewriten цца,[54] e.g.:

ОТМЕ́ТИТЬСЯ	ОТМЕ́ТИТСЯ	УДА́СТСЯ	ЗАБО́ТЬСЯ
от/мье́тьитьсьа	от/мье́тьитсьа	у/да́стсьа	за/бо́тьсьа
→от/мье́тьи<u>цца</u>	от/мье́тьи<u>цца</u>	у/да́с<u>цца</u>	за/бо́<u>цца</u>

(see 3N for further changes to the string цц under some circumstances).

3M: In the reflexive morpheme сьа (as it now appears), the soft sign ь is omitted when the sequence follows any "Hard" consonant, *except in participial forms.* Thus,

НЁССЯ	ВЗЯ́ЛСЯ	БОЙ́ШЬСЯ	БОЙ́МСЯ	ЗАДО́ХСЯ
ньо́ссьа	взья́лсьа	боййшсьа	бойймсьа	за/до́хсьа
→ньо́с<u>са</u>	взья́л<u>са</u>	бойй<u>ша</u>	бойй<u>мса</u>	за/до́х<u>са</u>

When the preceding consonant is not a C_h there is no change, e.g.:

ПЛА́ЧЬСЯ   СДАВА́ЙСЯ

пла́ч<u>сьа</u>   з/дава́й<u>сьа</u>

n/c   n/c

There is no change if the word is a participle, e.g.:

ВЗЯ́ВШИМСЯ   СОБИРА́ЮЩИХСЯ

взьа́фшым<u>сьа</u>   со/бьира́йущих<u>сьа</u>

n/c   n/c

And when the сьа is not the *reflexive* particle, there is no change:

ВСЯ́   ЛОСО́СЯ

ф<u>сьа</u>́   лосо́<u>сьа</u>

n/c   n/c

Stylistic Variations (3L, 3M)

In the *CSR* prescribed by Avanesov, 3M is *optional* except after the two consonants л and с. Hence, of the five examples given above, нь<u>о́сса</u> and взьа́<u>лса</u> are the only pronunciations he accepts; but in the other cases he is less stringent, and allows both бойй<u>ша</u> and бойй<u>шсьа</u>; both бойй<u>мса</u> and бойй<u>мсьа</u>; both за/до́х<u>са</u> and за/до́х<u>сьа</u>.

As for the reflexive particle сьа after "Soft" consonants, he is quite rigorous; 3M does not apply, with *one* optional exception, namely, after ч; thus УЛЕ́ЧЬСЯ may be pronounced both as у/льé<u>чсьа</u> and as у/льé<u>чса</u>.

Further, Avanesov mentions the "rare" pronunciation of the other reflexive particle, СЬ, as с. This is especially uncommon, he says, after the "soft" vowels, И and Е. So, for example, for НЕСЛА́СЬ he prescribes нь<u>еслá</u>сь, and notes the rare variant нь<u>еслá</u>с; and for НЕСЛИ́СЬ, he prescribes нь<u>есльú</u>сь, and notes the *very* rare variant нь<u>есльú</u>с.

Panov describes four varieties of pronunciation, and ranks them as four historical stages, as follows:[55]

STAGE	STYLE	сьа	сь	(RO)
I	OM	са	с	
II		са	с (exc. after и, е)	
III	CSR	са (only after Cₕ)	n/c	
IV		n/c	n/c	

Thus, where *OM* had "hard" с(а) in all positions, there has been a gradual development over the past 75 years towards a style with "soft" сь(а) in all positions. There is much individual variation between the two extremes, but stage IV is very noticeable in the speech of the youngest generation. The *OM* style persists to a large extent in theatrical speech. The intermediate stages II and III demonstrate a phenomenon which is unusual (though not unique) for Russian: namely, PROGRESSIVE ASSIMILATION.[56]

Note that the norm prescribed by Avanesov corresponds to Panov's stage III; and pronunciations which he characterizes as "rare" are typical of Panov's stage II.

This is another example of "orthographic pronunciation" (see sections 1.1. and 3.16.). When and if stage IV becomes the norm for literary Russian, rule 3M will be unnecessary; and speakers will once again--as, it is assumed, they did until the 19th Century--be pronouncing most reflexive particles as they are spelled.

3.10. DEGEMINATION

The *SO* of *CSR* presents a large number of double, or GEMINATE, consonants. In alphabetical order, for example, we may cite АББА́ТСТВО, ВВЫ́СЬ, ЛЕГГО́РН, ПОДДА́ТЬ, ЖУЖЖА́ТЬ, ИЗЗЯ́БНУТЬ, АККУМУЛЯ́ТОР, ГУЛЛИ́ВЫЙ, ПРОГРА́ММА, ЦЕ́ННЫЙ, ГРУ́ППА, ТЕРРОРИ́СТ, РУ́ССКИЙ, ОТТАСКА́ТЬ, ЭФФЕ́КТ, ПАЛА́ЦЦО, ПИЧЧИКА́ТО. As can be seen from this list, *all* the *SO* consonant letters occur geminate except ЙЙ, ХХ, ЩЩ and ШШ; this last *does* occur in strings derived by 3H1, e.g., НЁСШИЙ → ньо́шшый.

Some of these geminate consonants are indeed pronounced long (for phonetic details, see 4.3.), but many are simplified to a single consonant (DE-GEMINATED). Before the rules are presented which specify degemination, two preliminary points should be made.

Firstly, in native *CSR* words, geminate consonants occur (for the most part) only at the point of contact between:

(a) a stem and a suffix (e.g., ЦЕ́Н-НЫЙ,* ГУЛ-ЛИ́ВЫЙ, РУ́С-СКИЙ; note also ВИ́ТЬ-СЯ → вьи́ц-ца, НЁСШИЙ → ньо́ш-шый)

---

*The boundary between stem and suffix shown here by a hyphen.

(b) a prefix and a stem (e.g., ВВЫСЬ → в/вы́сь, ПОД-
    ДА́ТЬ → под/да́ть, ИЗЗЯ́БНУТЬ → из/зьа́бнуть; note
    also СШИ́ТЬ → ш/шы́ть)

(c) a preposition and a noun or adjective (e.g.,
    ОБ БЕ́РЕГ, В ВОДЕ́, ПОД ДА́ЧЕЙ, ИЗ ЗИМЫ́, ОБ ПОЛ →
    о́п/пол, БЕЗ СО́ВЕСТИ → бьес/со́вьестьи, ОТ ТО́ПОРА,
    ИЗ ША́ПКИ → иш/ша́пкьи).

The only exceptions to this general rule (that geminate consonants in native words occur only at stem-
suffix boundaries and at / boundaries) are presented
by words spelled with жж or зж in the *SO*, e.g.,
МОЖЖЕВЕ́ЛЬНИК, ЕЗЖА́ТЬ → йежжа́ть.* Now Avanesov (*RLP*
128-29) states that there is (with a few exceptions)
no degemination across grammatical boundaries in
native *CSR* words; and this general rule includes the
string -нн-. However, the 8 examples he gives with
-нн- (*RLP* 129) have these letters following a *stressed* vowel, and one can only guess what he has in mind
for -нн- following *unstressed* vowels; as can be seen
in 3N(a) and 3N(b) below, this stress difference is a
very important one.[57]   Other authorities describe the
degemination of -нн- even after *stressed* vowels,[58]
and one can assume that this degemination occurs much
more frequently after unstressed vowels. We have
written our rules so that -нн- is normally degeminated after unstressed vowels. Since Avanesov is not
fully explicit on this point, we may be contradicting
his intentions in this one instance.
    Secondly, some consonants occur geminate ONLY in
loanwords. If we consider strings as they appear at
the present stage of derivation, i.e., after 3M, we
see that бб, вв, дд, зз, жж, пп, сс, тт, цц, шш occur (often with an intervening /) in both native and
borrowed words; but that гг, кк, мм, рр, фф, чч are
only encountered in borrowed words (see 3.15. for a
discussion of this category).
    In the following rule, we use two new notational
devices: firstly, C_1C_1, which means a *string of two
consonant letters which are identical, or which differ only by the presence or absence of the soft sign*;
and secondly, V̆, which means an *unstressed vowel*.

---

*See also p. 142 re the (normal) geminate pronuncia-
tion of щ.

$$\text{N.B. This Rule does not Apply to жж}$$

N.B. This Rule does not Apply to жж
N.B. This Rule does not Apply Across
      the / Boundary

(3N) $C_1C_1 \rightarrow C_1$ /

(a) $\begin{Bmatrix} \acute{V} \\ \tilde{V} \end{Bmatrix}$ —— V (list)

(b) $\check{V}$ —— V (exc. list)

(c) $\begin{Bmatrix} C \\ \# \\ \#\# \end{Bmatrix}$ —— (exc. list)

(d) —— $\begin{Bmatrix} C \\ \# \\ \#\# \end{Bmatrix}$ (exc. (1) list
                                      (2) "by analogy")

Discussion and Examples (*RLP* 128-34)

Note that two general restrictions on 3N: it never applies to жж, and never applies across the / boundary. If these restrictions are correlated with our remarks above, it will be seen that gemination--generally speaking--*occurs less frequently in native words*, than in loanwords.

3N(a) and 3N(b): Geminate consonants are degeminated between vowels as follows:

(a) *rarely* when the preceding vowel is *stressed*, and
(b) *normally* when the preceding vowel is *unstressed*.

The rule therefore specifies degemination *only* in a list of specified words in (*a*), and *everywhere except* in a list of specified words in (*b*).
Thus 3N(a) does not apply to most words such as:

КО́ННЫЙ   КА́ССА   ГРУ́ППА   ВА́ННА

ко́нный   ка́сса   гру́ппа   ва́нна

n/c   n/c   n/c   n/c

But 3N(a) does apply in a relatively short list of exceptional words, including, e.g.:

ОДИ́ННАДЦАТЬ   ТЕ́ННИС   КЛА́ССА

одьи́ннатцать   тэ́нньис   кла́сса

→одьи́натцать   тэ́ньис   кла́са

А́ФФИКС   МАШИ́ННОТРА́КТОРНЫЙ

а́ффьикс   машы̆нно#тра́кторный

→а́ф̱ьикс   машы̆но#тра́кторный

3N(b), on the other hand, applies to the majority of such words as:*

ОТМЕ́ТИТЬСЯ   ГРАММА́ТИКА   СКА́ЗАННЫЙ

от/мье́тьицца   грамма́тьика   ска́занный

→от/мье́тьиц̱а   грама́тьика   ска́зан̱ый

СУМАСШЕ́ДШИЙ   ОБЩЕ́СТВЕННЫЙ

сумашше́тшый   о́пще戁ствьенный

→сумаш̱е́тшый   о́пще戁ствьен̱ый

But 3N(b) fails to apply to a relatively short list of words, including, e.g.:

ГУЛЛИ́ВЫЙ   ЭЛЛИНИ́ЗМ   АССИМИЛЯ́ЦИЯ

гулльи́вый   элльиньи́зм   ассьимьиля́цыйа

n/c   n/c   n/c

According to the general restrictions, 3N(a) and 3N(b) do not apply to жж, or across the / boundary; thus,

Е́ЗЖУ   ЖУЖЖА́НИЕ   ИЗЖЕ́ЧЬ   О́ТТЕПЕЛЬ

йе́ж̱жу   жуж̱жа́ньийе   иж/жэ́ч   о́т/тьепьель

n/c   n/c   n/c   n/c

РО́ССЫПЬ   ПОДДЁВКА   ИЗЗЕЛЕНИ́ТЬ

ро́с̱/сыпь   под̱/дьо́фка   из̱/зьельеньи́ть

n/c   n/c   n/c

3N(c) and 3N(d): Geminate consonants are degeminated when contiguous to the phrase-boundary ##,** the word-boundary #, or another consonant.

*Cf. our remarks on geminate -нн- on p. 69 above.

**All examples given for word-initial and word-final position are valid also for phrase-initial and phrase-final position, of course.

There are very few exceptions.

3N(c) applies in word-initial position, e.g.:

ССО́РА

ссо́ра

→с̲о́ра

But 3N(c) does not apply across the / boundary, nor
to жж:

ССА́ДИТЬ	СЗА́ДИ	ВВО́Д	ЖЖЁТ	СЖЁГ
с/с̲а́дьить	з/з̲а́дьи	в/в̲о́т	жж̲о́т	ж/ж̲о́к
n/c	n/c	n/c	n/c	n/c

3N(c) applies after another consonant, e.g.:

ПОПА́СТЬСЯ	УДА́СТСЯ	ШЕСТЬДЕСЯ́Т
по/па́сцца	у/да́сцца	шездьдьесья́т
→по/па́с̲ца	у/да́с̲ца	шездьесья́т

Exceptions to 3N(c): The sequences -лзш- and -рзш-
do not show any degemination; a few other words are
also exceptional, e.g.:

УПО́ЛЗШИЙ	ЗАМЁРЗШИЙ	ЛАНДТА́Г
у/по́л̲ш̲ый	замьо́р̲ш̲ый	лантта́к
n/c	n/c	n/c

3N(d) applies before another consonant, e.g.:

РУ́ССКИЙ	МАСШТА́Б	КЛА́ССНЫЙ	АФФРИКА́Т
ру́сскьий	машшта́п	кла́ссный	аффрьика́т
→ру́с̲кьий	машта́п	кла́с̲ный	аф̲рьика́т

But 3N(d) does not apply across the / boundary:

РАЗЗНАКО́МИЛСЯ	БЕССПО́РНЫЙ	РАСШВЫРЯ́ТЬ
раз/знако́мьилса	бес/спо́рный	раш/швырья́ть
n/c	n/c	n/c

3N(d) applies in final position, e.g.:

ВА́ТТ	ГРУ́ПП	КЛА́СС	СТРЕПТОКО́КК
ва́тт	гру́пп	кла́сс	стрьептоко́кк
→ва́т	гру́п	кла́с	стрьептоко́к

Exceptions to 3N(d):

(i) *before another consonant*, specified words with the string -сск- show no degemination, e.g.:

МАТРО́ССКИЙ	ЭСКИМО́ССКИЙ
матро́сскьий	эскьимо́сскьий
n/c	n/c

(ii) *in final position*, "by analogy": if a word preserves geminate consonants when these occur before a vocalic ending, then gemination is preserved when there is *no* ending, if, AT THE SAME TIME, these consonants are fricatives or resonants (*RLP* 135).[59]

So, for example, whereas gemination is preserved in

КА́ССА	ВА́ННА
ка́сса	ва́нна
n/c	n/c

it is also preserved in final position:

КА́СС	ВА́НН
ка́сс	ва́нн
n/c	n/c

But when gemination is lost before a vowel, as in, e.g.:

КЛА́ССА	ГРА́ММА
кла́сса	гра́мма
→кла́са	гра́ма

then gemination is also lost in final position:

КЛА́СС	ГРА́ММ
кла́сс	гра́мм
→кла́с	гра́м

Although there is no degemination in

ГРУ́ППА

гру́<u>пп</u>а

n/c

there *is* degemination in final position:

ГРУ́ПП

гру́пп

→гру́<u>п</u>

since the final consonant is neither resonant nor
fricative. In view of the complexity of rule 3N,
dictionary look-up is recommended, especially where
loanwords are concerned. One minor rule-of-thumb may
be helpful: Avanesov states (*RLP* 132) that the
string -pp- is *always* degeminated.[60]

Stylistic Variations (3N)

The above rules, while complex, are still *generalizations* of Avanesov's often very specific recommendations. However, Avanesov does allow some lati-
tude in the pronunciation of geminate consonants,
especially in borrowed words.

Variations on the above rules can mostly be
covered by another general statement: careful speech
has less degemination, and ordinary conversational
CSR shows more.

The string -нн- (which, so Avanesov implies, is
never degeminated in native words: see our remark on
p. 69) is often degeminated, *even after stressed vowels*, when occurring in past passive participial
forms. This is common *even in slow careful styles*.

If the / boundary is "opaque" (see the discussion on page 35), then the rules will often apply,
even in careful speech; thus,

РАССТАНО́ВКА

рас?/стано́фка

→ра<u>ст</u>ано́фка

In conversational *CSR*, there is often degemination
even across "transparent" / *boundaries*, when two more
consonants follow, e.g.:

РАССТРÓЙСТВО

рас/стрóйство

→ра<u>с</u>трóйство   in this style

In a recent study of the pronunciation of gemi-
nates in loan words,[61] it was found that degemination
is LESS frequent when the consonants in question are
тдсзнц. The suggestion is that there is some correlation with the fact that in *native* words, these
are the most familiar geminate groups (see our remarks, page 69 above and general discussion of
loanwords, 3.15.).

Finally, note a form of degemination in conversational *CSR*: the string тц is simplified to ц in
the numerals ДВÁДЦАТЬ, ТРИДЦÁТЬ and their derivatives.[62]

3.11. PALATALIZATION ASSIMILATION

When a "hard" Paired Consonant is followed by a
"soft" consonant, the former may be "softened"
(PALATALIZED) in anticipation of the latter; or,
schematically, $C_p \rightarrow C_{p\flat}$ / — C_s. Like most assimilations in *CSR*, this is a REGRESSIVE assimilation: a
feature of a following consonant is adopted by a preceding consonant.[63]

However, there is a great deal of stylistic
variation with regard to this assimilation. It can
be characterized, in very general terms, as fluctu-
ating between two extremes: one where the palatalization assimilation rule is applied in all but a
few cases, and the other where it is almost never applied. There are very many complicating factors; and
the complete derivation of the pronunciations recommended by Avanesov (*RLP* 108-128) would require a
plethora of very intricate rules.

So that the rules should be reasonably compre-
hensible, we have abstracted from Avanesov's recommendations, firstly, three *general rules*; secondly,
the most important *restrictions* which must be placed
upon these; and thirdly, two of the most important
extensions to them.

3.11.1. GENERAL PALATALIZATION RULES AND RESTRICTIONS

1. P → Pь / — Pь ⎫
2. K → Kь / — Kь ⎬ (iterative)
3. T → Tь / — C$_S$ ⎭

restrictions*

(3P)

1. $\begin{bmatrix} п \\ б \\ к \\ г \\ т \\ д \end{bmatrix} \not\to \begin{bmatrix} пь \\ бь \\ кь \\ гь \\ ть \\ дь \end{bmatrix}$ / — / C$_S$ unless geminate

2. T $\not\to$ Tь / — $\begin{Bmatrix} pь \\ Kь \end{Bmatrix}$

3. н $\not\to$ нь / — Pь

4. $\begin{bmatrix} л \\ р \end{bmatrix} \not\to \begin{bmatrix} ль \\ рь \end{bmatrix}$ / — C$_S$ unless geminate

Discussion and Examples

The three general rules (3P1, 3P2, 3P3) can be summarized as follows: whereas *labials* and *velars* are normally only palatalized before *HOMORGANIC* soft consonants (i.e., labials are normally palatalized only before soft labials, and velars are normally palatalized only before soft velars), *paired dentals* are generally palatalized before ANY soft consonant.

The first restriction (3P restriction 1) affects consonants at all three major points of articulation (labial, dental, velar) but only involves the *stops*. This restriction states that stops are never palatalized by assimilation before the / boundary, i.e., in prefixes and prepositions, UNLESS they are the first consonant of a geminate cluster--that is, unless *the same stop* is repeated on the right hand side of the

*Note the use of the *barred arrow*, $\not\to$, in the restrictions. This symbol is to be read: "is NOT rewritten as".

/ boundary.*

Since the other three restrictions involve only dental consonants, we now exemplify the first two general rules (3P1, 3P2), and the first restriction insofar as it affects labials and velars.

To take labial consonants first: if the labial in question is not a stop, then 3P1 will apply, e.g.:

ЛИВМЯ	ДА́МБЕ	ВВЕДЁШЬ	В МИ́РЕ
льивмьа́	да́мбье	в/вьедьбш	в/мьи́рье
→льивьмьа́	да́мьбье	вь/вьедьбш	вь/мьи́рье

If it is a stop (п or б), it will be palatalized if the / boundary does not intervene, e.g.:

ЛЮБВЙ

льубвьй

→льубьвьй

When the / boundary intervenes, however, labial stops are not palatalized, e.g.:

ОБВЙТЬ	ОБМЕ́Н
об/вьйть	об/мьéн
n/c	n/c

If, however, *the same stop* occurs on the right hand side of the / boundary, then palatalization will still occur, e.g.:

ОББЕ́ГАЛ	ОБ ПÉНЬ
об/бьéгал	оп/пьéнь
→обь/бьéгал	опь/пьéнь

The velar consonants behave in the same way as the labials. If the velar is not a stop, then 3P2 will apply, e.g.:

---

*The inclusion of VELAR STOPS in this restriction is not warranted by any remarks made by Avanesov. They are included because (a) the inclusion makes the rule more general, and (b) the available evidence justifies it.[64]

ЛЁГКИЙ   МЯ́ГКИЙ

ль́бхкьий   мья́хкьий

→ль́бх<u>ьк</u>ьий   мья́х<u>ьк</u>ьий

If it is a stop (к or г), it will be palatalized, provided that the / boundary does not intervene, e.g.:

Э́ККЕР

э́ккьер

→э́к<u>ьк</u>ьер

When the / boundary intervenes, however, velar stops are not palatalized, unless *the same stop* occurs on the other side of the / boundary, e.g.:

К ХИ́ТРОМУ	К ХЕ́РЕСУ	К ГИ́ДУ	К КЕ́МПИНГУ
<u>к</u>/хьи́трому	<u>к</u>/хье́рьесу	г/гьи́ду	<u>к</u>/кье́мпьингу
n/c	n/c	<u>гь</u>/гьи́ду	<u>кь</u>/кье́мьпьингу

(This last example also shows the palatalization of м before пь by 3P1).

Note that we have only been considering HOMORGANIC clusters (labials before labials, velars before velars, etc.). If the cluster is not homorganic, labials and velars are not palatalized; thus:

Labials before soft dentals:

ХРЕ́БТИ	ФА́ВНЕ	О́БЩИЙ
хрье́<u>пт</u>ьи	фа́<u>вн</u>ье	о́<u>пщ</u>ий
n/c	n/c	n/c

Labials before soft velars:

СЁМГИ	КРЕ́ПКИЕ	СТА́ВКИ
сьо́<u>мг</u>ьи	крье́<u>пк</u>ьийе	ста́<u>фк</u>ьи
n/c	n/c	n/c

Velars before soft labials:

ХОРУ́ГВИ

хору́<u>гв</u>ьи

n/c

Velars before soft dentals:

ФРУ́КТЕ	НИГДЕ́
фру́<u>кть</u>е	ниг<u>дь</u>е́
n/c	n/c

We now move on to the consideration of *dentals*. The general rule, which states that paired dentals are palatalized before ANY soft consonant, is limited by *all four* of the restrictions. We exemplify these restrictions first.

3P restriction 1 states that the paired dental stops т and д are not palatalized before the / boundary, unless *the same stop* occurs to the right hand side of this boundary. Thus, e.g.:

ОТЛИ́ЧНО	ПОДБИ́Л	ОТЧЁТ
о<u>т</u>/льи́чно	по<u>д</u>/бьи́л	о<u>т</u>/чо́т
n/c	n/c	n/c

But with geminate dental stops, rule 3P3 applies, e.g.:

О́ТТИСК	ОДДЕ́Л
о́т/тьиск	од/дье́л
→о́<u>ть</u>/тьиск	о<u>дь</u>/дье́л

3P restriction 2 states that paired dentals are not palatalized either before рь, or before soft velars.* For example, before рь:

ТРИ́	ДРЕ́ВНИЙ	ЗРЕ́ЛЫЙ
<u>тр</u>ьи́	<u>др</u>ье́вньий	<u>зр</u>ье́лый
n/c	n/c	n/c

*Since neither labials nor velars are palatalized before soft dentals, this means that NO consonants become palatalized before рь; thus,

БРИ́ТЬ	ХРИ́ПЛЫЙ	ТРЕ́СК	СРЕДА́	ДО́МРЕ
<u>бр</u>ьи́ть	<u>хр</u>ья́плый	<u>тр</u>ье́ск	<u>ср</u>ьеда́	до́<u>мр</u>ье
n/c	n/c	n/c	n/c	n/c

Examples of paired dentals before soft velars:

ВÉТКИ	ЛÉССКИЙ	МОЗГИ́
вьѐткьи	льѐскьий	мозгьи́
n/c	n/c	n/c

3P restriction 3 states that the dental nasal н is not palatalized before soft labials, e.g.:

КОНВÉРТ	НА КАНВÉ	КОНФЕРÉНЦИЯ	САНБЕРНА́Р
конвьѐрт	на/канвьѐ	конфьерьѐнцыйа	санбьерна́р
n/c	n/c	n/c	n/c

3P restriction 4 states that the two liquids, л and р, are never palatalized by regressive assimilation, unless they are geminate.[65]   In fact р is sometimes palatalized, but under particular circumstances which require the special rule 3R below. We therefore only exemplify the fate of non-geminate л here:

ЖÉЛЧЬ	МÓЛВИТЬ	ЖЕЛТÉТЬ
жóлч	мóлвьить	желтьѐть
n/c	n/c	n/c

When the geminate strings лль and ррь occur, 3P3 applies:

ГУЛЛИ́ВАЯ	Э́ЛЛИН	ИРРЕГУЛЯ́НО
гулльи́вайа	э́лльин	иррьегульа́рно
→гульльи́вайа	э́льльин	ирьрьегульа́рно

Having presented examples of instances where regressive palatalization does *not* affect paired dentals, we now may exemplify instances where 3P3 DOES apply.

This involves clusters with dentals before soft labials, e.g.:

ЗВÉРЬ	ЧÉТВЕРТЬ	ПОСПÉЕШЬ
звьѐрь	чѐтвьерть	по/спьѐйеш
→зьвьѐрь	чѐтьвьерть	по/сьпьѐйеш

СФÉРЕ	РАЗМÉТИЛИ
сфьѐрье	раз/мьѐтьильи
→сьфьѐрье	разь/мьѐтьильи

3P3 applies in a very large number of words which have homorganic dental clusters (dentals before soft dentals), e.g.:

ЛЁ́ТЧИК	В КА́ССЕ	КОНЧА́ТЬ	МЕ́ДЛИТЬ
льо́тчик	ф/ка́ссье	конча́ть	мье́длить
→льо́тьчик	ф/ка́сьсье	конрьча́ть	мье́дльлить

АНТИ́К	С НИ́МИ	ЧЕРЕЗ НЕВУ́	С ТЁТЕЙ
антьи́к	с/ньи́мьи	черьез/ньеву́	с/тьо́тьей
→аньтьи́к	сь/ньи́мьи	черьезь/ньеву́	сь/тьо́тьей

Note that all the palatalization assimilation rules in 3P are ITERATIVE; i.e., they are to be repeatedly applied from right to left throughout all consonantal clusters, e.g.:

ЖЕ́НСТВЕННОСТЬ

→жэ́нствьеность

→жэ́нстьвьеносьть

→жэ́нсьтьвьеносьть

→жэ́ньсьтьвьеносьть

3.11.2.   EXTENSION OF PALATALIZATION ASSIMILATION RULES

Discussion and Examples

This extension to the palatalization assimilation rule 3P states that the fricative letter в is palatalized when occurring before й, e.g.:

ВЪЕЗДНО́Й	ВЪЯ́ВЕ	В Ю́БКАХ
в/йездно́й	в/йа́вье	в/йу́пках
→вь/йездно́й	вь/йа́вье	вь/йу́пках

Review: Palatalization of Consonants Before й

Since the rules for palatalization assimilation are very complex in Russian, it will be useful to review them in connection with the letter й, which is a

particularly interesting case. In strings of letters
as derived by the rules up to and including 3N, eight
different "hard" consonant letters occur before й in
native *CSR* words.* In every case, the prefix- and
preposition-boundary / intervenes between the consonant and the letter й. The letters involved are:
the four stop letters б, т, д, г and the four fricative letters в, с, з, х.

Our rules and restrictions block the palatalization of the four stops before й. б is not palatalized, since labials are only softened before soft
labials (3P1). г is not palatalized, since velars
are only softened before soft velars (3P2). т and д
would be palatalized before й by rule 3P3, but the
palatalization is blocked by 3P restriction 1, since
the / boundary intervenes. Hence, *NO STOPS ARE PALA-
TALIZED BEFORE* й.

The fricative letters, however, present a different picture. с and з are palatalized before й by
3P3; and в is palatalized before й by the latest
rule, 3Q. On the other hand, х is not palatalized
before й by rules 3P or 3Q.[66] To summarize: *LABIAL
AND DENTAL FRICATIVES ARE PALATALIZED, AND VELAR
FRICATIVES ARE NOT PALATALIZED, BEFORE* й.

Examples, showing derivation through 3N and then
by 3P and 3Q.

Stop letters: no palatalization before й:

	ОБЪЯВЛЯ́ТЬ	ОТЪЕ́ХАТЬ	ПОДЪЯРЕ́МНЫЙ
(3N)	об/йавльа́ть	от/йе́хать	под/йарье́мный
(3P, 3Q)	n/c	n/c	n/c

	ОТ Я́МЫ	НАД ЁЛКОЙ	ВОКРУГ Ю́НОШИ
(3N)	от/йа́мы	над/йо́лкой	вокруг/йу́ношы
(3P, 3Q)	n/c	n/c	n/c

Fricative letters: palatalization for в, с, з before
й:

---

*The many "soft" consonant letters occurring at this
stage before й--e.g., ч (КОША́ЧЬИ → коша́чйи), ль
(БЕЛЬЁ → бьельйо́), ть (ПИТЬЯ → пьитьйа́)--present no
problems for us here, since they are already palatal
or palatalized.

	ВЪЕ́ЗД	СЪЕ́СТЬ	БЕЗЪЯЗЬ́ЧНЫЙ
(3N)	в/йе́ст	с/йе́сть	бьез/йазы́чный
(3P)	n/c	→сь/йе́сьть	бьезь/йазы́чный
(3Q)	→вь/йе́ст	n/c	n/c

	ЧЕРЕЗ Я́МУ	НАПРОТИВ Я́ХТЫ
(3N)	черьез/йа́му	напротьив/йа́хты
(3P)	черьезь/йа́му	n/c
(3Q)	n/c	→напротьивь/йа́хты

But no palatalization for х before й:

	ДВУХЪЯ́РУСНЫЙ
(3N)	двух/йа́русный
(3P)	n/c
(3Q)	n/c

The above remarks apply to NATIVE *CSR* words only. In LOANWORDS, where there is no / boundary,[67] all paired dental letters will be palatalized by 3P3 before й, e.g.:

	АДЪЮТА́НТ	ИНЪЕ́КЦИЯ	ДИЗЪЮ́НКЦИЯ
	адйута́нт	инйе́кцыйа	дьизйу́нкцыйа
(3P)	→адьйута́нт	иньйе́кцыйа	дьизьйу́нкцыйа

The б in the following example, however, remains unpalatalized, since labials are softened only before soft labials (3P1):

	СУБЪЕ́КТ
	субйе́кт
(3P, 3Q)	n/c

Stylistic Variations (3P, 3Q)

Rules 3P and 3Q generate, by and large, the style of pronunciation prescribed by Avanesov. He further allows a large number of options for certain consonantal combinations under certain circumstances, and makes a number of very fine distinctions.[68]

The style of pronunciation prescribed in *RLP* for regressive palatalization assimilation can be placed about half-way between the *OM* style and the one which

recent investigations have ascertained for speakers
of conversational *CSR*.[69] Investigations have been
numerous, and their results not always in agreement;
but the general concensus can be summarized in two
tables, as below.

In these tables, C_2 and C_1 denote the following
and preceding consonants, respectively. The plus
sign + signifies that C_1 is palatalized; the minus
sign - that C_1 is not palatalized; and ±, that palatalization is optional.

OM style

C_1 \ C_2	Pь	Tь	Kь
P	+	-	±
T	±	+	±
K	-	-	+

Conversational
CSR style

C_1 \ C_2	Pь	Tь	Kь
P	±	-	-
T	±	±	±
K	-	-	+

Most investigators agree about most of the nine
combinations tabulated here for each style; but there
is considerable disagreement about the combination
TPь, and there are minor dissensions about the combinations PPь, TTь, and TKь.

It may be noted that in *OM* our general rules 3P1
and 3P3 are obligatory; and that in conversational
CSR, only 3P3 is obligatory.

If the general tendency which is apparent in the
above tables is to continue, only those consonants
which are spelled "soft" in the *SO* will be pronounced
"soft" by speakers of *CSR*; i.e., we have another apparent example of the trend towards "spelling pronunciation" (see 3.16.).

Regressive palatalization assimilations appear to
occur more frequently under certain circumstances.
These fall into four groups:

A. Stylistic: in the *OM* style, and those close to it (see above).

B. Phonetic: when the articulatory nature of the consonants concerned, and of the preceding and following vowels, is of a certain kind; and in slower, more careful speech.[70]

C. Grammatical: when there are no grammatically related forms not showing palatalization assimilation; and when there is no grammatical boundary, or when the boundary is of a more "opaque" nature.[71]

D. Lexical: in certain lexical classes.[72]

Each scholar who has studied this phenomenon emphasizes a different combination of factors.[73] It should be noted that, whatever the eventual consensus may be, the factors are numerous and often competing; hence, precise specifications will probably be out of the question.

Note that a large number of LOANWORDS have been observed to show palatalization assimilation in *geminate* clusters.[74]

Since so many factors are involved, OBSERVATION OF THE GENERAL RULE 3P IS RECOMMENDED FOR MOST PRACTICAL PURPOSES.

3.11.3. SPECIAL RULE FOR p

In 3P above, the letter p is not palatalized except in those rare instances where the string ppь occurs (see 3P restriction 4). In fact, p is sometimes palatalized, but the circumstances are idiosyncratic and require a special rule.

Avanesov (*RLP* 120-22) is far from precise on this matter. Firstly, he distinguishes between "soft", "half-soft", and "hard" p; and secondly, he allows some words to be pronounced with two or even all three of these varieties of p. Since we are aiming at a set of relatively simple and general rules, we have had to extract some regular statement from this confusion. Our rule 3R specifies palatalization for those forms which Avanesov says must have, or may have, "soft" p, and excludes those forms which he says are "hard" or "half-soft" but never "soft".

$$(3R) \quad \text{р} \rightarrow \text{рь} \; / \; \begin{cases} (a) \begin{Bmatrix} \text{é} \\ \text{э́} \end{Bmatrix} \text{---} \; C_s \\[6pt] (b) \begin{Bmatrix} \text{и} \\ \text{е} \end{Bmatrix} \text{---} \; C_s \begin{Bmatrix} \text{и} \\ \text{е} \end{Bmatrix} \\[6pt] (c) \hspace{4cm} (\text{list}) \end{cases}$$

Discussion and Examples

Note that in 3R(a) and 3R(b), not only do the *following* letters have to be specified, but *preceding* letters also figure in the specification of the environment.

3R(a): The letter р is rewritten рь when it occurs before any soft consonant if, at the same time, it is *also* preceded by stressed é or э́:

ВЕ́РФЬ	СМЕ́РТЬ	ПЕ́РСИК
вье́рфь	сьмье́рть	пье́рсьик
→вье́рьфь	сьмье́рьть	пье́рьсьик

ПЕ́РВЕНЕЦ	ВЕ́РСИЯ
пье́рвьеньец	вье́рсьийа
→пье́рьвьеньец	вье́рьсьийа

Note that the unusual formulation of 3R(a) reflects a particular historical origin for most of the words concerned.[75]

3R(b): The letter р is rewritten рь if it is immediately preceded by an и or е and if it is immediately followed by a soft consonant and another и or е, e.g.:

МЕРСИ́	ТЕРПЕ́ТЬ	КИРПИ́Ч
мьерсьи́	тьерпье́ть	кьирпьи́ч
→мьерьсьи́	тьерьпье́ть	кьирьпьи́ч

3R(c): The letter р is rewritten рь in a list of three specified words, viz.:

БÓРЩ   СКÓРБЬ   ЦÉРКОВЬ

бóрщ   скóрпь   цэ́ркофь

→бóр̭ьщ   скóр̭ьпь   цэ́р̭ькофь

3R does not normally apply, however, when the preceding vowel is not е or и; thus,

ПÁРТИЯ   ÁРМИЯ   СГÓРБИЛСЯ   ШКÝРНИК

пáр̭тьийа   áр̭мьийа   э/гóрбьилса   шкýр̭ньик

n/c   n/c   n/c   n/c

3R does not normally apply, either, when the following consonant is "hard", thus,

ЧЕТВÉРГ   ПÉРВЫЙ

четьвьéр̭к   пьéр̭вый

n/c   n/c

Stylistic Variations (3R)

Panov insists that our rule 3R has been quite
eradicated from *CSR*; and that ЦÉРКОВЬ is the *only*
word now pronounced with р̭ before another consonant,[76] the word most typical of the archaic *OM*
style. In *OM*, palatalization of р was even more
widespread than in the style prescribed in *RLP*; for
example, it was normal after other vowels, e.g., in
ÁРМИЯ → áр̭мьийа in this style.

3.12. VOWEL-REDUCTION

Here, even more than in any preceding section,
there is a great deal of fluctuation between different varieties of pronunciation within *CSR*. The rules
given below (3S - 3X) derive one of the styles sanctioned by Avanesov (*RLP* 58-80, 152-68, 175-76),
namely that style which other Soviet scholars report
as being most widespread; in *Stylistic Variations*
other styles (both "permitted" and "nonpermitted"
options) will be briefly described.

In this book, vowel-reduction is dealt with in
two separate stages. The *first stage*, which appears
in the present section, is concerned only with instances where there is a loss of distinctions between
vowels (as they are represented in the *SO* and modi-
fied by rule-blocks 2A, 3J), i.e., when it is convenient to rewrite one vowel as a second vowel, since

both are pronounced in the same way. This phenomenon
is traditionally called NEUTRALIZATION, since a distinction is neutralized (or, eliminated) in a particular environment.

An example of the neutralization of a distinction between vowels in a particular environment in
English is provided by the words MELÓDIOUS and MIRÁC-
ULOUS (where the pronunciation of stressed Ó in one
word is different from the pronunciation of stressed
Á in the other), and the words MÉLODY and MÍRACLE
(where the O and A, now both unstressed, are pronounced the same). Here we may say that the distinction between O and A is *neutralized* when the stress
falls on the preceding syllable.[77]

A frequently-cited example in *CSR* is that of o
and a in, firstly, вол and вал (where the vowels are
stressed, and pronounced differently), and secondly,
волы́ and валы́ (where the vowels are unstressed and
pronounced the same); here we may say that the distinction between stressed o and a is *neutralized* when
the stress falls on the following syllable.[78]

This example illustrates the fact that the
choice of vowel-symbols in our rules is, to some extent at least, arbitrary. Since unstressed o and a
in pretonic position are pronounced the same, we may
do one of three things: (i) we may rewrite o as a;
(ii) we may rewrite a as o; or (iii), we may rewrite
both unstressed vowels as some third symbol--say, ь.

We have rejected options like (iii) in general
to avoid the unnecessary proliferation of symbols.
We have rejected options like (ii) in general, according to the popular procedure whereby the vowel-
letter chosen is the one which, under its most
straightforward phonetic interpretation, is closest
to the sound actually pronounced. In this way, we
shall derive a *PO* which will reflect the actual pronunciation of an utterance as faithfully as can be
achieved using the basic stock of letters in the *SO*.*

The *second stage* of vowel-reduction is presented
in 4.1., where a more detailed phonetic transcription
is developed.

3.12.1. SPECIFICATION OF VOWEL-STRENGTHS

In order to specify the phonetic quality of a
vowel in Chapter Four, we shall need to know its

---

*г' is the only non-standard letter appearing in the
PO.

tonic or stress position; to know, for example,
whether the vowel is in stressed position, in the
syllable immediately preceding the stressed vowel, or
in some other position. It is convenient to introduce this information now, and to take advantage of
it in the vowel-reduction rules proper (3T - 3X).

We already have two stress-markings present in
our transcription, namely the acute accent (´) which
indicates PRIMARY STRESS, and the grave accent (`)
which indicates SECONDARY STRESS. These markings
will remain unaltered, and will be carried over into
the Phonetic Transcription which is derived in Chapter Four.

With the unmarked, "unstressed" vowels, these
two markings constitute a three-member SCALE OF RE-
LATIVE DEGREES OF STRESS.[79] Such a relative scale
could be designed to show a number of fine distinctions; for example, a five-point scale has been suggested.[80] For our purposes, however, a *four-point
scale* is quite adequate; and this means that we shall
have to distinguish between two degrees of "unstressed" vowels, i.e., between what we shall henceforth
call HALF-STRESSED VOWELS and UNSTRESSED VOWELS proper.[81] *Half-stressed vowels* will be identified by
the accent (ˆ), according to their position and environment as specified in 3S below; *unstressed vowels*
proper will be left unmarked.[82]

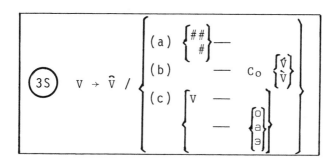

Discussion and Examples

3S states that vowels without primary or secondary stress are to be marked with a superscript ˆ in
three types of environment:

(a) when occurring in absolute word-initial position
(after the ## and # boundaries);

(b) in "immediate pretonic" position, that is, in a
syllable immediately preceding the stressed

syllable;* and

(c) when *either* following any other vowel, *or* preceding о, а or э. For further discussion of this environment, see NOTE ON VOWEL-CLUSTERS below.

 Note that 3S(b) and 3S(c) follow the general rule stated at the end of 3.2. (page 36), and therefore operate across the / boundary.

EXAMPLES

ГО́РОД	ГОРОДА́	ГОРОДОВО́Й	ЗА́ ГОРОДОМ	ИНОГОРО́ДНЫЙ
го́рот	города́	городово́й	за́/городом	иногоро́дный
→ n/c	горо̭да́	городо̭во́й	n/c	и̭ного̭ро́дный

ОДЕЯ́ЛО	ОБОРО́НОСПОСО́БНОСТИ	УРА́ЛМА̀ШЗАВО́Д
одьейа́ло	оборо̀но#спосо́бносьтьи	ура̀л#ма̀ж#заво́д
→о̭дьейа́ло	о̭боро̀но#спо̭со́бносьтьи	у̭ра̀л#ма̀ж#за̭во́д

ПОД ЛА́МПОЙ	ОТ ОДНОГО́	О ЯЗЫКЕ́
под/ла́мпой	от/однобо́	о/йазыкье́
→по̭д/ла́мпой	о̭т/одно̭во́	о̭/йазы̭кье́

ДОСТОПРИМЕЧА́ТЕЛЬНОСТИ	ВЫ́ТОПТАННОЕ
достопрьимьеча́тьельносьтьи	вы́/топтанойе
→достопрьимьэ̭ча́тьельносьтьи	n/c

Note On Vowel-Clusters (*RLP* 51-54)[84]

 The formulation of 3S(c) covers most, but not all, occurrent sequences of TWO VOWELS in *CSR*.
 3S(c) states first that, if it is unstressed, the SECOND member of such a sequence will always be marked ˆ, as in the following examples (note that changes due to 3S(b) are also included here):

---

*The symbol C$_O$ is to be read as "ANY NUMBER OF CONSONANTS, INCLUDING NONE." This device is used to indicate that only the vowels are important and that the number of intervening consonants is irrelevant.[83]

НА ОКНЕ́   У ОДНОГО́   НЕОБХОДИ́МО
на/окнье́   у/одново́   нье/опходьи́мо
→на̂/о̲кнье́   у̂/о̲дново̂   нье̂/о̲пхо̂дьи́мо

НЀОРЕАЛИ́ЗМ   ЗООПА́РК
нэ̀о#рьеальи́зм   зоопа́рк
→нэ̀о̲#рье̂а̲льи́зм   зо̂о̲па́рк

3S(c) also states that the FIRST member of a two-vowel cluster will however be marked ˆ *only* if the SECOND member is о, а or э. This would apply to the first vowel of each cluster in all of the examples just cited, as well as in, e.g.:

РЕАКЦИОНЕ́Р   СОЦИАЛИСТИ́ЧЕСКИЙ
рьеакцыонье́р   соцыальисьтьи́ческьий
→рье̂а̲кцы̂о̲нье́р   соцы̂а̲льисьтьи́ческьий

ПОЭТИ́ЧЕСКИЙ   ДЀАЭРА́ЦИЯ
поэтьи́ческьий   дэ̀#аэра́цыйа
→по̂э̲тьи́ческьий   дэ̀#а̂э̲ра́цыйа

If the SECOND member of a two-vowel cluster is *not* а, о or э (which means: if the second member is y*), then the FIRST member will be left unmarked, e.g.:

НЕУРЯДИ́ЦА   ПАУКООБРА́ЗНЫЙ   НА УГА́Д   ПОУБИРА́ТЬ
нье/урьадьи́ца   паукообра́зный   на/уга́т   по/убьира́ть
→нье/у̲рьа̂дьи́ца   па̂у̲ко̂о̲бра́зный   на/у̲га́т   по/у̲бьи̂ра́ть

Sequences of THREE VOWELS and of FOUR VOWELS are not discussed in *RLP*. These can be divided into two groups:

(i) Those which occur in compound words (cf. p. 32), and have an intervening # boundary because they do not all belong to the same *CW*. These pose no problem

*No other possibilities exist at this point. Post-vocalic и and е are rewritten ий and йе by 2A3; and ы does not occur after vowels in *CSR*.

in 3S, since each *CW* is considered separately, e.g.:

КВÀЗИАЭРОТЕРАПЍЯ   РÀДИОАУ́КАНЬЕ

квàзьи#аэротьерапьи́йа   рàдьио#ау́каньйе

→квàзьи#а͡эротьерап͡льи́йа   ра̀дьи͡о#а͡у́каньйе

(ii) Those which occur within *IW*'s or *CW*'s. Some of
these *will* pose problems when 3S is applied. For
example, the cluster вау in the word НЕАУТЕНТЍЧНЫЙ →
нье/аутэньтьи́чный will be marked е͡/а͡у by 3S(c), although it is to be doubted that this marking will
ensure the correct phonetic derivation. The same
applies to, e.g., ОУЭНЍЗМ → оуэньи́зм → о͡у͡эньи́зм; we
doubt whether this word is commonly pronounced as
four syllables in any style of *CSR*. To our knowledge
the only fully *native* *CSR* word with a three-vowel
cluster is the uncommon word ПРОАУ́КАТЬ.[85] Other
words with three-vowel clusters, and all words with
four-vowel clusters, are composed of loanword elements, either in part (e.g., НЕАУТЕНТЍЧНЫЙ, ДВУАУГ-
МЕ́НТНЫЙ, НЕОООЛЍТОВЫЙ) or in whole (e.g., КВÀЗИАЭРО-
ТЕРАПЍЯ, ДÀУЭСИЗÁЦИЯ, БРÀНДМÁУЭР).
     We do not provide special rules for three- and
four-vowel clusters for three reasons:

(i) Avanesov's silence on the subject;

(ii) The lack of data on how these words are normally pronounced, and data on the number of stressed
syllables they contain;

(iii) The fact that the necessary rules to derive
the most probable pronunciation would be extremely
complex.
     As a rule of thumb, we suggest that, when in
doubt, three or four unstressed vowels occurring con-
secutively should all be marked ⌃ but that the prob-
ability be borne in mind that one or more of them
should be considered as unstressed vowels proper
rather than as half-stressed vowels, or that part of
the cluster may be even elided in some way.

Stylistic Variations (3S)

     In rapid conversational Russian, not only are
some half-stressed vowels reduced to unstressed
vowels proper, and many unstressed vowels omitted altogether (see 5.2. and 5.4. respectively), but a
number of vowel-clusters are replaced by single vowels (see 5.2.8.).
     Avanesov (*RLP* 76-77) allows the optional

reduction of the cluster ôô to ô (but never, for *CSR*, to o) in five words: ВООБЩЁ, СООБРАЗИ́ТЬ, ВООБРАЗИ́ТЬ, СООБРАЖЕ́НИЕ, ВООБРАЖЕ́НИЕ, e.g.:

ВООБЩЁ

во/опщё

→вô/ôпщё by 3S above, or further → вôпщё

As an optional variant in *CSR*, vowels occurring after the / boundary may be treated as half-stressed rather than unstressed; i.e., 3S(a) is extended to apply after all boundaries, including the / boundary, e.g.:

ОТ ОДНОГО́

от/одново́

→ôт/одновô by 3S above, or optionally → ôт/ôднôго́

In loanwords, clusters of two vowels including и, ы or у may have this vowel unstressed, in contradiction to 3S(c).* Thus, according to 3S,

АУТЕНТИ́ЧНО	АССОЦИА́ЦИЯ	ПИАНИ́СТ	ДРЕДНО́УТ
аутэньтьи́чно	асоцыа́цыйа	пьианьи́ст	дрьедно́ут
→а̂у̲тэньтьи́чно	а̂соцы̲а́цыйа	пьи̲а̲ньи́ст	дрье̲дно́у̲т

However, the following derivations are probably to be preferred as more representative of *CSR*:

а̂у̲тэньтьи́чно а̂соцы̲а́цыйа пьи̲а̲ньи́ст дрье̲дно́у̲т

These vowels are frequently reduced EVEN FURTHER, without actually being elided; in other words, they are replaced by GLIDES:** и by й, ы by ы̌, and у by у̌;[86] thus,

а̂у̲тэньтьи́чно а̂соцы̲а́цыйа пьйа̲ньи́ст дрье̲дно́у̌т

As in all loanwords (cf. 3.15. below), there is considerable vacillation.[87] Avanesov (*RLP* 79-80) mentions only a dozen examples from the hundreds of

---

*For the fate of э in one word as prescribed in *RLPU*, see АЭРО- in 3Z below.

**For an example of this as a prescribed pronunciation, see ИУДАИ́ЗМ in 3Z.

loanwords involved, and is extremely imprecise as to
their recommended pronunciation.

     Note that for some of the words involved, there
are *alternative spellings* in the *SO*;[88] and that for a
few words, only one spelling is accepted, but alternative pronunciations are allowed.

3.12.2. REDUCTION OF ы

(3T) ы → а / —— ва   in verbal stems

Discussion and Examples

     The ы of -ыва- verbal stems is rewritten а;[90]
this applies also to nouns derived from -ыва- verbal
stems. Note that this rule applies only to unstressed ы and not to ы̂. Examples:

РАССКА́ЗЫВАЮ   СПРА́ШИВАЛИ   ВВЁРТЫВАНИЕ

ра̂с/ска́зывайу   с/пра́шывальи   в/вьо́ртываньийе

→ра̂с/ска́за̲вайу   с/пра́ша̲вальи   в/вьо́рта̲ваньийе

BUT   СРЫВА́Ю

        с/ры̲ва́йу

           n/c

Stylistic Variations (3T)

     In *OM* and the speech of older generations of *CSR*
speakers, this rule applies also to the adjectival
ending -ый,

ДО́БРЫЙ   СКО́ВАННЫЙ

до́брый   с/ко́ваный

→до́бр ай   с/ко́ван ай

        in this style

     Note that when in 3U below the unstressed ad-
jectival ending -ой is rewritten -ай, the result will
be a neutralization of the distinction between these
endings: the two orthographically different endings
will be pronounced the same. In other words, the *OM*
style does not distinguish in pronunciation between
the unstressed endings -ой and -ый, a fact which

corresponds to the historical origin of these endings
in *CSR*. The younger generations and speakers of the
style prescribed by Avanesov do, however, make this
distinction. This is another example of "spelling
pronunciation", since the ending -ый was first introduced orthographically (to the *SO*) in accordance
with Church Slavonic writing traditions.[91]

Similarly, the *OM* style pronounced the и in
-ива- verbal stems and the adjectival endings -ий,
AFTER VELARS, as if they were written -ава-, -ай; cf.
p. 61 above, where in Stylistic Variations to 3Л(a)
we suggest the rule for *OM*, и → ы in these contexts.
Following this suggestion, we now suggest the further
rule for *OM*: ы → а in -ива- verbal stems and the
adjectival ending -ий, e.g.:

РУ́ССКИЙ	СТРО́ГИЙ	ТИ́ХИЙ	ОТСКА́КИВАТЬ
ру́скый	стро́гый	тьи́хый	о̂т/ска́кывать
→ру́скай	стро́гай	тьи́хай	о̂т/ска́кавать
in this style		in this style	

РАЗДЁРГИВАЛ	СПИ́ХИВАЛИ
ра̂з/дьо́ргывал	с/пьи́хывальи
→ра̂з/дьо́ргавал	с/пьи́хавальи
in this style	in this style

In colloquial *CSR*, rule 3T is extended to unstressed ы in posttonic position (i.e., in syllables
following the stressed syllable) in a number of other
words, e.g.:

ПА́СЫНОК	НЕ́ БЫЛО
па́сынок	ньé#было
→па́санак	ньé#бала	in this style

(for о → а, see 3U); this pronunciation seems to be
particularly common in Leningrad.

In some varieties of colloquial *CSR*, the rule is
extended to cover the other "hard" vowel which is
phonetically high, namely у: e.g.:

О́БУВЬ
о́буфь
→о́бафь	in this style

The effect of this extension--if carried out with no
exceptions--would be that unstressed posttonic vowels
after hard consonants would be ALL pronounced in the
same way; in other words, that there would be *complete* neutralization between vowels in this environment. Instances of extreme neutralization are rare,
but, according to recent reports, may be becoming
more common.[92]

3.12.3. REDUCTION OF o

We now introduce the phenomenon traditionally
known as AKAN'E.

(3U) o → a / { $\widehat{—}$ / $—$ } (except list (loanwords))

Discussion and Examples

All o's, whether half-stressed or unstressed, are
rewritten a, except in a list of loanwords. The
vowels ô and o in *CSR* normally occur only after Hard
Paired Consonants (C_p), as in the following examples:[93]

ОКНÓ ГÓРОД ГОРОДÁ ОБОРÒНОСПОСÓБНОСТЬ   ПОД ЛÁМПОЙ

ôкнó гóрот горôдá ôбôрòно#спôсóбносьть пôд/лáмпой

→âкнó гóрат гарâдá âбâрòна#спâсóбнасьть пâд/лáмпай

In a small group of loanwords, ô and o occur after
Soft Paired Consonants (Cpь), Hard Unpaired Consonants (H), and Soft Unpaired Consonants (S). Rule
3U applies to ô and o *whatever* consonant precedes, as
long as the word concerned is not listed as being an
excepted loanword. Examples of reduction of o in
loanwords, where o occurs after consonants other than
C_p (see *RLP* 63):

Cpь:	H:	H:	S:
ГИЛЬОТИ́НА	ШОФЁР	ЖОНГЛЁР	МАЙОНÉЗ
гьильôтьи́на	шôфьóр	жôнгльóр	майôньéс
→гьильâтьи́на	шâфьóр	жâнгльóр	майâньéс

Avanesov distinguishes three groups of loanwords

in this context:

(i) those where the o is always reduced to ə;

(ii) those where the o may be optionally reduced to ə; and

(iii) those where the o is never reduced in the norm for *CSR*.

For example,

(i) with regular vowel-reduction:

    РОМА́Н   ПРОГРЕ́СС   КООПЕРАТИ́В   ПРОФЕ́ССОР

    рôма́н   прôгрьес   кôôпьерâтьйф   прôфьесор

→рəма́н   прəгрьес   кəəпьерâтьйф   прəфьесəр

    ВОЛЕЙБО́Л   МОНОПОЛИ́СТ

    вольêйбо́л   монопôльи́ст

→вəльêйбо́л   мəнапâльи́ст

(ii) with optional reduction:

    СОНЕ́Т   ФОНЕ́ТИКА   ПОЭТИ́ЧЕСКИЙ

    сôньет   фôньетьика   пôэтьическьий

→сəньет   фəньетьика   пəэтьическьий

    or n/c   or n/c   or n/c

(iii) without reduction:

    РА́ДИО ШОССЕ́ БОА́ ОТЕ́ЛЬ ДОСЬЕ́

    ра́дьйô шôссэ бôа́ ôтэль дôсье́

    n/c   n/c   n/c   n/c   n/c

    See 3.15. for a general discussion of loanwords. Dictionary look-up is recommended for students who wish to adhere to Avanesov's prescriptions.

Stylistic Variations (3U)

    Most Soviet scholars who have investigated the pronunciation of loanwords are not as restrictive as Avanesov; they report that many speakers of *CSR* "Russianize" the pronunciation of loanwords very much more frequently. As far as 3U is concerned, this means that they speak with reduction of o to ə very much more frequently.

    Investigators still distinguish three groups in

the way that Avanesov does, but they shift many words
from group (ii) to group (i), and many words from
group (iii) to group (ii).

One example: Avanesov places the word РА́ДИО in
group (iii); that is, he prescribes pronunciation
without reduction of the final o; other reports place
this word in group (ii), with optional reduction, or
even in group (i), with regular reduction → ра́дьйа̂.[94]

3.12.4. REDUCTION OF э AND a AFTER HARD UNPAIRED CONSONANTS

There are at this point only four unstressed
vowel letters occurring after Hard Unpaired Consonants (H): э, ы, у and a.* Two of these are concerned in our next rule: э, which is replaced by
another vowel in all unstressed and half-stressed
positions, and a, which is replaced when half-stressed in a short list of words only.

$$
\text{(3V)}\quad
\begin{aligned}
&1.\quad \text{э} \to \text{а} \;/\; \begin{cases} \text{(a)}\;\; \text{H} \!-\! \text{C} \\[4pt] \text{(b)}\;\; \text{H} \!-\! \begin{Bmatrix} \# \\ \#\# \end{Bmatrix} \text{only in n/a. sg.} \\ \hphantom{\text{(b)}\;\; \text{H}-}\text{neut. nouns} \end{cases} \\[18pt]
&2.\quad \text{э} \to \text{ы} \;/\; \begin{cases} \text{(a)}\;\; \text{H} \!-\! \begin{Bmatrix} \# \\ \#\# \end{Bmatrix} \text{exc. in n/a. sg.} \\ \hphantom{\text{(a)}\;\; \text{H}-}\text{neut. nouns} \\[4pt] \text{(b)}\;\; \text{H} \!-\! \widehat{\;\;} \end{cases} \\[18pt]
&3.\quad \text{а} \to \text{ы} \;/\; \qquad \text{H} \!-\! \widehat{\;\;} \qquad \text{list}
\end{aligned}
$$

Discussion and Examples (*RLP* 63-65, 71-72)

3V1 states that э is rewritten as a, after Hard
Unpaired Consonants when unmarked for stress in two
environments:

3V1(a): when occurring before another consonant,
e.g.:

     ШЕПТУНЫ́ ЖЕРЕБЁНОК   ВЫ́ШЕЛ ЦЕЛИКО́М   СЕ́РДЦЕМ

     шэптун̂ы́ жэрьѐбьо́нак вы́шэл цэльйко́м сьѐрцэм

   →шаптун̂ы́ жарьѐбьо́нак вы́шал цальйко́м сьѐрцам

---

*This results from (a) the restrictions on co-occur-
rence of H letters with vowels in the *SO* and from
(b) the effects of rule-block 3J.

3V1(b): when final, but ONLY in the Nominative or Accusative Singular of Neuter Nouns,[95] e.g.:

СЕ́РДЦЕ	*BUT*	НА́ШЕ
сье́рцэ		на́шэ
→сье́рца̲		n/c

n/c since this is not a noun (see 3V2(a) below)

3V2 states that э is rewritten ы in two circumstances (*RLP* 65, 71-72):

3V2(a): when unmarked for stress after Hard Unpaired Consonants and in final position, EXCEPT in the case endings specified in 3V1(b) above, e.g.:

МЕ́НЬШЕ	ВЫ́ШЕ	КО́ЖЕ	У́ЛИЦЕ	СЕ́РДЦЕ	(L. Sg.)
мье́ньшэ	вы́шэ	ко́жэ	у́льицэ	сье́рцэ	
→мье́ньшы̲	вы́шы̲	ко́жы̲	у́льицы̲	сье́рцы̲	

3V2(b): when marked ⌃ after Hard Unpaired Consonants, i.e., in pretonic position only, e.g.:

ПОЦЕЛУ́Й	ЖЕНА́	ОЦЕНИ́ТЬ	ШЕПТА́ТЬ
по/цэ̂лу́й	жэ̂на́	о/цэ̂ньи́ть	шэ̂пта́ть
→по/цы̲̂лу́й	жы̲̂на́	о/цы̲̂ньи́ть	шы̲̂пта́ть

Stylistic Variations (3V1, 3V2)

Final Position:

It will be noted that in these rules, generally speaking, the reduction of э in absolute final position (where э is not marked for stress) results in the same vowel, viz., ы, as the reductions of э when half-stressed. In other words, FINAL unstressed vowels are (in this respect at least) somewhat "stronger" than other unstressed vowels; one might wish, for example, to characterize final vowels as "quarter-stressed".[96]

The exception to this general statement is provided (3V1(b)) by the N/A. Sg. of Neuter Nouns; which are (according to Avanesov) to be treated as non-final unstressed vowels, and reduced to a. In this way, *CSR* is prescribed as distinguishing between the N/A. Sg. and the L. Sg. of Neuter Nouns whose stems end in Hard Unpaired Consonants.*

Many speakers of *CSR*, however, do not make this distinction, and have full reduction in *all* cases. Thus where the norm will have ə in the N/A. Sg. (and, of course, in the G. Sg.!) and ы in the L. Sg., many speakers will have the same vowel, ə, in all four cases:

	SO	*CSR* (Avanesov)	*CSR* (many speakers)
N/A. Sg.	СЕ́РДЦЕ	сье́рцə	сье́рцə
G. Sg.	СЕ́РДЦА	сье́рцə	сье́рцə
L. Sg.	СЕ́РДЦЕ	сье́рцы	сье́рцə

Loanwords

1.   *Loanwords with э after "Hard" (NOT Unpaired) Consonants:*

Many speakers of *CSR* extend the rules 3V1(a), 3V2(b) so that they apply to э occurring after ANY "hard" consonant in loanwords.[97]

In 3J2(b) above, we rewrite е as э within stems of specified loanwords. Most speakers follow Avanesov and, in many of these words, make no reduction of the э; our rules allow for this, since we specify reduction after H and omit any reference to reduction after C$_h$. In a number of words, however, reduction of э IS often heard; and it appears that, normally, it is rule 3V2(b) that is extended to apply in these instances; the э, whether half-stressed or unstressed, is reduced to ы, e.g.:

ДЕКОЛЬТЕ́   ДЕТЕКТИ́В

дэкальтэ́   дэтэ̂ктьйф

дыкальтэ́ in this style   дытэ̂ктьйф in this style

The application of 3V1(a) to those instances where it might be applicable, i.e., to unstressed э's, seems to be much more rare, e.g.:

ДЕТЕКТИ́В

дэтэ̂ктьйф

→датэ̂ктьйф in this style

---

*For an analogous situation with regard to neuter nouns whose stems end in "soft" consonants, see 3.12.5. below.

2. *Loanwords with initial* э:

No reduction of initial э in loanwords is prescribed in *RLP*; but many speakers do reduce the э to
ы, initially as after any C$_h$ (cf. above), e.g.:

> ЭЛЕКТРЍЧЕСКИЙ
>
> э̂льэ̂ктрьы́ческьий
>
> →ы̲льэ̂ктрьы́ческьий   in this style

3.   ТАНЦЕВА́ТЬ and ГАРЦЕВА́ТЬ

In these two words, the э (which is in pretonic
position and therefore half-stressed) may optionally
be reduced to а rather than to ы; this reflects the
fact that at one time these words were often spelled
with а in the *SO* (*RLP* 65).
3V3 states that, in a (short) list of specified
words, а (which, in this list, is always half-stressed) is to be rewritten ы; e.g.:

> ЖАЛЕ́ТЬ   ЖАНЕ́Т   РЖАНО́Й   ЛОШАДЕ́Й
>
> жа̂ле́ть   жа̂кье́т   ржа̂но́й   лаша̂дьей
>
> →жы̲ле́ть   жы̲кье́т   ржы̲но́й   лашы̲дьей

Stylistic Variations (3V3)

Avanesov (*RLP* 63-64) specifies only seven words
which (with their derivatives) are to be listed for
this rule.
In *OM*, ALL words with а̂ after Unpaired Hard Consonants were pronounced in this way. Among speakers
of *CSR* today, there is a vast amount of variation;
but recent studies generally corroborate Avanesov's
prescriptions.[98]
Some loanwords with о̂ after Hard Unpaired Consonants and in pretonic position do not show any reduction (cf. 3.12.3. above). However, if they are
"Russianized" to the extent that vowel-reduction
takes place, this о̂ will usually be pronounced as ы̂.
This pronunciation fits into the framework of our
rules as follows:

> ШОССЕ́
>
> шоссе́   by 3J2(b)
>
> →шо̂ссе́   by 3U
>
> →шы̲ссе́   by an extension of 3V3
>   in this style

3.12.5. VOWEL-REDUCTION AFTER "SOFT" CONSONANTS (NOT GRAMMATICAL ENDINGS)

We have, in 3T, 3U and 3V above, now covered the various types of vowel-reduction after "Hard" consonants (C_h); we now turn to vowel-reduction after "Soft" consonants (C_s). Note that, for this environment, grammatical endings are discussed SEPARATELY, in 3.12.6.

There are only four unstressed vowels which normally occur after "Soft" consonants at this stage of the rules: а, е, и and у.* They may be set out as follows:

The Three Steps of Vowel-Reduction After "Soft" Consonants

In *CSR*, two degrees, or STEPS, of vowel-reduction have to be considered. In conversational *CSR*, a third step has been noted (see Stylistic Variations below). We now introduce and compare the three steps.[99]

(i) Step-One Vowel-Reduction (VR-1)

The simplest instance of vowel-reduction after soft consonants involves the neutralization of only ONE of the distinctions between the four vowels set out above. In this step, which we shall refer to with the abbreviation VR-1, the distinction between а and е is neutralized; in other words (cf. pp. 87-88) unstressed а and е after soft consonants are pronounced identically. Their phonetic realization is different from that of и and from that of у,

---

*э and ы never occur after C_s (cf. 3.8.), with the exception of a very few loanwords such as БЕЛЬЭТÁЖ where э does occur; in these words (if they are not excepted, *qua* loanwords, from the relevant rules), э behaves in the same way as е. The vowel о does occur after C_s in some loanwords; in a few of these it is reduced to а by rule 3U above, and thus appears as C_sа at the present stage of derivation, and is treated normally, with reduction as in 3W1 (for exceptions to this, see ГИЛЬОТИНА, МАЙОНÉЗ in 3Z).

however. Thus:

$$C_s a = C_s e \mid C_s \text{и} \mid C_s y$$

(ii)   Step-Two Vowel-Reduction (VR-2)

The second step involves the neutralization of the three-way distinction between unstressed a, e and и after Soft consonants; i.e., all three vowels are pronounced in the same way; but their phonetic realization is still different from that of y in this environment. Thus:

$$C_s a = C_s e = C_s \text{и} \mid C_s y$$

(iii)   Step-Three Vowel-Reduction (VR-3)

The most extreme type of vowel-reduction after Soft consonants involves COMPLETE neutralization of all vowel-distinctions: i.e., a, e, и and y are all pronounced identically. Thus:

$$C_s a = C_s e = C_s \text{и} = C_s y$$

This step (VR-3) is not permitted in the norm for *CSR*, but see Stylistic Variations below.

A Note On Terminology

Step-One Vowel-Reduction (VR-1) is normally referred to as *EKAN'E*, and Step-Two Vowel-Reduction (VR-2) as *IKAN'E*.[100] We prefer not to use these terms because of the possible confusion which may arise from the fact that they have been used in two very different senses: the PHONOLOGICAL sense, where e.g., ekan'e refers to a particular type of vowel-reduction, and presupposes no facts of pronunciation; and the PHONETIC sense, where e.g., ekan'e is used to imply that the actual pronunciation is close to that of stressed é. We avoid the terms ekan'e and ikan'e altogether, since we consider it important that these two senses be clearly distinguished.[101]

VR-1 or VR-2?

For many years Soviet normative grammarians have been debating the problem as to which step of vowel-reduction, *VR-1* or *VR-2*, should be the basis for the norms of *CSR* pronunciation. (The debate has often been obscured by the terminological confusion described above.) The background to the problem is briefly described in Stylistic Variations below. We must now interpret Avanesov's recommendations in *RLP*.

This is not an easy task. The different editions of *RLP* have, over the years, shown a gradual shift from a position where *VR-1* was the ONLY permitted norm and *VR-2* was rejected, to the position in the latest edition where Avanesov appears to sanction BOTH *VR-1* and *VR-2*. On two points he is clear: the "conversational" style of *CSR* may have only *VR-2*; and the "elevated" style may have only *VR-1*. Where the "neutral" style is concerned (and it is this style that we are trying to derive here) he is unfortunately still too vague.[102]

A further complication is provided by two facts: (i) that one of the permitted *CSR* styles shows a *mixture of VR-1 and VR-2* (viz., *VR-1* in half-stressed syllables, and *VR-2* in unstressed syllables; in other words, less neutralization in the stronger syllables, and more neutralization in the weaker ones); (ii) that the distinction in *VR-1* between the realizations of unstressed и, on the one hand, and unstressed а and е, on the other, is normally a very fine phonetic nuance.

WE ADOPT VR-2 (IKAN'E) AS THE STANDARD NORM FOR VOWEL-NEUTRALIZATION IN OUR RULES. The particular rules for this, given in 3W and 3X below, represent the consensus of those linguistic and pedagogical authorities who have published on this subject;[103] and at the same time represent a pronunciation which is at least *acceptable* to Avanesov, even though he may seem not to prefer it.

Those readers who prefer to adopt *VR-1* as a style of pronunciation, will find hints for drawing up the necessary rules in STYLISTIC VARIATIONS below, and they should substitute these rules for those given in 3W.

N.B. This Rule-Block does *not* Apply to *Grammatical Endings*

(3W) 1. a → и / C_s {‸ / —} C

2. е → и / C_s {‸ / —} (except list (loanwords))

Discussion and Examples

3W1: Every â is rewritten û and every a is rewritten и when after a "Soft" consonant and before any other consonant,[104] e.g.:

ВЗЯЛА́	ПА́МЯТНИК	ЯЗЫ́К	ЯЗЫКА́	ЧАСЫ́	ЗА́НЯТ
взьа̂ла́	па́мьатьньик	йа̂зы́к	йазы̂ка́	ча̂сы́	за́ньат
→взьи̂ла́	па́мьитьньик	йи̂зы́к	йизы̂ка́	чи̂сы́	за́ньит

Note: 3W1 applies to C_sa which derives from C_sо, e.g.:

ГИЛЬОТИНИ́РОВАТЬ	ЙОДОФО́РМ
гьильатьи̂ньи́равать	йада̂фо́рм
→гьильитьи̂ньи́равать	йида̂фо́рм

In absolute final position, however, a is not changed, e.g.:

ИСПОДЛО́БЬЯ	ДОНЕ́ЛЬЗЯ
и̂спа̂дло́бьйа	да̂ньéльзьа
n/c	n/c

3W2: Except in a list of loanwords, every ê is rewritten û and every е is rewritten и when occurring after a soft consonant. This applies to non-final position, as in e.g.:

ВЕСНА́	МÉДЛЕННО	ПЕРЕВЕДЕНА́	ТЕПÉРЬ
вьесна́	мьéдьльена	пьерье/вьедьêна́	тьэпьéрь
→вьи̂сна́	мьéдьльина	пьирьи/вьидьи̂на́	тьи̂пьéрь

3W2 applies equally in absolute final position, as long as grammatical endings are not involved, e.g.:

КРО́МЕ   РА́ЗВЕ

кро́мье   ра́зьвье

→кро́мьи̲   ра́зьвьи̲

Examples of lack of reduction (non-application of 3W2) in loanwords (*RLP* 175):

АППЕРЦЕ́ПЦИЯ   БЕЛЬЭТА́Ж   АЛЛЕГРЕ́ТТО

а͡пь͡эрцэ́пцыйа   бьельэ͡та́ш   а͡льэ͡грьє́тта

n/c   n/c   n/c

Stylistic Variations (3W)

We discuss separately those styles of pronunciation which are variations on the scheme of *VR-2* set out above; and those styles which involve either *VR-1* or *VR-3*.

Variations: VR-2

In conversational *CSR* 3W1 may be extended to ә in absolute final position, e.g., ә is reduced to и at the end of the words ИСПОДЛО́БЬЯ and ДОНЕ́ЛЬЗЯ.

In "elevated" *CSR*, 3W1 may not be applied to ә when it occurs in final syllables before *hard* consonants (*RLP* 69). Thus, whereas the ә in ЛА́ЯТЬ → ла́йать will be rewritten и by 3W1, → ла́йить, the ә in ЗА́НЯТ → за́ньә̱т will be left unchanged (unreduced).

The list of loanwords which form exceptions to 3W2, as given in *RLP* and *RLPU*, is short; in conversational *CSR*, many of these words are pronounced with normal reduction of е to и. Similarly, the loanwords with э and o after soft consonants (cf. footnote, p. 102) may be pronounced with reduction of э and o to и.

See 3.15. for a general discussion of loanwords.

Variations: VR-1

The alternative style prescribed (and apparently still preferred) by Avanesov, and the "elevated" *CSR* style, is that of *VR-1* (traditionally, EKAN'E). This style of speech was the normal one in Leningrad at the turn of the century, and has lived on in the normative works not only of many Leningrad authorities, but also of some Muscovite ones, including Avanesov's teacher Ušakov.[105]

The rule to replace 3W by *VR-1* would be comparatively much simpler. In the first place, е would not be changed. Secondly, ә would have to be rewritten е in the environment specified in 3W1; thus,

$$a \rightarrow e \; / \; C_s \left\{ \begin{array}{c} \smallfrown \\ \underline{} \end{array} \right\} C$$

The examples given above for 3W1 would all have their
a's rewritten as e; and in final position, a would be
left unchanged.

It is possible, though unlikely [since this
variation is typical of faster speech, and fast
speech is atypical of *VR-1* speakers] that this rule
for *VR-1* would be extended to absolute final position
as well, and that a would be reduced to e in such
words as ИСПОДЛÓБЬЯ and ДОНÉЛЬЗЯ.

On the other hand, it is very likely [since this
variation is typical of more careful speech] that
VR-1 speakers would except from this rule such words
as ЗÁНЯТ, with a before hard consonants in final syllables.

Variations: VR-3

In some varieties of fast colloquial *CSR* the extreme step of vowel-reduction has been noted, especially in fully unstressed syllables, namely, the
neutralization of ALL vocalic distinctions after Soft
consonants. What happens is that unstressed y is
also reduced to и, e.g.:

ИМÉЮЩИМСЯ

и̂мьéйущимса

→и̂мьéй<u>и</u>щимса   in this style

The effect of this extension to the vowel-reduction rules--if carried out with no exceptions--would
be that unstressed vowels after Soft consonants would
ALL be pronounced identically. Since at the same
time unstressed vowels after *Hard* consonants might
also, in this style of *CSR*, have their distinctions
neutralized (cf. pp. 87 - 88) the net effect might be
that ALL unstressed vowels would have a predictable
form: и after soft, and a after hard consonants. At
the present, such a style of pronunciation is conjec-
tural; but it should be pointed out that there is
some evidence that a tendency *towards* this style has
been established.[106]

3.12.6. VOWEL-REDUCTION AFTER SOFT CONSONANTS IN GRAMMATICAL ENDINGS

Our rule for Vowel-Reduction after Soft consonants in grammatical endings is based on *VR-2* (IKAN'E) rather than on *VR-1* (EKAN'E) (cf. pp. 102-04). Rules for this latter style are suggested in Stylistic Variations below.

Here, perhaps more than in any other section of the Rules, there is a great deal of variation among *CSR* speakers. There are, moreover, a number of instances where Avanesov himself refrains from being dogmatic and allows optional pronunciations. Where Avanesov allows a choice between two or more pronunciations, we have been guided by two criteria: (i) if an option is characterized as *OM* or as "older" in style, we have rejected it; (ii) in all other cases, we have made those choices which tended to simplify rule-block 3X. In every case, the other options are discussed below in Stylistic Variations, as are recent investigations whose results, in part, strongly disagree with Avanesov's prescriptions.

Note that, in 3X, the only vowel affected is е;[107] the three other vowels occurring in this environment, а, и, and у, are left unchanged.

N.B.   This Rule-Block Applies to Grammatical endings *Only*

$$1. \quad e \to a \ / \quad C_s - \left\{\begin{matrix} \# \\ \#\# \end{matrix}\right\} \text{only in n/a. sg. adjectives}$$

(3X)

$$2. \quad e \to \text{и} \ / \left\{\begin{matrix} \text{(a)} \ C_s - \left\{\begin{matrix} \# \\ \#\# \end{matrix}\right\} \text{except in n/a. sg. adjectives} \\ \\ \text{(b)} \ C_s - C \end{matrix}\right.$$

Discussion and Examples

3X1: In the Nominative/Accusative singular of adjectives, i.e., of neuter adjectives, the ending -е is rewritten -а, e.g.:

ДО́БРОЕ	СИ́НЕЕ	КОША́ЧЬЕ	ДВО́Е
до́брайе	сьи́ньейе	ка͡ша́чйе	дво́йе
→до́брай<u>а</u>	сьи́ньий<u>а</u>	ка͡ша́чй<u>а</u>	дво́й<u>а</u>

(Note: the second vowel in the second example above,*
and in the fourth example below is, rewritten by 3X2
(b)):

3X2(a): Absolute final -e in all endings *other than*
the one specified in 3X1, is rewritten и, e.g.:

ДÓБРЫЕ	СИЛЬНÉЕ	ДЕШÉВЛЕ	ÉДЕТЕ
дóбрыйе	сь͡ильньéйе	дьэ͡шэ́влье	йéдьетье
→дóбрыйи	сь͡ильньéйи	дьэ͡шэ́вльи	йéдьитьи

СИ́НИЕ	ПÓЛЕ	КРЕСТЯ́НЕ	РАБÓТЕ	ДÓМЕ
сь͡иньийе	пóлье	крь͡исьтьáнье	ра͡бóтье	дóмье
→сь͡иньийи	пóльи	крь͡исьтьáньи	ра͡бóтьи	дóмьи

3X2(b): -e in ALL other endings, i.e., in all endings before a consonant (be this hard or soft), is
also rewritten и, e.g.:

УЧИ́ТЕЛЕМ	СИ́НЕГО	СИ́НЕМУ	СИ́НЕМ
у͡чи́тьильем	сь͡иньева	сь͡иньему	сь͡иньем
→у͡чи́тьильи͡м	сь͡иньи͡ва	сь͡иньи͡му	сь͡иньи͡м

ÉДЕШЬ	ÉДЕМ	ÉДЕТ	ÉДЕТЕ	КРАСИ́ВЕЙ
йéдьеш	йéдьем	йéдьет	йéдьетье	кра͡сь͡ивьей
→йéдьиш	йéдьи͡м	йéдьи͡т	йéдьитьи	кра͡сь͡ивьи͡й

СОСÉДЕЙ	КÁПЛЕЙ	КÁПЛЕЮ	БРÁТЬЕВ
са͡сьéдьей	кáпльей	кáпльейу	брáтьйеф
→са͡сьéдьи͡й	кáпльи͡й	кáпльи͡йу	брáтьйи͡ф

Note that the style of speech derived by 3X thus distinguishes between all instances of e and a in grammatical endings (e being rewritten и, and a being
unchanged), *with the exception of* the Nominative/
Accusative Singular Neuter of Adjectives, where final
e is pronounced the same as final a. This means that
for example, there is neutralization between the two
adjectival forms ДÓБРОЕ and ДÓБРАЯ:

---

*The unstressed N/A. Sg. Neuter adjectival ending -EE
is not discussed in *RLP*; the pronunciation given here
is the most likely given the prescriptions for -OE
and for -ЕГО, -ЕМУ.

ДО́БРОЕ   ДО́БРАЯ

до́брайе   до́брайа

→до́бра<u>йа</u>   до́бра<u>йа</u>

Stylistic Variations (3X)

As for 3W above (p. 106), we provide separate discussion of stylistic variations which fall under *VR-2*, and those which belong to *VR-1*.

Variations: VR-2

Four optional variations on the above rules are sanctioned by Avanesov, as follows:

1. The words ДВО́Е, ТРО́Е, which show reduction of
   e to ə by 3X1, may also be pronounced with final
   -и, especially if they precede the # boundary;
   thus ДВО́Е СУТОК → ##дво́йи̲#су́тəн##. Before the
   ## boundary, however, -ə is more normal: НА́С
   БЫ́ЛО ДВО́Е → ##на́с#бы́лə#дво́й<u>а</u>##.

2. The comparative forms, e.g., СИЛЬНЕ́Е and the N/A.
   Sg. of neuter nouns, e.g., ПО́ЛЕ, may follow 3X1
   rather than 3X2 and thus end in ə rather than in
   и; thus, СИЛЬНЕ́Е → сьи̲льнье́й<u>ə</u>, ПО́ЛЕ → по́ль<u>ə</u>.

   Note that this style, which is typical of *OM*,
   makes a distinction between the N/A. Sg. (по́ль<u>ə</u>)
   and the L. Sg. (по́ль<u>и</u>). Cf. our remarks on p.
   100 concerning s̲imilar distinctions between forms
   of words like СЕ́РДЦЕ.

3. The adjectival endings -ЕГО, -ЕМУ, -ЕМ may follow
   3X1 rather than 3X2, and be pronounced, e.g.,
   сьи̲нь<u>ə</u>ва, сьи̲нь<u>ə</u>му, сьи̲нь<u>ə</u>м rather than сьи̲нь<u>и</u>ва,
   -<u>и</u>му, -<u>и</u>м. This style is̲ also typical of *OM*.

4. The I. Sg. ending -ЕМ[108] and the G. Pl. ending
   -ЕВ may follow 3X1 rather than 3X2, and be pronounced, e.g., учи́тьиль<u>ə</u>м, бра́ть<u>ə</u>ф rather than
   учи́тьиль<u>и</u>м, бра́ть<u>и</u>ф.

Avanesov also sanctions one optional extension
to rule 3X2: the I. Pl. ending -ЯМИ, -АМИ (which is
not affected by 3X) may show reduction of -a- to -и-,
thus, e.g., КА́ПЛЯМИ → ка́пльамьи → ка́пльимьи. Note
that this is the only *CSR* ending with -Я̄- before a
soft consonant.

Recent investigation[109] points to a much simpler
system of pronunciation than the one given above, a
system which also fits into the *VR-2* style. This
system can be described without any reference to

grammatical categories. The necessary rules would be
as follows:

$$1. \quad e \rightarrow a \; / \; C_s \; \text{---} \; \#$$
$$2. \quad e \rightarrow и \; / \; C_s \; \text{---} \; C$$
$$3. \quad a \rightarrow и \; / \; C_s \; \text{---} \; C_s$$

Comparison of these rules with 3X presents the following chief differences: (a) 3X1 is extended (at
the expense of 3X2(a)) to cover *all* final -e endings;
this parallels the optional pronunciations listed as
nos. 2, 3, 4 above; (b) 3X2(b) is unchanged; and (c)
the I. Pl. ending is rewritten with an и, as in the
optional pronunciation of КА́ПЛЯМИ, as discussed
above.

Variations: VR-1

On p. 105 above we suggested simplified rules
for *VR-1* for vowels after soft consonants *outside*
grammatical endings. Parallel to this, Avanesov
still recommends *VR-1 within* grammatical endings for
"elevated" *CSR* and more careful speech generally.
Here, an -e will *not* be pronounced the same as an -и:
there will be no neutralization. Thus, for example,
the I. Sg. and the D. Pl. of adjectives with "soft"
stems, e.g., СИ́НЕМ and СИ́НИМ, will NOT be pronounced
in the same way.

The set of rules to derive *VR-1* within grammatical endings would be much simpler than 3X, for only
one rule would be needed; specifically, a rule identical to 3X1. 3X2 would be unnecessary, since e
would be left unchanged.

The minor stylistic variations for *VR-1* would
however involve a list as long as the one given above
for *VR-2* (points 1 to 4, page 110), to allow for
all these optional pronunciations of e as a and of a
as и.

3.13. SYNCOPE AND EPENTHESIS OF й

There are now two measures to be taken with respect to the letter й. Firstly, it must be deleted
in certain environments; and secondly, it must be inserted in certain environments.

In 3I (pp. 57-58) й was dispensed with when occurring in initial position before и. We now remove

this letter from two other environments where it is
not pronounced.

$$\text{(3Y1)} \quad \text{й} \to \emptyset \; / \; \begin{cases} \text{(a)} \; \text{V} \text{ — } \text{и} \\ \text{(b)} \; \text{V} \text{ — } \text{е (list (loanwords))} \end{cases}$$

Discussion and Examples

3Y1(a): The letter й is deleted intervocalical-
ly before и.* This applies not only to words which
have и in the *SO*, e.g.:

БОЙШЬСЯ	МОЙ	ФАМИ́ЛИИ	ПОЦЕЛУ́И
ба̂й̲й̲шса	ма̂й̲й̲	фа̂мьи́льийи	пацы̲лу́й̲и
→ба̂йшса	ма̂й̲	фа̂мьи́льии	пацы̲лу́и

but also to words in which the и is derived from
another vowel by 3W or 3X,[110] e.g.:

НОЯБРЯ́	ВОЕВА́ТЬ	ТРАЕКТОРИЯ	ПОЯВИ́ТЬСЯ
най̲й̲брьа́	вай̲й̲ва́ть	трайинта̂рьй̲йа	па/й̲й̲вьи́цца
→най̲брьа́	вай̲ва́ть	траинта̂рьй̲йа	па/й̲вьи́цца

ВЫ́ЕЗД	НЕЕСТЕ́СТВЕННО	НА ЯЗЫКЕ́	ДЕ́ЛАЕТ
вы́й̲ист	ньи/й̲йсьтьé сьтьвьина	на/й̲изы̲кьé	дьé лай̲ит
→вы́ист	ньи/й̲сьтьé сьтьвьина	на/изы̲кьé	дьé лаит

ПО́ЯС	ПЛЮ́ЕТ	БОЛЬШИ́Е	СИ́НИЕ
по́й̲ис	пльу́й̲ит	ба̂льшы̲́й̲и	сьи́ньий̲и
→по́ис	пльу́ит	ба̂льшы̲́и	сьи́ньии

3Y1(b): The letter й is deleted also intervo-
calically before е in a list of loanwords,[111] e.g.:

КЛИЕ́НТ	ГА́ЕР
кльй̲й̲é нт	га́й̲ер
→кльй̲é нт	га́ер

*The symbol V is used to represent *any* vowel, regardless of stress.

Stylistic Variations (3Y1)

   3Y1(a) may be ignored in careful, "elevated" *CSR*, especially across the / boundary. (Note that careful speech is normally characterized by *VR-1* (cf. p. 104), and with this step of vowel-reduction very few or no instances of derived и may be observed, e.g., ПОЯС would be rewritten пойес in this style, and 3Y will not be applicable.)

   For syncope of й in other environments in fast conversational *CSR*, see 5.4. below.

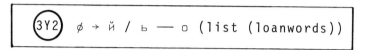

(3Y2)   ∅ → й / ь — o (list (loanwords))

Discussion and Examples

   The letter й is inserted between ь and o in a specified list of loanwords. This rule reflects an anomaly in the *SO* of these words, which--if consistency with native spellings were to be maintained-- would be spelled with Ё instead of О, e.g.:

ФЬОРД	СИНЬОР	БАТАЛЬОН
фьорт	сьиньбр	баталльон
→фьйорт	сьиньйбр	баталльйон

3.14. "AD HOC" FORMULAE: RULE-BLOCK 3Z

   We now have a few odds and ends to clear up. These constitute a list of words or stems which are best considered as MISSPELLED in the *SO*. These words could have special idiosyncratic rules devised for them; but each such rule would apply to a very few words--in most cases, to one word only--and none would have any of the wider implications or generality of the rules considered so far.

   In the following list, which we shall refer to as RULE-BLOCK 3Z, the words and stems are presented in three columns:

(1) the *SO*;

(2) the form as derived by all rules up to and including 3Y; in other words, the form which would normally be expected by the general rules;

(3) the *PO* which is actually required if the pronunciation derived will be that prescribed in *RLP* (or, if the word or stem is not mentioned there, in

RLPU).

In the fourth column are explanatory notes and/ or cross-references to sections where related phenomena are discussed.

Note that all the words listed below are also to be found (in their normal alphabetical position) in the LEXICON OF EXCEPTIONS, where the notation 3Z is to be understood to refer the student to the list here.

Rule-Block 3Z

(1) *SO*	(2) by rules thru 3Y	(3) by 3Z = *PO*	(4) Remarks
ÀЙ-ÀЙ-ÁЙ	àй#àй#áй	àй#йàй#йáй	As if spelled ÀЙ-ÀЙ-ЯЙ
АЛЛО́	а̂ло́	а̂льб	See *RLP* 169-70 *re* "European л".
А́НГЕЛ	а́нгьил	а́нь̲гьил	The sole exception to 3P restriction 2. Also in АРХА́НГЕЛ.
АЭРО- e.g. АЭРО- ДРО́М	а̂зра̂дро́м	а̂йра̂дро́м	*RLP* 282. Cf. p. 93.
БЛИ́З	бльи́с	бльи́сь̲	*RLP* 98, 398.
БРАНДВА́ХТА	бра̂ндва́хта	бра̂нтва́хта	As if a compound word, *SO* БРА̂НДВА́ХТА, with two stresses.
БЮСТ- ГА́ЛЬТЕР	бьу̂здга́ль- тэр	бьу̂зга́ль- тэр	Cf. the cluster стн in 3B (Stylistic Variations).
ГАЛО́ШИ	га̂ло́шы	к̲а̲ло́шы	Note alternative *SO* КАЛО́ШИ.
ГИЛЬОТИ́НА	гьильйтьи́на	гьильатьи́- на	Note: 3U applies but 3W1 does *not* apply.

(1) *SO*	(2) by rules thru 3Y	(3) by 3Z = *PO*	(4) Remarks
ДЕВЯТЬСО́Т	дьивьй̂тьсо́т	дьивьи͟цсо́т	Cf. 3G2. *RLP* 407; note that *RLPU* has дьивьй̂т͟со́т.
ДЗЕ́КАНЬЕ	дзэ̇́каньи	д͟ь͟з͟ь͟е́каньи	The only example of "soft" дзь (see p. 29).
ЖЮРИ́	жу̂рьи́	ж͟ь͟у̂рьи́	*RLP* 87. The only example of "soft" жь (apart from Proper Names).
ИЕЗУИ́Т	й̂йезу̂и́т	й͟е͟зу̂и́т	As if *SO* ЕЗУИ́Т.
ЛАНДША́ФТ	ла̂нтша́фт	ла̂н͟ша́фт	Cf. 3B1.
МАДЕМУАЗЕ́ЛЬ	мадэму̂азэ́ль	мад͟ма̂зэ́ль	*RLP* 403.
МАЙОНЕ́З	майй̂ньес	май͟а̂ньес	Note: 3U applies but 3W1 does *not*.
МАЙОРА́Т	майй̂ра́т	май͟а̂ра́т	Note: 3U applies but 3W1 does *not*.
МАНЬЧЖУ́Р-	ма̂ньджжу́р	ма̂нь͟жу́р	Cf. 3B1, 3N3.
МАРАБУ́	мара̂бу́	ма͟а̂ра̂бу́	*RLPU*, not in *RLP*.
МАТИНЕ́	матьйн͡э	ма͟а̂тьйн͡э	*RLPU*, not in *RLP*.
МИЛЛИОНЕ́Р	мьильйа̂а̂ньер	мьильйа̂͟а̂ньер	Cf. 3S (Stylistic Variations) and note 88.
МУНДШТУ́К	мунтшту́к	мун͟шту́к	Cf. 3B1.
ПОЖА́ЛУЙСТА	па̂жа́луйста	па̂жа́лы͟ста	See special note re *PT* in 4.1. (p. 134).
ПО́ЙНТЕР	по́йньтьир	по́͟ньтьир	*RLPU*, not in *RLP*.

(1) SO	(2) by rules thru 3Y	(3) by 3Z = PO	(4) Remarks
ПОЛИЦЕЙ-МЕЙСТЕР	пальицӗй-мӗйсьтьир	пальӗцмӗй-сьтьир	Note alternative *SO*. ПОЛИЦМЕЙСТЕР.
ПРИЙТИ́	прьӣйтьй	прьӣтьтьй	As if *SO*. ПРИДТИ́; cf. *SO* ИДТИ́.
ПРОТОИЕРЕЙ	пратаӣӣрьей	пратаӣрьеи	Cf. 3S (Stylistic Variations).
-ПРЯ́Г-	-прьа́к-	-прьо́к-	As if *SO* ВПРЁГШИ, РАЗПРЁГСЯ, etc.[112]
-ПРЯ́ЧЬ	-прьа́ч	-прье́ч	As if *SO* ЗАПРЕ́ЧЬ, etc.[112]
ПШЮ́Т	пшу́т	пшьу́т	The only example of "soft" шь (apart from щ, see 4.3.).
ПЯТЬСО́Т	пьӣтьсо́т	пьӣцсо́т	Cf. 3G2. *RLP* 400. Note that *RLPU* has пьӣтсо́т (= пьӣцбт).
СО́ЛНЦЕ	со́лнца	со́нца	See special note re *PT* in 4.1. (p. 134).
ТЮ́БИНГЩИК	тьу́бьинкщик	тьу́бьиньщик	Cf. 3B2; note that 3P3 has also applied.
ТЯГЧА́ЙШИЙ	тьӣхча́йшый	тьӣкча́йшый	Sole exception to 3G1.
ФЕ́ЛЬДШЕР	фье́льтшар	фье́льшар	Cf. 3B1.
ЦЕЙХГА́УЗ	цэӣгга́ӯс	цэӣха́ӯс	As if there were no г in the *SO*.
ШЕСТЬСО́Т	шӗсьтьсо́т	шӗссо́т	*RLP* 410.
ЯГДТА́Ш	йӣнта́ш	йӣгда́ш	*RLP* 411. N.B.: in *RLPU* the "expected" йӣнта́ш!

Stylistic Variations (3Z)

The above "ad hoc" changes all apply to the *CSR* style as prescribed by Avanesov. If we turn to other styles of Russian close to *CSR*, we can draw up similar lists: in each case, words which would have to be dealt with in an "ad hoc" manner because they do not follow the "rules" for that particular style.

Such an approach would clearly require that the "rules" for the style in question had been set out in the first place; and this we have not attempted to do in a rigorous manner. For this reason, we are in no position to present "ad hoc" lists for any style other than Avanesov's *CSR*. However, there are a number of words which are mentioned by Avanesov and other authorities as having unusual pronunciations (or, as they are usually called, *mis*pronunciations) in one or another non-standard variety of Russian. Since many of these often occur in the speech of Russians who use *CSR*, and since many of them are everyday items of vocabulary, we present some of them below.

It is to be understood that IF the "rules" for the style in question were to be properly worked out, some (or indeed all) of our examples might be found to be--for the style in question, if for no other-- perfectly "regular". It is also to be understood that these words are given as examples, and that these lists have no pretensions to exhaustiveness.

We present these examples in a similar layout to 3Z above; note, however, that column (3) now refers to a different style.

"Ad Hoc" Formulae: Old Moscow Style

(1) *SO*	(2) *PO*	(3) *OM*	Remarks
БЛА́ГО‑	блага‑	бла́га‑	Cf. p. 42.
БОГА́ТЫЙ	бага́тый	бага́тый	Cf. p. 42.
ДО́ЖДЬ	до́шть	до́щ	Cf. p. 56.
ДОЖДЯ́	даждьа́	дажжьа́	Cf. p. 56; also in the other oblique cases.
ЦЕЛУ́Ю	цылу́йу	цалу́йу	*RLP* 65; cf. 3V1, 3V2.

The *OM* style has been well described,[113] for which reason there are numerous references thereto in the paragraphs on Stylistic Variations in this book.*

One other major feature of *OM* must be mentioned --a feature which, in a set of Reading Rules for the *OM* style, would perhaps call for a special rule: namely, the pronunciation of the 3rd Pl. ending of second-conjugation verbs (-ат in the *RO*) and of the Present Active Participial marker of these same verbs (-ащ in the *RO*). In *OM*, these forms are pronounced with -y- instead of the -a-,[114] e.g.:

(1) SO	(2) PO	(3) OM
ХО́ДЯТ	хо́дьат	хо́дь<u>у</u>т
СЛЫ́ШАТ	слы́шат	слы́ш<u>у</u>т
СЛЫ́ШАЩИЙ	слы́шащий	слы́ш<u>у</u>щий

"Ad Hoc" Formulae: Conversational *CSR*

(1) SO	(2) PO	(3) Conversational *CSR*	Remarks
БУХГА́ЛЬТЕР	бўг'га́льтьир	бў<u>х</u>а́льтьир	Cf. ЦЕЙХГАУЗ in 3Z. *RLP* 399.
ДЕКА́БРЬ-СКИЙ	дьйка́брь-скьий	дьйка́бр-<u>скьий</u>	Vinogradov 1965: 211-13; (so also НОЯ́БРЬСКИЙ, ОКТЯ́БРЬСКИЙ, СЕНТЯ́БРЬСКИЙ).
ОТСЮ́ДА	ӑт/сьу́да	ӑ<u>цу́</u>да	*RLP* 405 ⎱ cf. 3G2.
СЮДА́	сьўда́	с<u>ў</u>да́	*RLP* 409 ⎰

The above suggestions are but a few of the many that could be made. *Conversational CSR*, as a style, is normally less well-defined than the official norm, and, *qua* a faster style of speech, is discussed at length in Chapter V below.

The three words cited above from *RLP* are said there to have the above pronunciations with *specific* reference to the "conversational" style. In *RLPU* and in

*See pp. 30, 41, 42, 51, 56, 58, 61, 67, 83-85, 87, 94-95, 101.

RLP a number of other words are listed with the comment "*not* . . ."; e.g., ВЕРОЯ́ТНО is given as "not ВИРИЯТНА" (i.e., in terms of our *PO*, not вьирья́йа́тна). No reference is however made as to what style this and other pronunciations typify; no doubt many of them figure in "conversational" *CSR* as well as in "*prostorečie*" ('vulgar speech'), but little attempt is made in these works to distinguish the two.[115]

3.15. REMARKS ON LOANWORDS

It will have been noticed that LOANWORDS are mentioned very often in the 25 blocks of rules which appear in this chapter; indeed, if it had not required these specific notes, the whole of this third chapter would have been very much shorter--as would have been our LEXICON OF EXCEPTIONS.

In five instances, loanwords are mentioned *explicitly* in the wording of the rule itself, namely in:

3J2(b) е→э / PC —— within stems of loanwords (list)

3U о→а / $\left\{\begin{smallmatrix} \frown \\ = \end{smallmatrix}\right\}$ except list (loanwords)

3W2 е→и / C_s $\left\{\begin{smallmatrix} \frown \\ = \end{smallmatrix}\right\}$ except list (loanwords)

3Y1(b) й→∅ / V —— е list (loanwords)

3Y2 ∅→й / ь —— о list (loanwords)

In five more instances, the rule is designed exclusively or predominantly for words containing borrowed elements; namely,

3B1(b),(c): the simplification of the clusters стсн, ндсн, нтсн, мтсн, нтн and ндн, all of which involve borrowed stems;

3B2: the simplification of the clusters снсн and ргсн, which occur in words whose stems were originally borrowed;

3N: the four degemination rules all require the specification of a LIST; and in all four cases, loanwords predominate in the lists;

3S1(c): the specification of vowel-strengths in vowel-clusters involves a large number of loanwords;

3Z: the "ad hoc" list is composed for the greater part of loanwords.

The remaining rules fall into two groups:

(1) those which apply in the same way to all *CSR* words, be they native or borrowed; and

(2) those which are designed for specific problems arising in *native* words; thus the question of their applicability to loanwords does not arise.

Furthermore, loanwords have called for special discussion, at some length, on eight separate occasions.*

From the summary just presented, three conclusions are to be drawn:

(1) SOME RULES APPLY *ONLY* TO CERTAIN LOANWORDS,
(2) SOME RULES APPLY EVERYWHERE *EXCEPT* IN CERTAIN LOANWORDS, and
(3) SOME RULES APPLY GENERALLY TO BOTH NATIVE WORDS AND LOANWORDS.

If the three groups are examined, we see that two different processes or phenomena are involved. In some instances, special provision has to be made so that loanwords are treated *differently* from native Russian words; and, in other instances, we have to ensure that loanwords are pronounced--in some respects--as if they were ordinary Russian words, i.e., we have to ensure that loanwords receive *the same* treatment as native Russian words.

To put this another way: in some respects, loanwords are RUSSIANIZED, that is, absorbed into the Russian system; while in other respects, loanwords are left UN-RUSSIANIZED, or unabsorbed. Thus, of the rules which apply only to loanwords, some are required so that the pronunciation of what would otherwise be awkward, NON-RUSSIAN sound-combinations is eased and made "more Russian". An example of such *Russianizing rules* is rule 3B1(b),(c).

Similarly, the rules which apply indifferently to native words and to loanwords have the effect of *Russianizing* the pronunciation of the latter. Two very important examples of such rules are 3E and 3P, whereby (respectively) VOICING ASSIMILATION and PALATALIZATION IN CONSONANT CLUSTERS are applied to all words, regardless of origin.[116] (Note that these rules are among the ones which are *iterative*, as well.)

On the other hand, some of the rules which apply only to loanwords are designed so that these words will be written in a NON-RUSSIAN form. For

*See pp. 64, 69, 75, 83, 92, 96-98, 100-01, 106.

example, in 3J2(b), the spelling of loanword stems is
rendered NON-RUSSIAN by rewriting е as э; as a consequence, the normal *CSR* rule which palatalizes consonants before е (rule 3K) will not apply to these
loanword stems. The words are thus left UN-RUSSIAN-
IZED.

Similarly, the rules which apply everywhere
EXCEPT in certain loanwords have the effect of leav-
ing these words UN-RUSSIANIZED. Thus, for example,
certain loanwords are left without VOWEL-REDUCTION,
when they are excepted from 3U and/or 3W2; and certain loanwords are left with geminate consonants
when they are excepted from 3N(b).

Specifically, two problems require comment. We
may put these in the form of questions: (1) WHICH
LOANWORDS are involved and (2) WHICH RULES apply (or
do not apply) to each particular loanword?

(1) The first question involves the problem of
defining the term 'loanword' as we have used it so
far, namely, as a borrowed word which in some way or
another has not been completely RUSSIANIZED, i.e.,
absorbed or assimilated into the native system of
Russian pronunciation. We might attempt an *external*
definition here, in which case we would have to refer to such cloudy criteria as the date at which a
word was first borrowed, the frequency of its use,
and the class of people who use it.[117] Alternatively, we might attempt an *internal* definition and use
as criteria the very rules which relate to the words
in question; but in this case we run the risk of
circularity (i.e., "these rules apply to that list
of words which we define as being the words to which
these rules apply"). Since we have decided to base
our rules on the official prescriptions of Avanesov,
however, we can circumvent this problem simply by
referring the reader to our LEXICON OF EXCEPTIONS,
which is drawn directly from *RLP* and *RLPU* and which
consists largely of words of foreign origin. Real-
istically, we have very little choice in the matter,
since *factual data* about the actual pronunciation of
these words by a majority of speakers of Russian is
in very short supply;[118] at the very least, it is
known that a great deal of *variation* in pronunciation
occurs. For our purposes, therefore, recourse to the
prescriptive lists is the only practical alternative
available.

(2) Our answer to the second question must also
necessarily be unsatisfactory. There would be no
problem if it were true that, for any one borrowed
word, *either* it was fully Russianized, *or* it was left

totally unabsorbed and "foreign-sounding". However,
many loanwords fall somewhere in between the two
extremes: they are Russianized in some respects, but
not in others. Furthermore, it is often very difficult to say for any one word in *which respects* it is
Russianized, or whether it is even *consistently*
Russianized in the *same* respects when it is used on
different occasions.

We may take the word ДЕМОНТА́Ж as an example.
Six rules come into consideration for this word:*

3E	(final ж→ш)
3J2(b)	(е→э)
3K	(д→дь, if 3J2(b) has *not* applied)
3U	(о→а)
3V	(э→ы, if 3J2(b) *has* applied)

(Note that 3V only applies to э after д in *non-standard* speech; but this pronunciation is very common.)
Cf. Stylistic Variations, pp. 99-100.

3W2	(е→и, if 3J2(b) has *not* applied)

All of these rules except 3E and 3K apply to
some loanwords and not to others. If it is not known
whether 3J2(b), 3U, 3V and 3W2 apply to this word
(if, for example, a student has available neither our
LEXICON OF EXCEPTIONS nor a reference-manual such as
RLPU), then the derivation of the *PO* for ДЕМОНТА́Ж
could proceed from *RO* to *PO* along no fewer than *EIGHT*
different paths, as shown on p. 123. Thus, EIGHT
different *PO*'s for this one word could theoretically
be derived, as follows:

(1) ДЕМОНТА́Ж

    демонта́ш (3E)
    дэмонта́ш (3J2(b))
    дэма̂нта́ш (3U)
    дыманта́ш (3V)

PO(1): дыма̂нта́ш

(2) ДЕМОНТА́Ж

    демонта́ш (3E)
    дэмонта́ш (3J2(b))
    дэма̂нта́ш (3U)
    n/c (3V)

PO(2): дэма̂нта́ш

*Apart from 3S, which, of course, applies in *every*
derivation of this word!

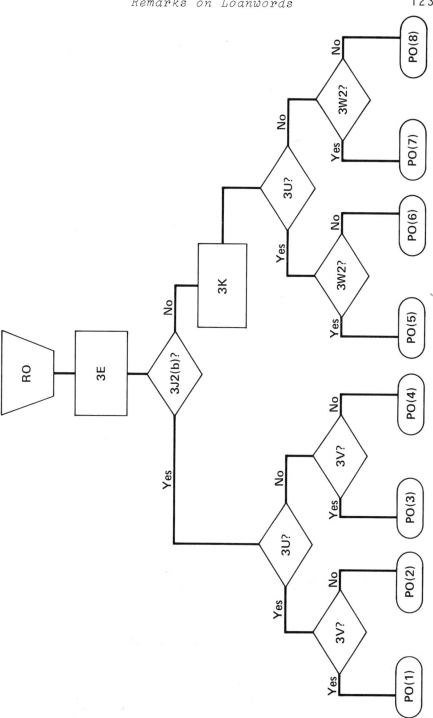

(3) ДЕМОНТА́Ж

     демонта́ш   (3E)

     дэмонта́ш   (3J2(b))

       n/c   (3U)

     дымо̂нта́ш (3V)

    PO(3):   дымо̂нта́ш

(4) ДЕМОНТА́Ж

     демонта́ш   (3E)

     дэмонта́ш   (3J2(b))

       n/c   (3U)

       n/c   (3V)

    PO(4):   дэмо̂нта́ш

(5) ДЕМОНТА́Ж

     демонта́ш   (3E)

       n/c   (3J2(b))

     дьемонта́ш (3K)

     дьема̂нта́ш (3U)

     дьима̂нта́ш (3W2)

    PO(5):   дьима̂нта́ш

(6) ДЕМОНТА́Ж

     демонта́ш   (3E)

       n/c   (3J2(b))

     дьемонта́ш (3K)

     дьема̂нта́ш (3U)

       n/c   (3W2)

    PO(6):   дьема̂нта́ш

(7) ДЕМОНТА́Ж

     демонта́ш   (3E)

       n/c   (3J2(b))

     дьемонта́ш (3K)

       n/c   (3U)

     дьимо̂нта́ш (3W2)

    PO(7):   дьимо̂нта́ш

(8) ДЕМОНТА́Ж

     демонта́ш   (3E)

       n/c   (3J2(b))

     дьемонта́ш (3K)

       n/c   (3U)

       n/c   (3W2)

    PO(8):   дьемо̂нта́ш

For our purposes, it is enough to know what is prescribed in *RLP* (or, failing a mention there, in *RLPU*) for each loanword. Look-up in the LEXICON OF EXCEPTIONS will provide this knowledge, insofar as our lexicon is adequate.

To know, however, how loanwords are pronounced by speakers of *CSR* and of styles close to *CSR*, a great deal more data is required. In this one instance, for example, are ALL EIGHT *PO*'s equally possible? And, of the pronunciations which do occur, which are most likely, given, say, a series of successive stages of Russianization from the least Russian-sounding дэмо̂нта́ш *(PO(4))* to the most Russian-sounding дьима̂нта́ш *(PO(5))*? The literature on the subject indicates that not all versions are equally likely; at the present stage, we can not go much further than this statement.[119]

In *RLP*, Avanesov normally recommends either that consonantal palatalization before э and vowel-reduction rules ALL apply, or that NONE of these rules apply, i.e., that in our example, ДЕМОНТА́Ж be pronounced either as (*PO(5)*) or as (*PO(4)*). He gives very little discussion to possible intermediate stages. Elsewhere in the literature on this subject, it has been stated that consonantal palatalization presupposes vowel-reduction--i.e., that pronunciations with the former but without the latter occur only rarely or not at all. This would mean, in our example, that (*PO(6)*), (*PO(7)*) and (*PO(8)*) are all unacceptable. This "loanword-rule" could be summarized as a slogan: "NO PALATALIZATION WITHOUT VOWEL-REDUCTION".[120]

3.16. REMARKS ON "SPELLING PRONUNCIATION"

We have made frequent references in this chapter to the apparent *TREND TOWARDS SPELLING-PRO-NUNCIATION*. This subject now requires review and further commentary.

The fundamental effect of the vast majority of our Rules is to transform the *SO* into a special orthography, the *PO*, which reflects as faithfully as possible the actual pronunciation of *CSR* as prescribed in *RLP*. (For the very few exceptions to this general statement, see below.) We have thus been saying that, to the extent that this *PO* differs from the *SO*, *CSR* is *NOT* pronounced as it is spelled.

In our notes on Stylistic Variations, we have made frequent reference to either the *OM* style, or the style of the Younger Generation (here: the *YG* style), or both, with a comment that the rule in question would have to be extended or restricted for one or the other style. When we are dealing, as in most instances, with rules which make the orthography more similar to the pronunciation, then it is true to make the following interpretations: a style for which a rule must be *extended* is a style in which the orthography and the pronunciation are even more dissimilar; and, conversely, a style for which a rule must be *restricted* is a style in which the orthography and the pronunciation are even more alike.

Now in each of the following nine instances to which a few others might also be added,[121] the necessary rule for *OM* would affect *many more words* than

the necessary rule for *YG*; that is to say, in these
instances, the *OM* style is much *less* similar to the
SO, and the *YG* style is *more* similar to it.   From
this it follows that, over the passage of time and
the succeeding generations between *OM* and *YG*, many
more words have come to be pronounced as they are
spelled.   This is precisely what is meant by the
TREND TOWARDS SPELLING-PRONUNCIATION.[122]
     The nine cases are as follows:

     (1)   In 3B, certain consonants are deleted.   In
OM, more are deleted; in *YG*, fewer are deleted.   *RLP*
takes up a position intermediate between the two (see
comments on pp. 40-41).

     (2)   In 3C2, г is replaced by г'.   In *OM*, this
occurred in several words; in *YG*, the rule is essentially optional, except for a few "interjectional"
words.   *RLP* is close to *YG* in this respect.

     (3)   In 3G1, к is replaced by х before к and ч.
In *OM*, this rule was extended in three respects:
(a) to the voiced stop г; (b) to the position before
dental stops; and (c) to apply even across the /
boundary.   In *YG*, there are reports that the rule is
applied even less than stated in *RLP*, and perhaps not
at all.[123]

     (4)   In 3H2, ДО́ЖДЬ → до́шть is rewritten до́щ for
the *OM* style.   Similarly, in 3H3, ДОЖДЯ́ → дождьа́ is
rewritten дожжьа́ for the *OM* style.   In *YG*, as in *RLP*,
these forms are pronounced much more as they are
spelled (*PO*:   до́шть, даждьа́).

     (5)   In 3H2, the clusters сч, сщ and шч are re-
written щ; it is further stated that for *CSR* this
rule is often to be regarded as optional.   In *OM*, the
rule applies consistently; in *YG*, the rule is applied
very inconsistently.

     (6)   In 3J1(a) and 3T, the adjectival ending ий
and the verbal affix ива, when occurring after *velars*, are given special rules for the *OM* style, so
that the *PO* for *OM* would be derived with, e.g.,
стро́гай and о̂т/ска́кавать, instead of the *RLP* (and *YG*)
pronunciation стро́гьий and о̂т/ска́кьивать.
     In 3T, further, the adjectival ending ый (which
occurs after "hard" consonants other than velars) is
given a special rule for the *OM* style, so that the
PO for *OM* would be derived as (for example) до́брай
rather than the *RLP* (and *YG*) pronunciation до́брый.
     The verbal affix ыва after "hard" consonants
other than velars, on the other hand, is rewritten

ава for the style prescribed in *RLP*, and (though perhaps not consistently?) for *YG*. Thus, in the relevant environments:

SO	PO(OM)	PO(RLP)	PO(YG)
ИЙ	ай	ьий	ьий
ИВА	ава	ьива	ьива
ЫЙ	ай	ый	ый
ЫВА	ава	ава	ыва

(7)   In 3J1(b), и is rewritten ы after the #
and / boundaries if a "hard" consonant precedes.
This applies equally well to *OM* as to the *RLP* style.
In *YG*, however, this rule is often suspended, especially after words ending in velars and after·pre-
positions.

(8)   In 3M, special rules are given for rewriting съа as са when it is the reflexive particle. It
is also explained how *RLP* takes up an intermediate
position between *OM*, in which both particles ся and
сь are pronounced with "hard" с, and *YG*, where they
are both pronounced with "soft" сь.

(9)   In 3P, 3Q, and 3R, complex rules are presented for regressive palatalization assimilation in
consonant clusters. In *OM*, this phenomenon is much
more widespread; in *YG*, it is much less noticeable.

As stated at the beginning of this section, some
rules are exceptional in that they make the *PO* MORE
(and not less) like the *SO*; this is because they are
required to correct instances of over-regularization
in the *RO*. A case in point is rule 3I, where the й
which is introduced in 2A is deleted in initial
position. In this particular instance, however, it
turns out that for *OM* we have to make exceptions; in
other words, that the *OM* style of pronunciation is
(again) LESS like the spelling than the style prescribed in *RLP* and the *YG* style (the words affected:
ИМ, ИМИ and ИХ).

To summarize, we may say that there are at least
ten instances where the *YG* style of pronunciation is
closer to the spelling than is the *OM* style. In
three of these instances, the pronunciation recommended by Avanesov is that of the *YG* (namely (4) and
(6) above, and rule 3I); in the other instances, *RLP*
takes up a sort of compromise position between the
two extremes. It would thus appear that the *OM* is

going decidedly out of style in the contemporary
Russian language.

When faced with a discernable tendency such as
this, it is tempting to speculate about a continua-
tion of the tendency in the future. Where pronunciation is concerned, any kind of forecasting is normally to be regarded as irresponsible. However, we may
indulge in a forecast if we insure ourselves with a
conditional introduction, as follows:

IF ALL THE TRENDS NOTED ABOVE FOR THE PAST 75
YEARS CONTINUE IN THE SAME WAY, then, at some (non-
specifiable) future date, a set of Reading Rules for
Russian will take the form of the rules presented
here, with the following simplifications:

(1) rules 3B, and 3J1(b) and perhaps 3I will be
restricted to some extent;
(2) rules 3P, 3Q and 3R will also be restricted
to some extent, and perhaps greatly restricted;
(3) rules 3C2, 3G1, 3H2 and 3M will be omitted
altogether, or at the very least will be extremely
restricted in scope.

A forecast such as the above can be justified
for *CSR* on the following grounds; that *all* the items
listed follow the same *general* tendency, that is, of
pronouncing words more as they are spelled. To this
we may add that there is very little evidence of the
reverse tendency, i.e., of pronouncing words *less* as
they are spelled.[124]

Two final cautionary notes merit attention.
Firstly, a distinction must be made between the general tendency towards spelling-pronunciation as an
observed fact, and possible *causes* for this tendency.
As a factual description, there is nothing wrong in
saying that more and more words are coming to be pronounced more as they are spelled; however, it does
not follow that they are pronounced in this way
BECAUSE they are spelled in this way, i.e., that the
orthography has *caused* the change in pronunciation.
As a hypothesis of cause, this suggestion may have
its merits (and, in a country like Russia where the
spread of literacy is a matter of especial prestige,
its attractions); this is nonetheless a hypothetical
matter.[125]

Secondly, it must be emphasized that *the vast
majority* of our rules (and the phenomena they reflect) show NO evidence of a trend towards spelling
pronunciation. Even if the observed tendency con-
tinues, indeed, even if it is hastened, there are as
yet no grounds for supposing that future generations

of Russians will restrict or suspend the other rules
--that they will, for example, cease and desist from
reducing unstressed vowels, or will renounce their
voicing assimilations.[126] Indeed, most of our rules
reflect features of the sound system of Russian which
(although of course not immutable) are nevertheless
much more firmly embedded and constant than the
transitory ten which we have listed here. If speech
and writing are in conflict, the Russian example suggests that speech still has the upper hand.

CHAPTER FOUR

FROM PHONETICIZED ORTHOGRAPHY TO PHONETIC TRANSCRIPTION

4.0. INTRODUCTION

In this chapter we convert our phoneticized orthography (*PO*) to a phonetic transcription (*PT*). For the latter, we use a style of transcription which is current in North America and common among Slavists on the European Continent; in 4.8. we give, for reference, a conversion chart from this style to other common styles of transcription, particularly the International Phonetic Alphabet (IPA) and the styles current in the Soviet Union.

In any *PT*, a more a less arbitrary choice has to be made concerning the *degree of delicacy*. A less delicate, "*broad*" transcription shows fewer phonetic distinctions; a more delicate, "*narrow*" transcription shows more phonetic niceties. Our own *PT*, while fairly narrow, does not take a number of fine distinctions into account; for these, students are referred to such standard works as Jones & Ward (1969), Boyanus (1965), Panov (1967), and Avanesov (*RLP*).

For clarity, we subdivide the rules into seven blocks. We deal with vowel-letters in 4A, digraphs in 4B, and single consonant-letters in 4C; we delete the boundary symbols in 4D. Application of these first four rule-blocks will result in a broad *PT*. Note that they are *all* to be applied to the same input string in the *PO*; it is not necessary to rewrite the input string four different times, once for each block; instead, it can be rewritten just once, in piecemeal fashion, according to the instructions for each individual character. For the sake of clarity, only one unit is rewritten at a time in the examples provided.

Our remaining three rule-blocks, 4E, 4F and 4G, give some of the more outstanding predictable phonetic features for consonants and vowels. If these blocks of rules are applied to the results of the first four, a much more narrow *PT* will be derived.

4.1. PHONETIC INTERPRETATION RULES FOR VOWEL-LETTERS

We now make final use of the distinction, made

in 3S, between *half-stressed* vowels and *unstressed vowels proper.*

Note particularly that the components of each of the rules in block 4A are ORDERED.*

$$
\boxed{4A}
\begin{aligned}
1. \ \ \text{a} \rightarrow &
\begin{cases}
\text{æ} \ / \ C_s \ \text{´or`} \ \ C_s \\
\text{a} \ / \ \text{other ´or`} \\
\text{Λ} \ / \ \underline{\ \ \frown\ \ } \\
\text{ə} \ / \ \text{elsewhere}
\end{cases} \\[2em]
2. \ \ \text{o} \rightarrow &
\begin{cases}
\text{ö} \ / \ C_s \ \underline{\text{´or`}} \ \ C_s \\
\text{o} \ / \ \text{elsewhere}
\end{cases} \\[2em]
3. \ \ \text{y} \rightarrow &
\begin{cases}
\text{ü} \ / \ C_s \ \text{´or`} \ \ C_s \\
\text{u} \ / \ \text{other ´or`} \\
\text{ʉ} \ / \ \text{other } C_s \ \underline{\quad\quad} \ C_s \\
\text{ʊ} \ / \ \text{elsewhere}
\end{cases} \\[2em]
4. \ \ \text{ы} \rightarrow &
\begin{cases}
\text{ɨ} \ / \ \underline{\text{´or`}} \\
\text{ɪ} \ / \ \text{elsewhere}
\end{cases} \\[2em]
5. \ \ \text{и} \rightarrow &
\begin{cases}
\text{i} \ / \ \underline{\text{´or`}} \\
\text{I} \ / \ \text{elsewhere}
\end{cases} \\[2em]
6. \ \begin{Bmatrix} \text{e} \\ \text{э} \end{Bmatrix} \rightarrow &
\begin{cases}
\text{e} \ / \ \underline{\quad\quad} \ C_s \\
\text{ε} \ / \ \text{elsewhere}
\end{cases}
\end{aligned}
$$

Discussion and Examples

In the rules in this chapter, we use the notation OTHER. This can be exemplified with reference to 4A1: if e.g. ɑ occurs with primary (á) or

---

*Note the symbol ´or`, which signifies "under primary or secondary stress."

secondary (à) stress between Soft Consonants (C_S),
then it is rewritten [æ]; if it occurs in any *other*
environment, it is rewritten [a].

Examples of stressed vowels:

ПЯ́ТЬ	ЧА́Й	ЧА́ШКА	ДА́ЧА	БРА́Т	ДА́
пьа́ть	ча́й	ча́шка	да́ча	бра́т	да́

→ · · ǽ · ·   · ǽ ·   · á · ·   · á · ·   · · á ·   · á

ТЁТЕ	ПЬЕ́ТЕ	ТЁТКА	ПЛО́ТЕ	СО́Т
тьо́тьи	пьйо́тьи	тьо́тка	пло́тьи	со́т

→ · · ŏ́ · ·   · · ŏ́ · ·   · · ó · ·   · · ó · ·   · ó ·

ЛЮ́ДИ	ЧУ́ТЬ	ЛЮ́Т	ЧУ́ДНО	УГЛУ́
льу́дьи	чу́ть	льу́т	чу́дна	̆углу́

→ · · ú · ·   · ú · ·   · · ú ·   · ú · ·   · · ú

ВЫ́	ВЫ́ТЬ	БЫ́Т	ШИ́ЛО
вы́	вы́ть	бы́т	шы́ла

→ · ɨ́   · ɨ́ · ·   · ɨ́ ·   · ɨ́ · ·

НИ́	НИ́М	НИ́МИ
ньи́	ньи́м	ньи́мьи

→ · · í   · · í ·   · · í · ·

ЦЕ́ПЬ	ЧЕ́СТЬ	ШЕ́СТЬ	ВЕ́ТЕР	Э́ТИ
цэ́пь	че́сьть	шэ́сьть	вье́тьир	э́тьи

→ · é · ·   · é · ·   · · é · ·   · · é · ·   é · ·

ШЕ́СТ	ЦЕ́П	ЧЕ́М	ВЕ́К	ЖЕ́	СТРОКЕ́	Э́ТОТ
шэ́ст	цэ́п	че́м	вье́к	жэ́	стра̂кье́	э́тат

→ · é · ·   · é ·   · é ·   · · é ·   · é   · · é   é · ·

Examples for unstressed vowels:

КАРАНДА́Ш	ОБОРО̀НОСПОСОБНОСТИ
кара̂нда́ш	а̂ба̂ро̀на#спа̂со́бнасьтьи

→ · ə · ʌ · ·   ʌ · ʌ · · · ə · · ʌ · · · ə · · · · ɪ

ЛЮДЕЙ	ЮБИЛЯР	ЛЮТОВА́ТЬ	СКА́ЖУТ
лью̈дьей	йу̲бьи̲льа́р	льу̲та̂ва́ть	ска́жу̲т
→ ··ü··	·ü··ɪ··	··ʊ·ʌ··	··ʊ·

УСУГУБЛЮ́	НЕ́ БЫЛО	УНЫ́ЛЫМИ	ПЕРЕНЕСУ́
у̂су̲гу̲́бльу́	нье́#бы̲ла̲	у̂ны́лымьи̲	пьирьиньи̂су́
→ ʊ·ʊ·ʊ··	··ɨ·ə	ʊ···ɨ··ɪ	··ɪ··ɪ··ɪ··

ОТЕ́ЛЬ	ДОСЬЕ́
о̂тэ́ль	до̂сье́
→ о··	·о··

ДЕТЕКТИ́В	БЕЛЬЭТА́Ж
дэтэ̂ктьий̃ф	бье̲ль эта́ж
→ ·ɛ·ɛ··	··e··ɛ··

The rules set out in 4A above result, for the vowels, in a compromise between the "broad" phonetic transcriptions suggested in some pedagogical manuals, and the "narrow" ones put forward in others. Reference to the standard manuals is strongly urged in any case, both for the necessary articulatory descriptions and explanations, and for practical hints and exercises.

Stylistic Variations (4A)

There are for the vowels of *CSR* two important distinctions which the student should be aware of, even if he either prefers not to make them, or never succeeds in making them, himself.

1. Speakers of *EKAN'E* (see pp. 102-04, and cf. the suggested rule on p. 107), who distinguish between three different unstressed vowels after Soft Consonants (*VR-1*), are best represented in a *PT* by the vocalic symbol [I^v] for the third vowel in question; thus, for speakers of this style, we would have to rewrite the phonetic interpretation rules for e, so that at least in *native* Russian words,

$$e \to I^v \; / \; \left\{ \overline{\underline{}} \right\}$$

For example, in this style:

ВЗЯЛА́	ВЕСНА́	*BUT*	ВИНА́
взье̲ла́	вь̲е̲сна́		вьйна́
→ · · ɪᵛ ·	· · ɪᵛ · ·		· · ɪ · ·

2. Many speakers of *CSR* make a distinction between two varieties of unstressed ы, as it appears in our *PO*, as follows:

If the ы in our *PO* represents ы or и in the *SO*, it is pronounced in a way that is best transcribed as [ɨ];

If the ы in our *PO* is derived from *SO* а (by 3V3), or from э (either by 3V3 or by the extension to 3V2 described in STYLISTIC VARIATIONS on p. 100), then it is pronounced in a different way, which we can transcribe as [ɨᵛ].

For example, IN THESE STYLES:

МЫЛА́	ЖИЛА́	*BUT*	ЖАЛЕ́ТЬ	СЕ́РДЦЕ (L. Sg.)
мы̲ла́	жы̲ла́		жы̲льє́ть	сьє́рцы̲
→ · ɨ · ·	· ɨ · ·		· ɨᵛ · ·	· · ɨᵛ

ШЕПТА́ТЬ	ДЕТЕКТИ́В	*AND* (cf. 3Z)	ПОЖА́ЛУЙСТА
шы̲пта́ть	ды̲ты̲ктьый̇ф		па̂жа́лы̲ста
→ · ɨᵛ · ·	· ɨᵛ· ɨᵛ · ·		· · ɨᵛ · ·

3. The second part of rule 4A6, ${e \atop э}$ → ε / elsewhere, involves the environment "before the word-boundary #"; and, indeed, normally stressed é is realized as [ε] in final position. *If, however, the following word begins with a Soft Consonant*, then the final é may be realized as [é]. This is particularly frequent when the # occurs before a *particle*. Thus ПО ГОРЕ́ ЛИ → *PO* ##па/га̂рьє́#льи## may be pronounced either [pəgʌr'έl'ɪ] or [pəgʌr'él'ɪ]. In fast speech, the pronunciation of [é] instead of [έ] occurs even when a stressed word follows the # boundary; thus, ДВЕ́ ДЕ́ВОЧКИ → ##дьвьє́#дьє́вачкьи## is normally pronounced [d'v'έ d'évəčk'ɪ], but in fast speech may be pronounced [d͡v'é d'évəčk'ɪ].[1]

4. A final note may be made concerning the one word СОЛНЦЕ (cf. 3Z), which is normally pronounced with a velarized [ɵ]:[2]

СО́ЛНЦУ

со́нцу

→ ·**ó**··

4.2. PHONETIC INTERPRETATION RULES FOR DIGRAPHS

The three *digraphs* introduced and discussed in 3.1. are dealt with separately, in rule 4B, before single consonant letters are interpreted in 4C. It may be helpful for the student to recall that these three digraphs represent *single phonetic units*.[3]

Certain combinations of the single consonant letters listed in 4C may also be realized as *single units* in certain styles and in certain circumstances; see STYLISTIC VARIATIONS (4C) for details. The reader is also referred to the NOTE ON DIGRAPHS on page 30, and to the NOTE ON GEMINATE CONSONANTS in 4.3.

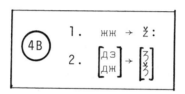

4B1:   жж is rewritten ž̌: in all environments, e.g.:

Е́ЗЖУ	ЖУЖЖА́Л	МОЖЖЕВЕ́ЛЬНИК	С ЖА́РУ
йе́жжу	жӯжжа́л	мажжы̆вье́льньик	ж/жа́ру
→··ž̌:·	··ž̌:··	··ž̌:··	·ž̌:··

See, however, STYLISTIC VARIATIONS below.

4B2:   дз is rewritten ʒ̪* except when the two letters are separated by a boundary, e.g.:

ОТЕ́Ц БЫ	ДЗО́Т	*BUT*	ОТ ЗУ́БА
атье́дз#бы	дзо́т		ад/зу́ба
→ ··ʒ̪··	·ʒ̪··		·d/z··

*Note that [ʒ] is equivalent to [d͡z], and [ž̌] is equivalent to [d͡ž̌]. If preferred, [d͡z] and [d͡ž̌] may be used, to avoid confusion with the I.P.A. notation (cf. the table in 4.8.). Note also that [ž̌] is an inherently "soft" *palatal* sound, and does not require the symbol ['].

ДЖ is rewritten ž̌* except when the two letters are separated by a boundary, e.g.:

НО́ЧЬ БЫ	А́ЛЧБА	ДЖА́З	*BUT*	ОТ ЖУ́НА
но́дж#бы	а́лджба	джа́з		ад/жу́на
→ ··ž̌··	··ž̌··	ž̌··		·d/ž··

Stylistic Variations (4B)

As discussed above in Chapter Three (pp. 30, 56, 61, 63 and 65), ЖЖ is interpreted as a "soft" consonant in a number of styles and circumstances.[4] The appropriate *PT* in this instance is [ž':], as for example, in:

Е́ЗЖУ	БРЫ́ЗЖЕШЬ
йе́жжу	бры́жжиш
→··ž':·	··ž':·· in these styles

In the latter example, the normal *CSR PO* has a after ЖЖ, derived by rule 3V1(a); in this style and in this word, however, ЖЖ is "Soft"; hence, 3V1(a) does not apply, and 3X2 applies.

In conversational *CSR*, ДЗ and ДЖ may be pronounced in a slightly different way from that given above; namely, as [ʒz] and [ž̌ž'] respectively (*RLP* 146-47).

4.3. PHONETIC INTERPRETATION RULES FOR SINGLE CONSONANT LETTERS AND Ь

We now complete the interpretation rules for the letters in our *PO* as far as our "broad" transcription is concerned.

---

*Note that [ʒ] is equivalent to [dʐ], and [ž̌] is equivalent to [dž̌]. If preferred, [dʐ] and [dž̌] may be used, to avoid confusion with the I.P.A. notation (cf. the table in 4.8.). Note also that [ʒ] is an inherently "soft" *palatal* sound, and does not require the symbol ['].

1.	п	→	p
2.	б	→	b
3.	т	→	t
4.	д	→	d
5.	к	→	k
6.	г	→	g
7.	ц	→	c
8.	ф	→	f
9.	в	→	v
10.	с	→	s
11.	з	→	z
12.	х	→	x
13.	г′	→	$\begin{cases} ɦ & / \text{list} \\ ɣ & / \text{elsewhere} \end{cases}$
14.	ч	→	č
15.	щ	→	š':
16.	ш	→	š
17.	ж	→	ž
18.	м	→	m
19.	н	→	n
20.	л	→	l
21.	р	→	r
22.	й	→	j
23.	ь	→	'

(4C)

Discussion and Examples

Most of these interpretation rules require no comment; the few that do so require are mentioned first.

4C7, 4C14: See STYLISTIC VARIATIONS below for frequent alternative pronunciations for ц, ч in two
idiosyncratic words. Note also that [č] is a *palatal*
sound; like its voiced counterpart, [ž], and like
[j], its phonetic "softness" is inherent and the

symbol ['] is not required.

4C15: See STYLISTIC VARIATIONS below for a very common alternative pronunciation for щ.

4C13: The non-standard character ѓ was introduced in 3C2 and 3G1 and must be distinguished from the standard character г. ѓ is rewritten as [ɦ] in three categories of words: (1) in the "interjectional" words АГА́, ОГО́, ГÓП, ГÓПЛЯ; this pronunciation is extremely common; (2) in the two loanwords БУХГА́ЛЬТЕР and БЮСТГА́ЛЬТЕР,* where again, [ɦ] is the normal pronunciation; and (3) in the noun ГОСПÓДЬ, particularly in its V. Sg. form ГÓСПОДИ, and in oblique cases of the word БОГ; in this third category, the sound [γ] is normally substituted. Thus,

```
      АГА́       БУХГА́ЛЬТЕР      СЛА́ВА БÓГУ

      а͡ѓа́       бу͡ѓа́льтьир      сла́ва#бо́ѓу

  →   ·ɦ·       ··ɦ··            ··ɦ·
```

or, more often, γ

ѓ → γ:

```
      ГА́БИТУС      МÓГ БЫ

      ѓа́бьитус      мо́ѓ#бы

  →   γ··          ··γ··
```

4C22: й is rewritten [j] in all environments. If a more precise, "narrow" transcription is required, the following alternative rule may be substituted:[5]

$$ й \rightarrow \left\{ \begin{array}{l} j \ / \ \left\{ \begin{array}{c} \text{\_́\_} \\ \text{\_̆\_} \end{array} \right\} \\ y \ / \ \text{elsewhere} \end{array} \right\} $$

For example:

```
      Е́ЗДИТЬ         ЕЗЖА́ТЬ        ПЛА́ТЬЕ        ПИТЬЁ

      йе́зьдьить      йе͡жжа́ть      пла́тьйе      пьйтьйо́

  →   j··            y··           ··y·          ··j·
```

4C21: Similarly, the following rule may be substituted for the one given for р, if a "narrower" transcription is required:[6]

---

*See 3Z.

$$p \rightarrow \begin{cases} \check{r} \ / \ v \text{---} v \\ \tilde{r} \ / \ \text{elsewhere} \end{cases}$$

For example:

ПОРА́   ПО́РТ   ПРА́Х   ПО́Р   РА́К

па̂р̱а́   по́р̱т   пр̱а́х   по́р̱   р̱а́к

→ ··ř··   ··r̃·   ·r̃··   ··r̃   r̃··

Finally, we must discuss the rule ь → [']. Although this apostrophe is written separately, it is not to be interpreted as a distinct segment, but rather as indicating that a feature of PALATALIZATION is co-articulated with the preceding consonant. Even at this, however, we are still taking certain liberties with the phonetic facts, for we are using the word *palatalization* as a cover-term for what are really diverse articulations. For example, [p] differs from [p'] primarily in terms of secondary articulation; the main difference between [t] and [t'] relates to the primary articulator employed; while the difference between [k] and [k'] is primarily one of place of articulation.[7]

Examples of consonantal interpretation rules not so far exemplified, in order:

4C1: ПА́ПЕРТЬ

па́п̱ьирть

→ p·p'··

4C2: БЕЗБО́ЖИЕ

бьи̂збо́жыйа

b'··b··

4C3: ТЯГОТА́

тьига̂та́

t'···t·

4C4: ДОДЕ́ЛКА

да̂дье́лка

→ d·d'··

4C5: КЕ́МПИНГ

кье́мьпьинк

k'·· ··k

4C6: ГИГРОГРА́Ф

гьигра̂гра́ф

g'·g··g··

4C7: ОТЕ́Ц

а̂тье́ц

→ ··c

4C8: ФИЛОСО́Ф

фьила̂со́ф

f'·· ··f

4C9: ВЫ́ВИХ

вы́вьих

v·v'··

4C10: СО́СЕН

со́сьин

→ s·s'··

4C11: ЗИГЗА́Г

зьигза́к

z'··z··

4C12: ХЛЕ́Б

хльеп

x··

4C12: ХИТРЕ́Ц

хьитрье́ц

→ x'··

4C14: ПЕ́ЧЬ

пье́ч

··č̌

4C15: ЩЁКОТ

що̄кат

š'̄:··

4C16: ШИ́ШКА

шы́шка

→ š·š··

4C17: ЖЕ́ЧЬ

же̄ч

ž̄··

4C18: МА́МЕ

ма́мьи

m·m'·

4C19: НЮА́НС

нь у͡а́нс

n'··n·

4C20: ЛИЛОВЕ́ТЬ

льила͡вье́ть

l'·l··

A Note on Geminate Consonants

There are basically two ways of transcribing geminate consonants phonetically; as a sequence of two consonants (thus, cc → [ss]), or with a diacritic mark such as a macron or a colon (thus, cc → [s̄] or [s:]). We recommend, and use, the colon; thus, in 4B above for жж → [ž:], and here in 4C for щ → [š':].

When the consonant in question is a fricative (as in the examples in the preceding paragraph) or a resonant, there is no possibility of confusion; phonetically, the transcriptions [ss] and [s:] are homophonous.

If the consonant is however a stop, confusion can arise. A "geminate *t*", for example, may be articulated as a single stop (with a long time-lag between implosion and explosion) or as a double stop (as a sequence of two separate stops). If this distinction were valid for *CSR*, the difference could be shown by distinguishing between [tt] and [t:]. Since geminate stops in *CSR* are always phonetically *long single stops*, either transcription could be used; but the use of "[t:]" is more precise.

When the consonant is an affricate, the same remarks also apply. Thus, цц → [c:], with only the stop element of the affricate lengthened; i.e., just as [c] can be represented as [t̯s], so can [c:] be equated with [t̯:s]. Similarly in the case of чч → [č:]; this is to be interpreted as equivalent to [t'̯:š']. The effect of this interpretation is that *both* цц and тц are in fact pronounced the same; and that *both* чч and тьч are pronounced the same.[8]   For example,

ОТЦА́	ВИ́ТЬСЯ	ЛЁТЧИК	ПИЧЧИКА́ТО
а̂тца́	вьи́цца	льо́тьчик	пьиччи̂ка́та
·tc·	··c:·	··t'ч̌··	··ч̌··
or ··t͡s··	or ··t͡s:··	or ··t'͡:ш̌'··	or ··t'͡:ш̌'··

The foregoing remarks concern representation of what are phonetically combinations of *lengthened stop and fricative release*. These are not to be confused with combinations of *stop and lengthened fricative release*. Examples of this latter combination are discussed in STYLISTIC VARIATIONS below.

Stylistic Variations (4C)

1. On pp. 53-55, the following combinations of consonants were mentioned as occurring in certain styles of Russian pronunciation: чш, джж, цс, дзз. All are combinations of *stop plus lengthened fricative release*, and are distinct from the combinations just discussed. For example, *in some styles*:

МЛА́ДШИЙ	О́ТЖИЛ	ОТСЫ́ПАЛ	ПОДЗО́Р
мла́чшый	о́дж/жыл	а̂ц/сы́пал	па̂дз/зо́р
→ [мlа́č̌š̌ɪj]	[ó ž̌ ž̌ɪl]	[ʌc sʲpəl]	[pʌ ʒ zór]

(cf. *in CSR*)

мла́тшый	о́д/жыл	а̂т/сы́пал	па̂д/зо́р
→ [мlа́tš̌ɪj]	[ód ž̌ɪl]	[ʌt sʲpəl]	[pʌd zór]

In all four cases, the phonetic combination is one of an affricate plus a fricative, and is identical to a combination of stop plus lengthened fricative release; thus, [č̌š̌] is the same as [t͡š̌:]; [ž̌ž̌], the same as [ǯ:];* [cs] can be equated with [t͡s:]; and [ʒz] with [ʒ:].

2. The stem лу́чш- should be considered separately. Following *RLP* (cf. p. 53), this should be transcribed [lú́č̌š̌-] for the *CSR* pronunciation, i.e., with "soft" [č̌] and "hard" [š̌]. In conversational

---

*Note that, in these styles, [č̌] and [ǯ] (when occurring before [š̌] and [ž̌]) are "hard" (cf. 4E3)!

CSR, the pronunciations [lúč':-]* and [lúčš-] are reported, viz., one with "soft" [č':], the other with
"hard" [čš].[9]

3.   The stem цвёт is, according to some reports,[10] pronounced very commonly with a "soft" rather than "hard" [c'], thus [c'v'ét].

4.   щ, which we transcribe as [š':]--a lengthened palatal [š']--is pronounced as [š'č'] by many
speakers of *CSR*. The evidence now available shows
that [š':] has replaced [š'č'] (the *OM* norm) in the
speech of all but the oldest generations in Moscow,
and even in the speech of the younger generations in
Leningrad. There is much individual variation, however, especially when the щ of our *PO* is derived from
сч, сщ or шч (see 3H2). Moreover, [š':] may be
phonetically degeminated to [š'], especially in final
position and before another consonant; this style,
although not orthoepic, is very common.[11]

5.   The symbols y̌, ы̌, *as used for certain styles
on page 93,* can be transcribed in a *PT* for these
styles as [w] and [ŭ], respectively.

4.4. DELETION RULES FOR SUPERFLUOUS SYMBOLS

We may now delete all the remaining symbols
which have no phonetic realization in speech and supply square brackets to indicate a phonetic transcription.

(4D)	1. delete { (1) all boundary symbols (2) the "half-stressed" symbol ^ }	
	2. enclose all strings in square brackets	

Discussion

Our *PT* consists of articulatory phonetic symbols
only; the three boundary symbols ##, # and / are
therefore deleted. Although there are no rigorous

*We show the necessary distinction between [č'] and
[č] here, but do not mark [č'] elsewhere, since--
apart from this one case--every ч in *CSR* represents
a "soft" sound.

traditions with regard to the use of *spaces* in phonetic transcriptions, the following rule of thumb
corresponds to standard practice: ## should be replaced with a space; / should not be replaced with a
space; # may or may not be so replaced (and in the
latter case, the *RO* may be used as a convenient
guide).

Our "half-stressed" symbol ^ has also fulfilled
its function in the Reading Rules, and is to be deleted. Of course, a system of vowel-strength symbols
representing articulatory facts could be devised, but
such a system would not necessarily correspond to the
simplified scheme we have used here.[12]

4.5. SECONDARY FEATURE RULES FOR CONSONANTS: BLOCK 4E

If rule-blocks 4A - 4D are applied, a *PT* will be
derived which, though quite "broad", is quite adequate for most practical purposes.

A number of minor articulatory characteristics
of consonants are also predictable from their phonetic environments. If a "*narrow*" *PT* for *CSR* is required, some or all of these features may be shown;
however, since they are minor and "automatic" for
native Russian speakers, they are not normally shown
in popular pedagogical works.

The following rules are presented *informally*, to
save space.*

4E1: Aspiration

Voiceless stops are aspirated when occurring
before voiceless stops, before non-homorganic nasals
and before a pause. They may be written with the
raised symbol ʰ, e.g.:

ТКЕ́Т	ПНЁМ	КТО́	ЦЕ́ПЬ	ВГЛУ́БЬ
ТКЬО́Т	ПНЬО́М	КТО́	цэ́пь	вглу́пь
t k'ót	pn'óm	któ	cép'	vglúp'
t ʰ··	pʰ··	kʰ·	··p'ʰ	··p'ʰ

4E2: Labialization

All consonants are labialized (rounded) before
rounded vowels, and may be written with the raised

---

*In this way, we may refer to "consonants" rather
than enumerate all the consonant-symbols which 4B
and 4C have furnished.

symbol ᵂ in this position, e.g.:

КО́М	ЛЮ́ДИ	ДУ́Л	ЕЩЁ
ко́м	льу́дьи	ду́л	йищо́
kóm	lʼűdʼɪ	dúl	yɪš̌ʼːó
k̲ᵂ·	l̲ʼᵂ··	d̲ᵂ·	··š̲ʼᵂː

Labial consonants show lip-rounding before stressed [ɫ] also, e.g.:

МЫ́	БЫ́ТЬ	ВЫ́Л	ФЫ́РКАТЬ
мы́	бы́ть	вы́л	фы́ркать
mɫ	bɫtʼ	vɫl	fɫrkətʼ
m̲ᵂ	b̲ᵂ··	v̲ᵂ·	f̲ᵂ··

4E3: Retroflexion

"Hard" [š ž] are retroflexed; they may therefore be written [ṣ̌ ẓ̌], e.g.:

ШИ́ТЬ	ЖИ́ТЬ
шы́ть	жы́ть
ṣ̌ɫtʼ	ẓ̌ɫtʼ
š̱··	ẕ̌··

4E4: Velarization

All "hard" consonants are velarized; they may be written with the symbol ~, e.g.:

ЛЫ́ЖА	ВА́С	ЗУ́БЫ
лы́жа	ва́с	зу́бы
lɫžə	vás	zúbɫ
ɫ̱·ẕ̌·	v̱·s̱	ẕ·ḇ·

This feature, which is especially noticeable in the case of "dark" [ɫ], and can also be quite easily observed in the voiced fricatives, is so seldom marked that we recommend its omission in most practical transcriptions. A convenient rule of thumb for the student to remember is that most Russian consonants are either velarized or palatalized. If therefore any consonant sound in the *PT* is not followed by the apostrophe to indicate palatalization, that consonant may generally be assumed to be velarized.

4E5: Alveolar Articulation

"Dental" stops and nasals are true dentals in *CSR* under most conditions. An alveolar articulation is normal when one of these consonants is either preceded or followed by the alveopalatal fricatives [š ž]. If the dental-alveolar distinction is to be marked in a *PT*, by normal practice the dentals are given a distinctive mark and the alveolars left unmarked. For *CSR*, clearly the reverse procedure makes more sense. The symbols concerned may thus be marked ˌ when next to [š ž], e.g.:

ТУ́К	БО́Н	*BUT*	ШТУ́К	ВОНЖУ́
ту́к	во́н		шту́к	ва̃нжу́
tú͟k	vó͟n		štú͟k	vʌn͟žú
			·t··	··n··
			ˌ	ˌ

4.6. ALTERNATIVE FEATURE RULES FOR RESONANT CONSONANTS: BLOCK 4F

In addition to the *minor* feature rules given above, one rule concerning *alternative* feature rules may be applied. It concerns liquids and nasals only.

When liquids and nasals occur either between consonants, or in prepausal position after a consonant, one of three *alternative* phonetic realizations may result:

4F1. EITHER, *if* the environment consists of voiceless consonants, the liquid or nasal is *devoiced* (e.g., [m̥]);

4F2. OR,--whether these neighbouring consonants are voiceless or voiced--the liquid or nasal is syllabicized (e.g., [m̩]);

4F3. OR, a [ə] or [ɪ] is inserted.[13]

For example:

	ТЕА́ТР	РИ́ТМ	ВО́ПЛЬ
	тьйа̃тр	рьи́тм	во́пль
1.	t'ɪátr̥̃	r'i̊tm̥	vópl̥'
2.	t'ɪátr̥̩̃	r'i̊tm̩	vópl̩'
3.	t'ɪátər̃	r'i̊təm	vópəl'

РУ́БЛЬ   ЖИ́ЗНЬ   ОКТЯ́БРЬСКИЙ   (see 3Z)

ру́бль   жы́знь   а̂ктьа́брскьий

2. rúbl̩'   žɨz'n̩'   ʌkt'ábr̩sk'ɪj

3. rúbəl'   žɨz'ɪn'   ʌkt'ábərsk'ɪj

4.7. SECONDARY FEATURE RULES FOR VOWELS: BLOCK 4G

Some very minor articulatory characteristics of
vowels are also predictable from their phonetic environments. If a narrow *PT* for *CSR* is required, some
of the more precise vocalic distinctions may thus be
shown.

The application of the following informal rules
simultaneously with those in 4E will provide a *PT*
which is unusually narrow for both consonants and
vowels.

4G1: Length

Stressed vowels are lengthened slightly in preconsonantal position, as compared to prepausal position, where they are shorter.

Vowels may therefore be marked for length when
stressed and non-final, e.g.:

ХОРОШО́   *BUT*   ХОРОШО́М   ВЫ́   *BUT*   ВЫ́Л

харашо́   харашо́м   вы̂   вы̂л

··ó̲   ··o̲: ·ɨ̲   ·ɨ̲:

5G2: Minor Qualitative Distinctions

All vowels are assimilated to some degree by
the "soft" or "hard" quality of neighbouring consonants. Some of the resulting phonetic distinctions
are striking enough to be shown in a "broad" *PT*
(see 4A); others may be reserved for a "narrow" *PT*,
as here.

Rule 4G2 is subdivided into three sections,
partly for clarity, and partly for reasons inherent
in the phonetic symbols involved.

4G2(a): The non-front vowels [á ə ó ú ʊ] are slight-
ly fronted when occurring after Soft Consonants; in
4A, non-front vowels occurring *between* Soft Consonants are transcribed with special symbols; here,
then, we are dealing only with other environments
after Soft Consonants:

МЯ́Т   ГО́ЛУБЯ   ЛЮ́БО   СЁМГА

мьа́т   го́лубьа   льу́ба   сьо́мга

m'át   gólub'ə   l'úbə   s'ómgə

··ấ˂   ··ə˂   ··ǔ˂··   ··ǒ˂··

4G2(b): The non-front vowels [á ə ó ú ʋ ɟ] are
slightly fronted when occurring before Soft Consonants. (Again, the position *between* Soft Consonants
is either already covered, or else non-applicable.)

МА́ТЬ   ДУ́ТЬ   ТО́ПЬ   БЫ́ТЬ

ма́ть   ду́ть   то́пь   бы́ть

mát'   dút'   tóp'   bɟt'

·ấ˂·   ·ǔ˂·   ·ǒ˂·   ·ɟ˂·

4G2(c): The mid-front vowels [é ɛ́ e ɛ] are distinguished in 4A according to the softness of following
consonants. Preceding softness vs. hardness also
affects their vocalic quality; for ease of transcription, in this case we show the *backed* quality of
these vowels when occurring initially and after Hard
Consonants:

Э́ТИ   Э́ТОТ   ДЕТЕКТИ́В   ШЕ́СТ

э́тьи   э́тат   дэтэктьи́ф   шэ́ст

ét'ɪ   ɛ́tət   dɛtɛkt'íf   šɛ́st

é˃··   ɛ́˃··   ·ɛ˃ɛ˃··   ·ɛ́˃·

For further distinctions, reference to the standard manuals is recommended.

4.8. CONTRASTIVE TABLE OF PHONETIC SYMBOLS

For reference, we give below a table which cor-
relates each of the phonetic symbols which we use in
this chapter, with the symbols used in the standard
manuals on Russian phonetics and general phonetics.
Where the symbol used in a particular transcription-
system does not differ from ours, this is shown with
the word SAME. In the columns headed OTHERS, symbols
are entered only when they differ from those previously given.[14] Students more conversant with the
I.P.A. should practise converting one transcription
to the other.

4.8.1. VOWEL SYMBOLS

Ours	IPA	Others (Latin)	Avanesov (*RLP*)	Panov (1967)	Others (Cyrillic)	Examples* (*PO*)
æ	same		ӕ	ӕ		мья́ть
a	same		a	a		ма́т
ʌ	same		a	a		валы́
ə	same		ь	ь		са́да
ӧ	æ/ɔ+	:ɔ	ӱ	ӱ		тьо́тьа
o	ɔ		o	o		то́т
ü	y/u+/ɵ		ӱ	ӱ		ду́ны
u	same		y	y		ду́нуть
ü	ɵ+		:ӱ	:ӱ		льубльу́
ʊ	ɵ		y	y		лубо́к
ɨ	same	y	ы	ы		бы́т
ɨ	ɵ	Y	ы	ы		была́
ɨˇ	ɵˇ		ыэ/эы**	ыэ/эы**		жыльэ́ть (*)

*Where a symbol is used to represent one of a number of *alternative* pronunciations--either because there is free variation, or because of a stylistic variation--the example involved is marked with an asterisk in parentheses (*).

**A fine distinction which we do not represent. Check the original for details.

Ours	IPA	Others (Latin)	Avanesov (RLP)	Panov (1967)	Others (Cyrillic)	Examples (PO)
i	same		и	и		вЬи́ть
ɪ	ɪ		и/ь**	и		вЬила́
ɪ̌	ɨ̆		и̯е	из/эй**		взвела́ (*)
e	same		ê	э:		сЬе́ть
ɛ	same		e	э		сЬе́л

Minor Distinctions (Examples of Symbols)

Ours	IPA	Others (Latin)	Avanesov (RLP)	Panov (1967)	Others (Cyrillic)	Examples (PO)
ǎ	a		ȧ/a̤**	ȧ/a̤**		мЬа́т, ма́ть
ê	e		ɛ̂	•ɛ		э́ты
a:	same	a·	¦a	¦a		ма́т

4.8.2. CONSONANT SYMBOLS

Ours	IPA	Others (Latin)	Avanesov (RLP)	Panov (1967)	Others (Cyrillic)	Examples
p	same		п	п		по́т
b	same		б	б		ба́л
t	same		т	т		то́т
d	same		д	д		да́л

Ours	IPA	Others (Latin)	Avanesov (*RLP*)	Panov (1967)	Others (Cyrillic)	Examples (*PO*)
k	same		к	к		кóт
g	same		г	г		гáт
c	t͡s		ц	ц		цэпь
ʒ	d͡z		дз	дз		дзот
f	same		ф	ф		флóт
v	same		в	в		вóт
s	same		с	с		сóт
z	same		з	з		зол
x	same		х	х		хóт
ɦ	same	h	h	h		агá
ɣ	same	g	ɣ	ɣ		бóгу
č	tʃ		ч	ч		чóм
ǯ	d͡ʒ	j	dʒ	дж		джáс
š	ʃ		ш	ш		шóл
ž	ʒ		ж	ж		жэ
m	same		м	м		мóт
n	same		н	н		нóт
l	same		л	л		лóтка

Ours	IPA	Others (Latin)	Avanesov (*RLP*)	Panov (1967)	Others (Cyrillic)	Examples (*PO*)
r	same		r	r		рóт
j	same	y	j	j	й	йа́
Palatalization:						
pʼ	pʲ	ṕ/pj/py	пʼ	пʼ	пь/пʲ	пʲóс
bʼ	bʲ	б́/bj/by	бʼ	бʼ	бь/бʲ	бʲа́сь
nʼ	nʲ	ń/nj/ny	нʼ	нʼ	нь/нʲ	нʲóм
etc.	etc.	etc.	etc.	etc.	etc.	
kʼ	k, /k⁺	ḱ/kj/ky/ḵ	кʼ	кʼ	кь/кʲ	ткʲóт
gʼ	g, /g⁺	ǵ/gj/gy/ǵ	гʼ	гʼ	гь/гʲ	гʲи́т
Length:						
š:	same	š·	ш̄	ш̄		ш/шу́мам

Minor Distinctions (Examples of Symbols)

Ours	IPA	Others (Latin)	Avanesov (*RLP*)	Panov (1967)	Others (Cyrillic)	Examples (*PO*)
r̃	ɾ					napá
x̌	ɻ					ра́к
y	i̯		ꭓ			ма́йа
w	same					see p. 142
ɟ̈	ɰ̆					тньо́т
tʰ	tˤ					ту́
tʷ	tʷ					па́л
ɟ	same	⨍			т	шту́к
t	t̪				•т	ту́к
t̑ (alveolar)	t					ша́к
x̌ˎ	ʈ			Σ<	Σ<	
			Σo	Σo	ры́тм (*)
m̥ (voiceless)	same	m̥				
m̩ (syllabic)	same					

4.9. EXTENDED EXAMPLE OF DERIVATION

Below we present an example of the derivation of a complete sentence, from the *SO* to the *RO* (without the intermediate steps); then through every rule in Chapter Three to the *PO*; to the *PT* as derived in 4A, 4B, 4C and 4D (i.e., to the recommended "broad" *PT*); and, finally, to the *PT* as derived by 4E, 4F and 4G (i.e., to the recommended "narrow" *PT*).

The complete sentence is written out in full seven times, viz.: in the *SO*; in the *RO*; after 3A (where the boundaries are inserted); after 3S (where the "half-stressed" vowels are marked); in the *PO*; in the "broad" *PT*; and in the "narrow" *PT*. For all the other intermediate steps, only those words are written out which are affected by the rule in question. The sentence is:

РЫ́ЖИЕ ВНУ́КИ ГОЛЛА́НДСКОГО МОРЯКА́ РА́ДУЮТСЯ ТЕ́М, ЧТО О̀Н ВЧЕРА́ ПЕ́РЕД ВЗЛЁТОМ С АЭРОДРО́МА ИХ МЯ́ГКО ПОЦЕЛОВА́Л.

It should be noted that this very unlikely sentence was conceived as being particularly representative of the operation of our rules. Most ordinary Russian sentences will call for much less rewriting than is exemplified here.

	РЫ́ЖИЕ	ВНУ́КИ	ГОЛЛА́НДСКОГО	МОРЯКА́	РА́ДУЮТСЯ	ТЕ́М,	ЧТО О́Н
SO	РЫ́ЖИЕ	ВНУ́КИ	ГОЛЛА́НДСКОГО	МОРЯКА́	РА́ДУЮТСЯ	ТЕ́М,	ЧТО О́Н
RO	ры́жийе	вну́ки	голла́ндского	морьака́	ра́дуйутсьа	те́м,	что о́н
3A	##ры́жийе#вну́ки # голла́ндского#морьака́#ра́дуйутсьа#те́м, # что#о́н#						
3B			голла́ндского				
3C			голла́нсково				
3D		у́нуки					
3E		вну́ки					
3F		вну́ки					
3G							
3H							
3I							
3J1	ры́жыйе						
3J2							
3K		вну́ьки				тьём	што

	##рыжыйе#внукьи	голанскова	морбака	радуйуца	тьём	што#он#
3L				ра́дуйуцца		
3N		гол́анскова		ра́дуйуца		
3P				ра́дуйуца		
3S	##ры́жыйе#вну́кьи #	го́ланскова #	морба́ка#	ра́дуйуца #	тьбм #	што#бн#
3U		га́ланскава	марьба́ка			шта
3V			марьба́ка			
3W1	ры́жныйи					
3W2	ры́жны					
3X	ры́жныйи					
3Y	ры́жны					
3Z						
PO	##ры́жны #вну́кьи #	га́ла́нскава #	марьба́ка	ра́дуйуца #	тьбм #	шта#бн#
PT	[r̪í ž‡ɪ vnúk'ɪ	gʌlánskəvə	mer'ıkə	rádujuсə	t'ɛm	šte ón
PT*	[r̪í:ž‡ɪ vnǔ:k'ɪ	gʌɬá:nskəvə	mə́r'ıkə	r̪a:dʊiʋсə	t'ɛ:m	šte ón

*Velarization is exemplified in a few instances only.

	ВЧЕРА́ ПЕРЕД	ВЗЛЁТОМ	С АЭРОДРО́МА	И́Х	МЯ́ГКО	ПОЦЕЛОВА́Л
SO	ВЧЕРА́ ПЕРЕД	ВЗЛЁТОМ	С АЭРОДРО́МА	И́Х	МЯ́ГКО	ПОЦЕЛОВА́Л
RO	вчера́ перед	вэльо́том	с аэродро́ма	и́йх	мья́гко	поцелова́л
3A	вчера́#перед #	вз/льо́том	с/аэродро́ма #	и́йх##мья́гко #		по/целова́л##
3B						
3C						
3D						по/целоу́ал
3E	Фчера́				мья́кко	
3F						по/целова́л
3G					мья́хно	
3H						
3I				и́х		
3J1						
3J2	пьервьед					
3K						по/цэлова́л

3L

3N

3P   вьэь/льо́том

3S   фчера́#пльерьве́д#вьэь/льо́том # с/аэра̊дро́ма # и́х # мба́хно # по/цэло̊ва̊л##

3U   вьэь/льо́там   с/аэра̊дро́ма   мба́хна   па/цэла̊ва̊л

3V   па/цэла̊ва̊л

3M1

3M2 фчира̊ пьырьыд

3X

3Y

3Z   с/айра̊дро́ма

PO   фчира̊#пльырьыд#вьэь/льо́там # с/айра̊дро́ма # и́х # мба́хна # па/цала̊ва̊л##

PT (broad)   fčırå p'ır'ıd v'z'ı'ótem   sʌjrʌdróme   íx   m'áxke   pecelʌvál   ]

*PT**(narrow) fčırå p'ıř'ıd v'z'ı'ő:tem   sʌ' iř'ʌdró:me   íx   m'á':xke   pecelʌvá:t   ]

*Velarization is exemplified in a few instances only.

CHAPTER FIVE

RAPID RUSSIAN

5.1. INTRODUCTION

All our rules up to this point have been concerned with the norm prescribed by Avanesov for *CSR*. It is however undeniable that few native speakers of Russian actually speak according to the *CSR* norm much of the time. What is usually spoken instead is a style of speech which is often called "Colloquial Russian" and which we shall call "Rapid Russian" (*RR*). Since the prescribed *CSR* is, statistically speaking, not normal, it would perhaps be more sensible to call this style "Slow Russian" and allot more time and space in this volume to the more typical *RR*.

There is however so much variation involved, and so complex a system of interrelated optional rules would be needed, that the derivation of *RR* by a set of rules would be extremely difficult, even if the necessary data were available; and it is impossible because these data are for the most part lacking. So much effort has been expended on the description and prescription of *CSR* that *RR* is very poorly and incompletely described in the literature. Until recently, indeed, very little study had been made of the way in which Russians usually speak (unless, of course, they were dialect-speakers); and recent studies have been no more than exploratory.[1]

5.1.1. *RR*: A DEFINITION

Whereas a definition of an arbitrarily codified language such as *CSR* is relatively straightforward-- the definition follows from the codification--attempts at defining a more "natural" language such as *RR* involve some difficult problems. We shall tentatively define *RR* as the *informal, non-dialectal language of those Russians who also speak CSR*. This definition is at fault for at least two reasons. First, the term *non-dialectal* begs a vital question; for, since the informal speech of speakers of *CSR* has been so little studied, the range of possible regional variations is largely unknown. To take the most obvious example, the informal speech of Moscow *CSR*-speakers and that of Leningrad *CSR*-speakers

158

apparently differs; are both varieties, or is only one of the two, to be labelled *RR*? Second, it makes use of the term *informal*, and thus involves questions of sociology and psychology which cannot be properly answered at the present.[2]

In addition, we may also be at fault in using the term *rapid* in our label for this style. After all, it is possible for informal styles to be enunciated slowly, and for formal styles to be spoken very quickly. However, it is certainly true that most of the characteristics of the informal colloquial style are ones which may be equated with the effects of speaking fast--in particular, consonant- and vowel-elisions, i.e., what is usually called "slurring"--and for this reason we shall continue to use the label *RR*.[3]

Digression: Some Non-rapid Characteristics of
              Colloquial Russian

The following features of at least some styles of colloquial Russian have been noted.[4]   These features clearly have little or nothing to do with the effects of rapid speech (and, perhaps, constitute elements of what is often called "vulgar speech"?):

1. In prepausal position, unstressed (*SO*) A and O, which are represented as ə in our *PO* and which are pronounced [ə] in *CSR*, are pronounced [ʌ] in Colloquial Russian (and thus are pronounced the same as *initial* A and O (cf. our remarks on final position on pp. 99-100)). Thus, e.g.: CHÓPO → [skórʌ].

2. Stressed (*SO*) É and Э́ are pronounced [éˆ] rather than the *CSR* [é] in positions before soft consonants. Thus, e.g.: СВИДЕ́ТЕЛЬ → [s'v'ɪd'éˆt'ɪl'].

5.1.2.   THE RELATIONSHIP BETWEEN *RR* AND *CSR*

The relationship between *RR* and *CSR* is far from clear. It has been argued, for example, that the two are "separate languages";[5] and yet all the linguistic descriptions of the pronunciation of *RR* not only try to relate the *RR* forms to *CSR* forms, but for the most part derive the former from the latter.[6] This approach is of course very convenient since the pre-scribed pronunciation of *CSR* forms provide generally-accepted bases for the derivation of the less well-understood *RR* forms; but the approach involves an as yet unproven assumption--namely, that *RR* is a modification of *CSR*. The assumption, in other words, is that when speaking informally, a speaker of *CSR*

produces another variety of the standard language: a
variety which, for various reasons, happens to be a
"slurred", indistinct version of *CSR*.[7] If however
the two *are* separate languages, it will be more correct to say that when speaking informally a speaker
of *CSR* switches into a (to some degree at least) different language.

    This problem will not be solved, at least, until
RR has been adequately described. In 5.8. below we
point out some of the obstacles to the solution of
this problem; meanwhile, we follow the convenient
traditional approach, and derive our *RR* from *CSR*.
For simplicity, since Chapter 4 above terminates in a
phonetic transcription, we discuss *RR* in purely phonetic terms, and compare it with the *PT* for *CSR*. Our
examples normally consist of three entries, e.g.:

SO КАКЍЕ-ТО   *CSR* [kʌk'ĩyətə]   *RR* [k'ːĩytə]~[k'ĩytə]*

and we normally discuss the relationship between the
forms in the second and third columns only.

RR as a "Style"

    If the assumption we have just mentioned is a
correct one, then *RR* may be thought of as one of the
"styles" of *CSR*; or, alternatively, both *RR* and *CSR*
may be considered as "styles" of some large linguistic entity. Of the alternatives, the latter is preferable. It is convenient (although perhaps un-
justifiable) to think of a complete range of styles,
from the most careful and formal to the most informal
and careless, with "innumerable nuances between an
absolutely clear and distinct pronunciation and a
careless, rapid pronunciation."[8] *CSR* may then be
equated with the style of pronunciation located near
the distinct, formal end of the scale; and *RR* may
therefore be regarded as comprising all of the remaining styles along the scale.[9]
    If, eventually, *RR* is to be derived from *CSR*, a
system of rules will be required which incorporates a
measure of *optionality*; for *RR*, according to the
viewpoint just presented, includes styles very close
to *CSR*, and for these only a few rules will have to
be applied; and, at the end of the scale, where extremes of elision ("slurring") occur, it includes

*Note the symbol ~ which denotes "or" and may be read
as "varies with".

styles of pronunciation for which the application of
many rules (and/or the repeated application of some)
will be required.

The Feature of Optionality

There is clearly a great deal of contextual and
individual variation in *RR*. If we are to derive *RR*
by a set of rules from any basic representation
(whatever this may be), then we may say first that
there is to be variation in the *extent* to which the
rules are applied; and second that there is to be
variation in the *choice* of the rules which are applied, and/or in the *scope* of their application.

For example, *SO* НАКЙЕ-ТО may be pronounced in *RR*
as [k'ː ɪ̂ytə], [k'ɪ̂ytə] or even as [k'ɪ̂t]; and *SO*
ДЕЙСТВЙТЕЛЬНО as [d'ɪs't'v'ɪ̂t'nə] or as [d'ɪs'ɪ̂t'nə][10]
in these cases it is apparently a matter of applying
progressively more rules of elision which result in
the loss of several whole segments. On the other
hand, *SO* ИССЛЕ́ДОВАТЕЛЬ has been noted in *RR* both as
[ɪsːl'ɛ́dəvət'l'] and as [ɪsːl'ɛ́dvət'ɪl']; when we
compare the *CSR* pronunciation, [ɪsːl'ɛ́dəvət'ɪl'], we
note that a vowel-elision rule has applied in one
case to the second [ɪ] and in the other to the first
[ə]. A much more complex example of this kind of
variation is given in 5.7. below.

There would have to be many limits imposed on
the feature of optionality; the completely free application of vowel- and consonant-elision rules, for
example, could result in the derivation of total
silence. As we point out below, however, the optionality of the rules would be limited to a great degree
by various factors. In addition, the mutual ordering
of these optional rules (with due allowance for simultaneous ordering, if and wherever convenient)
would make the whole business very involved: see
5.7. below for some tentative remarks on ordering.

Further, it is clear that speakers of Russian do
not always adhere to the same "style" even for the
duration of such limited utterances as short phrases.
For example, the phrase КОНЕ́ЧНО ДО ОПРЕДЕЛЁННОГО ВОЗ-
РАСТА has been noted with the pronunciation [kʌɛ́ž
dəʌpr'ɪd'ɪl'ón:əvə vózrəstə] where only the first
word shows the features of "rapid" speech. In terms
of the *scale* just referred to, it might seem that
speakers dart about from one position to another as
they speak. Even in formal situations, indeed, a
speaker of *CSR* may well be less than distinct; this
is particularly in evidence when he utters a date or
when he pauses to address his listener by his first

name and patronymic. For the date ТЫ́СЯЧА ДЕ́ВЯТЬСОТ
ШЕСТЬДЕСЯ́Т ШЕСТО́ГО ГО́ДА he may say [tɨ́š'ɪ d'ɪəcót
šəys'át šstóvə gódə] rather than the *CSR* fully explicit [tɨ́s'ɪčə d'ɪv'ɪtsót šəz'd'ɪs'át šɪstóvə gódə];
for *SO* ПА́ВЕЛ БОРИ́СОВИЧ he may prefer [pál bʌr'iš'č']
to the distinct [páv'ɪl bʌr'ísəv'ɪč']; but the rest
of his speech may not show any elisions or "slurring"
at all.[11]

Limitations on Optionality

There seem to be a number of severe limitations
upon the extent to which a speaker may "dart about"
from one position to another on the "carefulness"
scale, and even more severe limitations upon the extent to which he may "slur" his speech. We make a
few tentative suggestions here, and list them in a
quite arbitrary order.

(1) *Vocabulary*. In the first place, there seem
to be certain lexical categories which are commonly
pronounced with an extra degree of "carelessness",
numerals and proper names being the most striking
ones, since the informal pronunciation of words in
these two categories is an accepted concomitant of
the neutral style of *CSR* (see below). Secondly, it
seems probable that there is a correlation between
textual frequency and susceptibility to indistinct
pronunciation; the more commonly a word is used, the
more likely it is to be pronounced indistinctly.
This factor will vary according to the extra-linguistic context; for example, the rendering of *SO* УНИВЕР-
СИТЕ́Т and БИБЛИОТЕ́КА as [ʊn'ɪrs't'ɛ́t] and [b':ɪl'ɪʌ-
t'ɛ́kə] is presumably more common among university
students and professors than among other people;
while the pronunciation of ЗАЙМСТВОВАННЫХ as
[zʌímsnɪx] may well be restricted to professors and
students of linguistics.[12]

(2) *Other linguistic factors*. The intonation
of the sentence, and the position of words in the
sentence, may also be assumed to influence the extent to which words are pronounced indistinctly.
Both of these factors are dependent on the overall
syntax of the utterance in question--and here we see
one reason why it may not be sensible to try to
derive the *PT* for *RR* from the *PT* for *CSR*, since this
approach will inevitably leave syntactic questions
out of consideration.[13]

(3) *Extra-linguistic factors*. Closely linked
to, indeed fundamental for the syntax of the

utterance, are various extra-linguistic factors which may eventually prove to severely restrict the freedom of choice among the rules for *RR*. Given a complete description of the communicative situation, the choice of what may be said to pass a message between two human beings is not very wide. Such a complete description--to take the simplest situation, that of two people conversing--involves something approaching a biography of the speaker and the listener, a precise analysis of the context in which this message is to be conveyed, and a study of the relationship of this message to its context. One datum to emerge from this description would be the time in which the whole message is to be passed; and, given this time-span, the "rapidity" of speech and the possible and probable sound-elisions would be at least partly predictable.[14]

Avanesov and the *RR:CSR* Distinction

As mentioned above, personal names and numerals are frequently pronounced indistinctly by Russians at times when they are in all other, or in most other, respects speaking a distinct *CSR* style. In *RLP*, Avanesov describes and allows for these as *part* of *CSR*. Certain other words--all of them very common-- must be added to this list. One very obvious example is *SO* СЕЙЧА́С, which, traditionally, is seldom if ever pronounced in its fully explicit *CSR* form [s'ıyčás], but rather shows at least elision of the [y], thus: [s'ıčás], if not further shortening to the form [š'ás]. In *RLP*, СЕЙЧА́С is discussed and other consonant-elisions are occasionally mentioned, but not approved. Avanesov speaks at some length about vowel-elisions (*RLP* 68-72): he disallows most of the examples he cites, e.g., [sхʌrkú] for *SO* САХАРНУ́, but he does allow elision in two instances:

(1) elision of [ə] and of [ɪ] in posttonic syllables between two [v]'s, but only as long as the first of these is syllabicized, thus *CSR* [ĭvəvɪy]~ [ĭvvɪy] for *SO* И́ВОВЫЙ.

(2) in a list of eight specific words, namely, СКО́ВОРОДА, ПРО́ВОЛОКА, НЕ́КОТОРЫЕ, ДВОЮ́РОДНЫЙ, ТРОЮ́РОДНЫЙ, ТЫ́СЯЧА, МЕ́СЯЦА, and the word СЕЙЧА́С discussed above.*

---

*In these eight words, the segments which Avanesov allows to be elided are underlined.

Since it is quite normal for a Russian speaking *CSR* to pronounce such words, including numerals and proper names, in an elliptic fashion, it is quite possible--and frequently preferred--to define *CSR* as a style of speech in which every word is enunciated with a certain degree of distinctness, except for words in these few categories, which may be pronounced less distinctly. Indeed, this is Avanesov's definition. We, on the other hand, prefer to define *CSR* as the distinct style of speech for *all* words, and to add that most communicative contexts that call for *CSR* also allow for words in these few categories to be pronounced in *RR*. This is a purely terminological matter, but our approach allows us to summarize in the present chapter the phenomena which apply to *RR*, and to relate them to all relevant categories of words in Russian; we thus avoid having to discuss these phenomena twice--firstly in our chapters on *CSR*, and then again here.[15]

Recommendation

The beginning student is advised to note the "indistinct" *RR* pronunciation of the words given by Avanesov, and of numerals and personal names, in order to achieve competence in the comprehension of Russian as it is spoken in formal situations; and to note that the phenomena which are apparent in the pronunciation of these words, together with other characteristics as described below, will also be observed in instances when Russians speak informally and conversationally. It is for this reason that we include a certain amount of discussion of *RR* phenomena here. This discussion may also be of use for reading works of drama and dialogues in fiction.

5.2. WEAKENING OF SEGMENTS

When *RR* is compared with *CSR*, all the examples cited above show loss of segments--elision of vowels or of consonants--and even loss of complete syllables.[16] It is characteristic that a segment that is present in *CSR* may disappear altogether in *RR*; and the more elliptic the style, the more segments may disappear. Normally, this segment-loss is complete. Occasionally, however, what may be called weakening or partial loss occurs rather than complete loss.

In some cases, a feature of the disappearing segment is left behind, attached to a neighbouring segment (this phenomenon is dealt with in 5.3. below). In other instances, certain segments are *weakened.* For consonants, weakening--traditionally called *lenition*--results in a less tense articulation; thus a stop can in theory be weakened (lenited) to a fricative, a fricative to a glide, or--to take a milder alternative--a voiceless obstruent can be weakened to a voiced one.[17] For vowels, weakening (reduction) involves a less tense articulation, usually a shortened duration, and often a more centralized articulation.

Apparently Russian tends to avoid lenition in consonants--although complete loss is common. For example, *SO* БА́БУШКА may be pronounced with the second [b], as in *CSR* [bábuškə]; or it may be pronounced without any consonantal phone in this position, as in *RR* [báuškə]; but no cases of a lenited consonant (either a fricative [β] or glide [w]) have been reported in this case. It seems indeed to be normally true that either a consonant is fully articulated, or it is elided (apart from the "trace-features" mentioned in 5.3.).

There are however two examples which do occur. The first, that of [v] and [v'], has not been noted very often; however, the two following pronunciations have been observed:

SO	В СОРОКО́ВОМ ГОДУ́	В МОСКВЕ́
CSR	[fsərəkʌvóm gʌdú]	[vmʌskv'é]
RR	[fsʌrʌkʌwóm gʌdú]	[vmʌskw'é]

The second, that of [j] to [y], appears to be very common. In 4.3. we rewrote as [j] but noted that, more precisely, the fricative [j] occurs only before stressed vowels; elsewhere, in *CSR*, the glide [y] is more normal. In *RR*, however, the fricative [j] occurring before stressed vowels may also be lenited to [y]:[18]

SO	É ХАТЬ	*CSR*	[jéxət']	*RR*	[yéxət']
	СТАТЬЯ́		[stʌt'já]		[stʌt'yá]

It should be pointed out that this limitation of lenition to the three consonants [j], [v'] and [v] is of interest because it supports the suggestion that these phones belong together in a hierarchy of segment-types; see 5.5. below.

While lenition of consonants in Russian is rare, we have already seen that reduction of vowels (cf. 3.10.) in unstressed position is quite normal and regular for *CSR*. It is characteristic of *RR*, however,

that although there may be further *phonological*
reduction (in the sense that the few remaining oppositions between unstressed vowels are neutralized),
there seems to be very little phonetic *weakening* (in
the sense of a reduction in time).

　　　More complete *neutralization*, as noted above
in 3.12.2. (pp. 95 - 96) and 3.12.5. (p. 107), is also
quoted as typifying *RR*. The final result would be
one of *complete* neutralization, in that the only unstressed vowel which may occur after a "soft" consonant is [ɪ], while the only unstressed vowel that may
occur after a "hard" consonant is [ə]. This state of
affairs may well occur only in *RR*, but available data
suggest that it is not by any means a general rule
even for this style of Russian.[19]

　　　As for *weakening*, i.e., an intermediate stage
between the normal reduced articulation and complete
loss, a few examples have been noted, where *RR* [ə]
replaces *CSR* [ʌ]--note that if weakening were a general rule, we might expect seldom to find [ʌ] in *RR*--
and with [ᵊ] (i.e., a very brief schwa) replacing *CSR*
[ə]:[20]

SO	СООБРАЖЕ́НИЕ	*CSR* [sʌʌbrʌžén'ɪyə]	*RR* [səbrʌžén'ə]
	КАРАНДАША́	[kərəndʌšá]	[kᵊrəndʌšá]
	ГОЛУБЦЫ́	[gəlʊpcɨ]	[gᵊlʊpcɨ]

5.3.　"TRACE-FEATURES"

　　　As is mentioned above, there are instances where
a consonant or vowel does not disappear entirely; the
segment may indeed be lost, but it may leave some
trace feature behind, attached to a neighbouring segment.[21] Some typical examples:

(1)　If a [j] or a [y] is lost, the following vowel
may be fronted:

SO	СДЕ́ЛАЮ	*CSR* [z'd'élƏyʊ]	*RR* [z'd'éləü]
	ОСТАЁТСЯ	[ʌstʌjóc:ə]	[ʌstʌöc:ə][22]

(2)　If a nasal is lost, the following vowel may be
nasalized:

SO	ПОЧЕМУ́	*CSR* [pəčɪmú]	*RR* [pəčɪű]
	НАПРИМЕ́Р	[nəpr'ɪm'ér]	[nəpr'ɪ̃ér]
	ПОНИМА́ЕТЕ	[pən'ɪmáyɪt'ɪ]	[pəȷ̃áɪt'ɪ]

(3) If a [v] is lost, the following vowel may be rounded:

> *SO* ОБНАРУ́ЖИВАЮТСЯ
>
> *CSR* [ʌbnʌrúžɪvəyʊcə]
>
> *RR* [ʌbnʌrúžəʊücə]²³

(4) If a vowel is lost, either the following or the preceding consonant may become syllabic. Available data are insufficient for specifying which consonant (the preceding or the following) will be affected:²⁴

SO ВИ́ДИМО	*CSR* [v'íd'ɪmə]	*RR* [v'íd'mə]
ОБЕ́ДАЛА	[ʌb'édələ]	[ʌb'édlə]
СЛИ́ВОВОГО	[s'l'ívəvəvə]	[s'l'íɣɣə]

(5) If a vowel is lost, the total syllabic struc-ture of the word may be maintained by the lengthening of another vowel:²⁵

SO	УНИВЕРСИТЕ́Т	ИНИЦИАТИ́ВА
CSR	[ʊn'ɪv'ɪrs'ɪt'ét]	[ɪn'ɪcəʌt'ívə]
RR	[ʊ:n'ɪrs't'ét]	[ɪn'cʌ:t'ívə]

(6) If two vowels are contracted into one, this one may show an amalgamation of the features belonging to the original two:

> *SO* ПО ИМЕНА́М *CSR* [pəɪm'ɪnám] *RR* [pɪm'ɪnám]

(Here, the resulting vowel has the tongue-height of the original [ɪ] and the central articulation of the original [ə].)

SO СТА́ЛКИВАЮСЬ *CSR* [stálk'ɪvəyüs'] *RR* [stálk'ʊüs']

(Here, we have [ɪvə]→[ʊ]: the latter vowel has the tongue-height of the original [ɪ] and the labializa-tion of the elided [v].)

5.4. LOSS OF SEGMENTS

Most of the *RR* data available show neither weakening (as in 5.2.) nor partial loss (with "trace-features" as in 5.3.), but rather show complete eli-sion of segments or of whole syllables. This phenom-enon is well-known in other languages, e.g., English *SO I would have* which in Colloquial English may be pronounced variously as *I would've, I'd've, I'd'a,* phonetically [áy wúdəv], [áy dəv], [áydə], instead of the explicit [áy wúd hǽv].

5.4.1. CONSONANT ELISION

CSR shows a limited amount of consonant-elision
(also called *syncope*). We have seen in 3I and 3Y1
that й is lost initially and after vowels when
followed by и; that certain consonantal sequences are
simplified (rule-block 3B); and that certain geminate
consonants are degeminated (rule-block 3N). All of
these phenomena are more extensive in *RR*. Indeed it
is true to say that almost any consonant may, on occasion, be lost; and that loss of consonants may occur in almost all kinds of environment (but see 5.6.
for a discussion of environmental factors). In this
section, we give examples of extensions of the *CSR*
rules 3I / 3Y1 and 3N; examples of other consonant-
elisions will be given in 5.6. and 5.7. below.
     We have seen above (5.2.) that [j] may be
lenited to [y]; we must now allow for [y] to be
elided altogether--whether it represents *CSR* [j] or
[y]:

SO	CSR	RR
СТАТЬЯ́	[stʌt'já]	[stʌt'y̱á]~[stʌt'á]
СТА́ЯМИ	[stáyɪm'ɪ]	[stáɪm'ɪ]
ЕМУ́	[y̱ɪmú]	[ɪmú]
ТРЕ́ТЬЮ	[trét'y̱ʊ]	[trét'ʊ]
ДЕ́ЙСТВИТЕЛЬНО	[d'ɪy̱s't'v'ít'ɪl'nə]	[d'ɪs'v'ít'nə]
А́РМИЙ	[árm'ɪy̱]	[árm'ɪ]
ПОЙДЁМ	[pʌy̱d'óm]	[pʌd'óm]

These examples show deletion of [y] in a number of
different positions. We doubt, however, that [y] is
ever deleted when occurring initially before a
stressed vowel:

      SO Е́ХАТЬ *CSR* [jɛ́xət']   *RR* [yɛ́xət']
                              but never   *[ɛ́xət']?

     The phenomenon of *degemination* is quite exten-
sive in *RR*. There are not enough data, but it appears that grammatical boundaries may still act as
inhibiting factors. In the example

SO	CSR	RR
БЕССМЫ́СЛЕННО	[b'ɪs:mf́s'l'ɪnə]	[b'ɪ̱s:mf́snə]

there is elision of the [l'] and of the [ɪ], but the
geminate [s:] remains geminate; cf. the *PO* бьис/
смысьльина. On the other hand, in the example

    SO С СА́ХАРОМ *CSR* [s:áxərəm] *RR* [sáxrəm]

the geminate [s] has been degeminated, in spite of
the preposition-boundary (*PO* с/cáxaрам).

    Examples of degemination when boundaries are
not involved (see also *RLP* 136-37):

SO	*CSR*	*RR*
КАКИ́Е-ТО	[kʌk'íyətə]	[k'ːíytə]~[k'íytə]
ЭКСПЕДИЦИО́ННЫЙ	[ɛksp'ɪd'ɪcɪón:ɪy]	[ɪksp'ɪɪcɪónɪy]

5.4.2. VOWEL-ELISION

    RR shows a considerable amount of vowel-elision.
Since there are no vowel-elision rules in our set
for *CSR*, we do no more here than give examples in
different kinds of environment. Further examples are
given in 5.6. below.

    Immediate posttonic position shows a great deal
of vowel-elision:

SO	*CSR*	*RR*
ВЫ́НЕСУ	[vín'ɪsʊ]	[vɨn'sʊ]
ПА́ВЕЛ	[páv'ɪl]	[pál]
С СА́ХАРОМ	[s:áxərəm]	[sáxrəm]
И́ВОВЫХ	[íivəvɪx]	[íivɣɪx]

Vowels are however elided in other positions relative
to the stress, e.g.:

SO	*CSR*	*RR*
ДОНОСИ́ЛИСЬ	[dənʌs'íl'ɪs']	[dnʌs'íl'ɪs']
НЕИЗВЕ́СТНО	[n'ɪɪz'v'ɛ́snə]	[n'ɪz'v'ɛ́snə]
БА́БУШКА	[bábʊškə]	[báʊšk]
КА́КИЕ-ТО	[kʌk'íyətə]	[k'íit]

Stressed vowels may on occasion be elided:

CSR	*RR*
[já vám dám]	[já m̩ dám]

5.5.   HIERARCHIES OF SEGMENT-TYPES

It appears that, generally speaking, some types of consonants are more frequently elided than others. On the basis of what appears to be a natural correlation between susceptibility to syncope and articulatory factors, we suggest the following hierarchy, which shows a progression from less to more tense and/or from lesser to greater occlusion:[26]

(6) [y j]

(5) [v v']

(4) [l l' r r' n n' m m']   (liquids and nasals)

(3) [z z' ž ɣ]   (voiced fricatives)

(2) [b b' d d' g g' f f'   (voiced stops,
         s s' š š' x]   voiceless fricatives)

(1) [p p' k k' t t' č c]   (voiceless stops,
                              affricates)

It is to be understood that the higher a consonant is placed on this scale, the more likely it is to be elided in *RR*.

It must be emphasized, first, that this hierarchy is extremely tentative; and second, that other relevant factors--lexical frequency, syntactic structure, type of environment, and so on--must always be taken into account (cf. 5.6.3. below).

We know of no discussion in the literature concerning possible hierarchies for *vowels* with respect to susceptibility to elision. The articulatory criteria which seem so important for consonants, when applied to vowels, would suggest that high vowels are more susceptible to elision than low vowels--i.e., since we are dealing for the most part with unstressed vowels, that [ʊÜɪi] are more likely to be elided than [əʌ]. This is however a matter of conjecture.[27]

5.6.   HIERARCHIES OF ENVIRONMENTS?

In conjunction with segment-type, the factor of segment-position must be considered. It is clear that certain environmental factors are more conducive than others to the weakening or loss of segments or syllables. So many variables can however co-occur with regard to any one segment that the proposal of environmental hierarchies is no easy matter. Only in one instance may a hierarchy be proposed at the present stage of research--a hierarchy of positions, valid for vowels, with reference to the position of the stressed vowels (cf., however, the importance of the stressed quality of the vowel on the pronunciation of [j] versus [y], treated above; and the reference to contiguity with a stressed vowel in 5.6.2.(4) below).

5.6.1. ENVIRONMENTAL FACTORS INFLUENCING THE ELISION OF VOWELS

(1)   In 3.12., vowel-reduction in *CSR* is discussed with reference to degrees of stress.   In *RR*, it appears that somewhat different factors are operating, for there is evidence that suggests that the hierarchy of positions for vowel-*elision* in *RR* does not fully correspond to the hierarchy of positions for vowel-*reduction* in *CSR*.[28]   In particular it should be noted that absolute final position is known to be more distinct in *CSR* than other fully unstressed syllables, but less distinct than immediate pretonic position; in *RR*, however, absolute final position is less susceptible to elision than immediate pretonic position.   In *RR*, further, the immediate posttonic position is apparently the weakest of all the positions.   We may draw up the following table*:

Position with Reference to Word-Stress	Vowel-Reduction Strength (*CSR*)	Vowel-Elision Strength (*RR*)
primary stress	5	5
secondary stress	4	5
absolute initial	3	4
immediate pretonic	3	3
absolute final	2	4
other pretonic	1	2
immediate posttonic	1	1
other posttonic	1	3

Some *consonantal environments* are also apparently more conducive to vowel-elision than others.   The following guidelines (2)-(5) may be suggested; it is to be understood that these environments are particularly conducive to vowel-elision.

(2) When the preceding consonant is very similar to or identical with the following consonant, e.g.:

*Note that the degrees of stress discussed in 3.12. for *CSR* are here transposed into "strengths" for *RR*.

SO БИБЛИОТЕ́КА *CSR* [b'ɪb|'ɪʌt'ɛ́kə] *RR* [b':|'ɪʌt'ɛ́ka]

(here, the two consonants are identical except for the feature of palatalization).

   SO ЗДОРО́ВОГО   *CSR* [zdʌró<u>vəv</u>ə]   *RR* [zdʌróɣvə]
   ВА́ША ША́ПКА   [vá<u>sə š</u>ápkə]   [váš:ápkə]

(in these instances, the consonants in each set are identical).

(3) When a neighbouring consonant is palatalized, e.g.:

      SO ВИ́ДИМО *CSR* [v'ɪ́d'ɪmə] *RR* [v'ɪ́d̦'mə]

(4) When preceded or followed by a consonant-cluster, e.g.:

SO ЕСТЕ́СТВЕННО *CSR* [ɪs't'és't'v'ɪnə] *RR* [ɪs't'és'nə]

(5) When a neighbouring consonant is susceptible to being syllabicized, e.g.:[29]

   SO СОРОКОВЫ́Х *CSR* [sərəkʌv̥x] *RR* [sər̩kʌv̥x]
      ДЕ́СЯТЬ   [d'és'ɪt']   [d'és̩'t']

   Finally, vowel-chains must be considered separately. *CSR* has a certain number of these (cf. pp. 90-92); elision occurs frequently in vowel-clusters, e.g.:[30]

SO	*CSR*	*RR*
ЗАОСТРИ́ТЬ	[z<u>ʌʌ</u>str'ɪ́t']	[zʌstr'ɪ́t']
НЕОБЫКНОВЕ́ННЫЙ	[n'<u>ɪʌ</u>bɨknʌv'ɛ́n:ɨy]	[n'ɪbɨknʌv'ɛ́n:ɨy]
НА УГОЛО́К	[n<u>ʌʊ</u>gʌló̞k]	[nʊgʌló̞k]
У ОГОРО́ДА	[<u>ʊʌ</u>gʌródə]	[ʊgʌródə]

5.6.2. ENVIRONMENTAL FACTORS INFLUENCING THE ELISION OF CONSONANTS

   The following four guidelines may be kept in mind. Consonants are most frequently deleted:

(1) When occurring in clusters, e.g.:[31]

      SO КОГДА́ *CSR* [kʌ<u>gd</u>á] *RR* [kʌdá]
         ТО́ ЕСТЬ   [tó̞yɪ<u>s't</u>']   [tó̞ɪs']

(2) When intervocalic, e.g.:[32]

    SO ТЕПЕ́РЬ *CSR* [t'ɪp̲'ér'] *RR* [t'ɪér']

(3) When the preceding vowel is very similar to or identical with the following vowel (cf. 5.6.1.(2)), e.g.:

SO	*CSR*	*RR*
УНИВЕРСИТЕ́Т	[ʊn'ɪv̲'ɪrs'ɪt'ɛ́t]	[ʊn'ɪɪrs'ɪt'ɛ́t]

(4) When contiguous to a stressed (rather than an unstressed) vowel, e.g.:[33]

SO	*CSR*	*RR*
ПРЕДСТАВЛЯ́ЕШЬ	[pr'ɪtstʌvl̲'áyɪš]	[pr'ɪstʌáɪš]
ПОЧЕМУ́	[pəčɪm̲ú]	[pəčɪű]

5.6.3. CO-OCCURRENCE OF FACTORS

It is important to note that these factors may be co-occurrent (in which case their combined influence will make a segment more likely to be lost), or--on the other hand--may act at variance with each other throughout a word (in which case they may tend to cancel out each other's effect). For example, in *SO* И́ВОВЫЙ, *CSR* [ívəvɪy] the [ə] is immediately post-tonic, *and* occurs between two identical consonants, and these consonants are easily syllabicized; the elision of the [ə] is therefore very likely (see p. 163 above). Similarly, the [g] in *SO* КОГДА́, *CSR* [kʌgdá], although a consonant which is seldom deleted, does occur in a cluster, and occurs between two very similar vowels. On the other hand, *SO* УНИВЕРСИТЕ́Т, *CSR* [ʊn'ɪv'ɪrs'ɪt'ét] demonstrates how many of the segments may be affected by the different factors listed above. Vowel-factor (2) affects the fourth vowel; vowel-factor (3) affects all the vowels; vowel-factor (4) affects the third and fourth vowels; vowel-factor (5) affects the first four vowels. Consonant-factor (1) affects the cluster [rs']; consonant-factor (2) is involved in all the consonants except the last; and consonant-factor (3) is pertinent to the [v'] and the [rs']. As a result, we may expect considerable variation in the ways in which this word is pronounced in *RR*; see 5.7. below.

5.7. THE PROBLEM OF ORDERING

So far we have listed various segment-weakening and segment-elision processes in an arbitrary order.

We now briefly consider the question whether any of
them should be *ordered* in any way.[34]

In many instances, examples of *RR* suggest no
reasons for any such ordering. For example, *SO*
ВЧЕРА́, *CSR* [fčɪrá], *RR* [črá] shows loss of two seg-
ments--the elision of the [f] and the elision of the
[ɪ]. There is no evidence to suggest that we should
order either of these before the other, or indeed
that we must exclude the possibility of simultaneous
application. Taking the *CSR* phonetic forms as our
starting-point, we have three equal alternatives:

Elision of [f] before
    elision of [ɪ]:   [fčɪrá]→[čɪrá]→[črá]

Elision of [ɪ] before
    elision of [f]:   [fčɪrá]→[fčrá]→[črá]

Elision of both seg-
    ments at once: [fčɪrá]   →   [črá]

Other examples in the data do however seem to
suggest ordering. Thus *SO* БА́БУШКА, *CSR* [bábuškə], is
noted in two forms: [báuškə] and [báušk]. Since the
former is more explicit than the latter, this would
seem to suggest that the [b] is elided before the
final [ə]. This ordering is supported by what we
know about environmental conditions--for we have
noted that consonants are lost more often in intervocalic position, and vowels are more seldom elided
in final position. The evidence therefore suggests
that any mutual ordering that does obtain among these
processes depends on, and is to be formulated in
terms of, the constraints which are imposed by the
environments and characteristics of the segments in
question.

Even when the data of *RR* do not provide us with
two or more forms of pronunciation for a single word,
there are instances where we may reasonably guess
what the ordering may be. For example, *SO* ШИШМАРЁВ,
CSR [šəšmʌr'óf], is noted in *RR* with elision of the
first syllable: *RR* [šmʌr'óf]. *If* this syllable is
lost in two stages--one segment before the other--it
is reasonable to assume that the [ə] is to be elided
before the [š]; for in this order, viz. [šəšmʌr'óf]→
[ššmʌr'óf]→[šmʌr'óf] we have a simple explanation for
the second elision, that of degemination in initial
position before another consonant (cf. 3N(c)-(d));
while the alternative order would involve a rather
improbable intermediate stage *[šəmʌr'óf].

There are however a number of examples of *RR* available where many or all of the possible intermediate stages between most explicit and very elliptic have been noted. Thus *SO* МЕНЯ́, *CSR* [m'ɪn'á] is noted in all three forms [m'n'á], [m'ɪá] and [m'á]; we may thus draw up a "flow-chart" as follows:

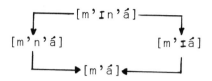

A much more complex example is provided by the word *SO* УНИВЕРСИТЕ́Т, *CSR* [ʊn'ɪv'ɪrs'ɪt'ét], which Barinova (1971a, 1971b and in Zemskaja 1973) notes in no fewer than twelve variant forms. On p. 173 above we noted how many of the segments appear to be more or less equally susceptible. We can now make a "flow-chart" of Barinova's forms, working from the *CSR* to the most elliptic form. See "flow-chart" on p. 176.

Examples like this last one (which, it may be assumed, happens to be noted in so many different forms because Barinova culled her data from a University environment) are probably typical of *RR*. In this case, many--but perhaps not all--of the possible orderings suggested by the extant data may not be necessary, and instead a variety of alternative orderings may have to be allowed.[35]

5.8. THE RELATIONSHIP OF *RR* TO *CSR*: FURTHER DISCUSSION

On pp. 159-160 above we explained that we relate the *RR* data to *CSR* forms for quite arbitrary reasons, and posed the question as to whether--given enough data for the formulation of a system of rules--*RR* should be derived from *CSR*, or whether both should be derived from some other (more abstract) representation. We now discuss this problem.

In the first place, it is clear that it is an uneconomical business to derive the *PT* for *RR* from the *PT* from *CSR*, for the simple reason that a number of the rules necessary to derive the phonetics of *CSR* will have to be repeated. For example, *SO* СКО́ЛЬКО ЖЕ, *CSR* [skól'kəžə]; the *RR* form shows not only elision of the [l'] and of the first [ə], but also voicing assimilation as in rule 3E2: [skog͡žə] rather than *[skokžə]. Similarly, *SO* ОСТАНОВИ́ТЬСЯ,

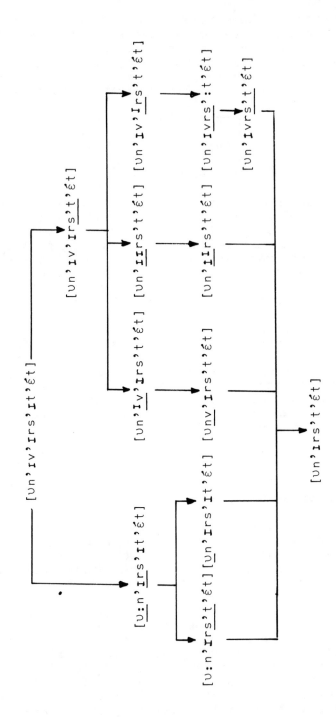

CSR [ʌstənʌv'íc:ə] shows elision of the first [ə] in *RR*, plus simplification of the resulting [stn] cluster to [sn], as in rule 3B1(f): [ʌsnʌv'íc:ə]. The *SO* word ФЕДОСЕВИЧ, *CSR* [f'ɪdós'ɪv'ɪč] shows loss of the segments between the [s'] and the [č] in *RR*, and further shows the change of this new cluster [s'č] to [š':], similar to rule 3H2: [f'ɪdóš':]. As a final example, *SO* ДОСТÁTОЧНО, *CSR* [dʌstátəčnə] shows elision of the first [ə] plus palatalization of the [t] to [t'] in its new position before [č], as in 3P3: [dʌstát'čnə].

On the other hand, some of the available evidence suggests that the application of at least some of these rules may not be obligatory in *RR*. For example, *SO* БЛЮДЕЧКО, *CSR* [bl'úḏɪčkə] occurs in *RR* with elision of the [ɪ]. It has been noted *without* devoicing of the [d']--thus, [bl'úḏ'čkə]--and with *partial* devoicing of this consonant--thus, [bl'ú-ḏt'čkə]*--and also, we may assume, occurs with *complete* devoicing, thus, [bl'út't'čkə]. It appears that a number of different nuances can be expected, ranging from non-application to complete application of this (and other?) rules.[36]

Secondly, we may have to extend our inventory of rules, to allow for such phenomena as the following:

Depalatalization Assimilation:

SO	CSR	RR
БЕССМЫ́СЛЕННО	[b'ɪс:mís'l'ɪnə]	[b'ɪsmísnə]

Here we must allow either for the loss of the syllable [l'ɪ] before the palatalization assimilation takes place, i.e., before с is rewritten сь as in rule 3P3; or we must have a new rule which states that [s'] is to be "hardened" before [n].[37]

Affricate Assimilation

	SO	ДВÁДЦАТЬ ЧЕТВЁРТОГО
CSR		[dvácət'čɪt'v'órtəvə]
RR		[dváč̱:órtəvə]

Here we see the loss of a number of segments which bring [c] and [č] together; there is assimilation from [cč] to [č:].

---

*[dt] denotes a dental stop with voicing at the beginning, but not at the end, and [td] the reverse.

Progressive Voicing Assimilation (?)

In a number of examples, Barinova notes this very unusual phenomenon, e.g.:

SO	CSR	RR
ДО СВИДА́НЬЯ	[dəs'v'ɪdán'yə]	[dəs'tdán'ə]

This phenomenon is so extraordinary in Russian that it is to be hoped that confirmatory data will soon be available.[38]

Thirdly, some forms noted for *RR* show phonetic sequences which, in the framework of the reading rules which we have proposed, can simply not be properly derived except by some unwarranted arbitrary device. (This may of course merely show that our reading rules, though suitable for teaching, are not linguistically satisfactory.) For example:

SO	CSR	RR
В ЕГО́ ДО́МЕ	[v' yɪvó dóm'ɪ]	[vɪvó dóm'ɪ]

In this case, if we are to derive *RR* from *CSR*, we are faced with the problem of deriving [vɪ] from [v'yɪ]; we could not find any reasonable grounds for the depalatalization of the whole syllable after the elision of the [y]. If, on the other hand, we go back to a more abstract representation, we will still have to allow for vowel-reduction (as in 3W2) before the change of и to ы (as in 3J1(b)).[39]

Fourthly, there are examples of *RR* data which suggest that allowance must be made for *RR* to be derived in such a way that information of a purely phonetic nature can be incorporated. For example:

SO ÉДУТ   CSR [jɛ́dʊt]   RR [yɛ́dᵂtᵂ]

Here the second vowel is elided, but the lip-rounding (which might be represented in a narrow phonetic transcription of *CSR* thus: [jɛ́dᵂʊtᵂ]) is maintained in the dental stops.

The evidence which at the present stage is available--and it is as yet very meagre--can be summarized as suggestive of a definite but very loose relationship between *RR* and *CSR*. If it should prove possible to derive both "styles" of Russian from one single common representation, using a system of rules, then it seems probable that a complex network of optional derivational routes will have to be posited, with (as an additional complexity) various optional orderings also allowed. Most scholars do not even discuss this problem; we suggest that until some kind of solution to it can be found, there can be no satisfactory or acceptable "phonology of Russian".[40]

LEXICON OF SPECIFIED WORDS

Listed below are the words and stems specified by Avanesov in *RLP* and *RLPU* which belong in the LISTS mentioned in the rules of Chapter Three. In cases where these two sources differ as to their recommendation, the more recent prescription in *RLP* has been followed.

To save space, only one of a number of related derivative words and stems are listed, if the same rule applies to the entire set. For example, АТЕЙЗМ, АТЕЙСТ, АТЕЙСТКА and АТЕИСТИ́ЧЕСКИЙ all come under rule 3J2(b), but only the first is listed. The same rule, 3J2(b), applies to ВА́ТЕР, ВА́ТЕРКЛОЗЕ́Т, ВА́ТЕР-ЛИ́НИЯ, ВА́ТЕРНЫЙ, ВАТЕРПА́С, ВАТЕРПРУ́Ф and ВА́ТЕРЩИК; again, only ВА́ТЕР is listed for this rule. As it happens, the related word ВА́ТЕРПО́ЛО is listed separately in the lexicon, but only because this particular word also constitutes an exception to rule 3U. Another example: the stem -МЕ́ЙСТЕР is listed with reference to rule 3J2(b); this rule applies equally to all compound words such as ХОРМЕ́ЙСТЕР, БАЛЕТ-МЕ́ЙСТЕР, ГРОССМЕ́ЙСТЕР and КУХМЕ́ЙСТЕР as well as to the simple word МЕ́ЙСТЕР itself.

The *letters* affected by the rule(s) in the word or stem are underlined, thus: ЛЕ́ЙДЕНСКИЙ 3J2(b). In this example, the second E is to be rewritten Э as in 3J2(b), but the first E--which is not underlined--is not to be changed. In a few instances, a specified word is listed twice to avoid ambiguity. This applies, for example, to the word БРЕТЕ́ЛЬКА, which is listed once as "БРЕТЕ́ЛЬКА 3J2(b)" and once as "БРЕ-ТЕ́ЛЬКА not 3W2". If these two entries were combined into one, it would not be clear which rule applied to which vowel.

When a word or stem is--according to our sources --to be *optionally* included in a list of specified words, this is shown by the dagger †. Thus, "3H4†" may be read "rule 3H4 applies, optionally"; and "not 3U†" is to be understood as "rule 3U may or may not apply".

A

АББА́Т	not 3N(b)	АБСОЛЮТИ́СТСКИЙ	3B1(b)
АБРЕ́К	3J2(b)	АБСЦЕ́ССА	3N(a)
АБСЕНТЕЙ́ЗМ	3J2(b)	АБХА́ЗСКИЙ	not 3N(d)

АВАНТЮРИ́СТСКИЙ	3B1(b)
А̀ВИАМОДЕЛИ́ЗМ	3J2(b)
АВИ́ЗО	not 3U
А̀ВТОГРЕ́ЙДЕР	3J2(b)
АВТОНОМИ́СТСКИЙ	3B1(b)
АГА́	3C2
АГРЕ́ССИЯ	3N(a)
АДА́ЖИО	not 3U†
АДАПТЕ́Р	3J2(b)
АДЕКВА́ТНЫЙ	3J2(b)
АДЕНИ́Т	3J2(b)
АДЕНО́ИД	3J2(b)
АДЕ́ПТ	3J2(b)
АДЮЛЬТЕ́Р	3J2(b)
АЗЕРБАЙДЖА́Н	3J2(b)†
АЙ-АЙ-А́Й	3Z
А́ЙСБЕРГ	3J2(b)
АКМЕИ́ЗМ	3J2(b)
АКТИВИ́СТСКИЙ	3B1(b)
АЛЛА́Х	not 3N(b)
АЛЛЕГРЕ́ТТО	3J2(b)
АЛЛЕГРЕ́ТТО	not 3W2†
АЛЛИТЕРА́ЦИЯ	not 3N(b)†
АЛЛО́	3Z
АЛЛО́	not 3N(b)†
АЛТЕ́Я	3J2(b)
АЛЬПИНИ́СТСКИЙ	3B1(b)
АЛЬТЕРНАТИ́ВА	3J2(b)
АМАРИ́ЛЛИС	3N(a)
АМБРЕ́	3J2(b)
АММОНА́Л	not 3N(b)†
АММО́НИЙ	not 3N(b)†
А́МПЕР	3J2(b)
АНА́МНЕЗ	3J2(b)

АНАРХИ́СТСКИЙ	3B1(b)
АНАРХОСИНДИ-КАЛИ́СТСКИЙ	3B1(b)
А́НГЕЛ	3Z
АНДА́НТЕ	3J2(b)
АНЕСТЕЗИ́Я	3J2(b)
АННА́ЛЫ	not 3N(b)
АННАМИ́ТКА	not 3N(b)
АННЕ́КСИЯ	3J2(b)†
АННЕКСИОНИ́СТ-СКИЙ	3B1(b) 3J2(b)†
АННОТА́ЦИЯ	not 3N(b)
АНТЕ́ННА	3J2(b) 3N(a)†
АНТИДЕТОНА́ТОР	3J2(b)
А̀НТИМАРКСИ́СТ-СКИЙ	3B1(b)
А̀НТИПАССА́Т	not 3N(b)
АНТИСЕ́ПТИКА	3J2(b)
АНТИТЕ́ЗА	3J2(b)
А̀НТИФАШИ́СТСКИЙ	3B1(b)
АНТРЕ́	3J2(b)
АНТРЕКО́Т	3J2(b)
АОРТА́ЛЬНЫЙ	not 3U
АПОСТЕРИО́РИ	3J2(b) not 3U
АППЕРЦЕ́ПЦИЯ	not 3W2†
АРАБЕ́СКИ	3J2(b)
АРИЕ́ТТА	3Y1(b)
АРИО́ЗО	not 3U
АРПЕ́ДЖИО	not 3U
АРХА́НГЕЛ	3Z
АСБЕ́СТ	3J2(b)
АСЕ́ПТИКА	3J2(b)
АСЕ́ССОР	3N(a)

АСПЕ́НТ	3J2(b)	БАЦИ́ЛЛО-	3N(a)
АССИМИЛЯ́ЦИЯ	not 3N(b)	БАЯДЕ́РКА	3J2(b)
АССИРИ́ЙСКИЙ	not 3N(b)†	БЕБЕ́	3J2(b)
АССОНА́НС	not 3N(b)	БЕДЕ́КЕР	3J2(b)
АСТЕНИ́Я	3J2(b)	БЕЖ	3J2(b)
АСТЕРО́ИД	3J2(b)	БЕЗВОЗМЕ́ЗДН-	not 3B1(f)
АТЕИ́ЗМ	3J2(b)	БЕЗДН-	not 3B1(f)
АТЕЛЬЕ́	3J2(b)	БЕЗЕ́	3J2(b)
АТО́ЛЛ	not 3N(d)†	БЕЗМЕ́ЗДН-	not 3B1(f)
АТО́ЛЛОВЫЙ	3N(a)†	БЕЙСБО́Л	3J2(b)
АТТИ́ЧЕСКИЙ	not 3N(b)	БЕ́К	3J2(b)
АУДИЕ́НЦИЯ	3Y1(b)	БЕКА́Р	3J2(b)
АУТЕНТИ́ЧНЫЙ	3J2(b)	БЕКО́Н	3J2(b)
А̀УТОДАФЕ́	3J2(b) not 3U	БЕЛОПОДКЛА́ДОЧ-НИК	3H4†
АФРИКА́НДЕРЫ	3J2(b)	БЕЛЬВЕДЕ́Р	3J2(b)
А́ФФИКС	3N(a)	БЕ́ЛЬКА́НТО	3J2(b)
АЭ́РО-	3Z	БЕЛЬФЛЁР	3J2(b)
		БЕЛЬЭТА́Ж	3J2(b)
Б		БЕМО́ЛЬ	3J2(b)
БАЗЕ́ДОВА	3J2(b)	БЕРБЕ́РСКИЙ	3J2(b)
БАКШТЕ́ЙН	3J2(b)	БЕРИ-БЕ́РИ	3J2(b)
БАЛАЛА́ЕЧНИК	3H4	БЕРСАЛЬЕ́Р	3J2(b)
БА́ЛЛА	3N(a)	БЕССЕМЕРОВА́НИЕ	not 3N(b)
БАНДЕРО́ЛЬ	3J2(b)	БЕ́ТА	3J2(b)
БА́НДЖО	not 3U†	БЕШАМЕ́ЛЬ	3V3
БАПТИ́СТСКИЙ	3B1(b)	БИЗНЕСМЕ́Н	3J2(b)
БАРА́НОЧНИК	3H4†	БИЛЬБОКЕ́	not 3U
БАРЕЛЬЕ́Ф	3J2(b)	БИОГЕНЕ́З	3J2(b)
БАРО́ККО	3N(a)†	БИССЕКТРИ́СА	not 3N(b)†
БАРОНЕ́ССА	3N(a)†	БИФШТЕ́КС	3J2(b)
БА́СКСКИЙ	3B2	БЛИЗ	3Z
БАТАЛЬО́Н	3Y2	БОА́	not 3U
БАТТЕРФЛЯ́Й	3J2(b) not 3N(b)	БОГ	3C2†

БОЛЕ́РО	not 3U†	В	
БОЛЬШЕВИ́СТСКИЙ	3B1(b)	ВАДЕМЕ́КУМ	3J2(b)
БОМО́НД	not 3U	ВА́ЛЬДШНЕП	3J2(b)
БОНАПАРТИ́СТ-СКИЙ	3B1(b)	ВАРЬЕТЕ́	3J2(b)
		ВАССА́Л	not 3N(b)
БОНВИВА́Н	not 3U†	ВА́ТЕР	3J2(b)
БОНМО́	not 3U	ВА̀ТЕРПО́ЛО	3J2(b)
БОНТО́Н	not 3U		not 3U
БОРДО́	not 3U	ВЕ́КТОР	3J2(b)
БОРЩ	3R(c)	ВЕНДЕ́ТТА	3J2(b)
БОТФО́РТЫ	not 3U†		3N(a)
БО́ЧЕЧНЫЙ	3H4†	ВЕРБЕ́НА	3J2(b)
БРАНДВА́ХТА	3Z	ВЕРЁВОЧНЫЙ	3H4†
БРЕТЕ́ЛЬКА	3J2(b)	ВЀСТГО́ТЫ	3J2(b)
БРЕТЕ́ЛЬКА	not 3W2	ВЕ́ТО	3J2(b)
БРИ́ТТЫ	3N(a)		not 3U†
БРОНХОАДЕНИ́Т	3J2(b)	ВЗЯ́ТОЧНИК	3H4†
БРУДЕРША́ФТ	3J2(b)	ВИКОНТЕ́ССА	3J2(b)
БРУ́СТВЕР	3J2(b)		3N(a)†
БРЮМЕ́Р	3J2(b)	ВОКАЛИ́ЗМ	not 3U†
БРЮССЕ́ЛЬСКИЙ	3J2(b)	ВОЛЬТЕ́РОВСКИЙ	3J2(b)
БУДДИ́ЗМ	not 3N(b)	ВОЛЮНТАРИ́СТ-СКИЙ	3B1(b)
БУ́ДОЧНИК	3H4†		
БУКВАЛИ́СТСКИЙ	3B1(b)	ВО́СЕМЬ	3C3†
БУЛА́ВОЧНЫЙ	3H4†	ВОСЕМЬСО́Т	3C3
БУ́ЛОЧНАЯ	3H4†	ВУНДЕРКИ́НД	3J2(b)
БУЛЬО́Н	3Y2	ВЫ́БОРГСКИЙ	3B2
БУРИМЕ́	3J2(b)	Г	
БУТЕРБРО́Д	3J2(b)	ГА́БИТУС	3C2
БУТЫ́ЛОЧНЫЙ	3H4†	ГА̀В-ГА́В	3C2
БУХГА́ЛТЕР	3C2	ГА́ЕР	not 3W2
БУШМЕ́Н	3J2(b)		3Y1(b)
БЮСТГА́ЛЬТЕР	3J2(b)	ГАЗГО́ЛЬДЕР	3J2(b)
	3Z	ГАЗЕ́ЛЛА	3J2(b)
		ГАЗЕ́ЛЬ	3J2(b)

ГАЛИФЕ́	3J2(b)
ГАЛЛОМА́Н	not 3N(b)
ГАЛЛОФО́Б	not 3N(b)
ГАЛО́ШИ	3Z
ГА́НГСТЕР	3J2(b)
ГАНТЕ́ЛЬ	3J2(b)
ГА́РШНЕП	3J2(b)
ГАСТРОЭНТЕРИ́Т	3J2(b)
ГЕДОНИ́ЗМ	not 3U
ГЕ́ЙЗЕР	3J2(b)
ГЕЛЕ́РТЕР	3J2(b)
ГЕЛЕ́РТЕР	not 3W2
ГЕЛИКОПТЕ́Р	3J2(b)
ГЕ́НЕЗИС	3J2(b)
ГЕНЕРА́ЦИЯ	3J2(b)
ГЕНЕ́ТИКА	3J2(b)
ГЕНОЦИ́Д	not 3W2†
ГЕОДЕ́ЗИЯ	3J2(b)
ГЕРМЕНЕ́ВТИКА	3J2(b)
ГЕТЕ́РА	3J2(b)
ГЕТЕ́РА	not 3W2†
ГЕТЕРОГЕ́ННЫЙ	3J2(b)
ГИББО́Н	not 3N(b)†
ГИГА́НТСКИЙ	3B1(b)
ГИЛЬОТИ́НА	3Z
ГЛИНТВЕ́ЙН	3J2(b)
ГЛИ́ССЕР	3N(a)†
ГОЛЛА́НДКА	3B1(c)
ГОЛЛА́НДСКИЙ	3B1(b)
ГО́П	3C2
ГО́ПЛЯ	3C2
ГО́РНИЧНАЯ	3H4†
ГОРТЕ́НЗИЯ	3J2(b)
ГОРЧИ́ЧНЫЙ	3H4
ГОРЯ́ЧЕЧНЫЙ	3H4
ГО́СПОДИ	3C2†
ГОСПО́ДЬ	3C2†
ГОФМАРША́Л	not 3U
ГОФМЕ́ЙСТЕР	3J2(b) not 3U
ГРАДИЕ́НТ	3Y1(b)
ГРЕ́ЙДЕР	3J2(b)
ГРЕ́ЧНЕВЫЙ	3H4†
ГРОТЕ́СК	3J2(b)
ГРУ́ППА	3N(a)†
ГРУППОВО́Д	not 3N(b)†
ГУА́НО	not 3U†
ГУВЕРНА́НТКА	3B1(c)
ГУЛЛИ́ВЫЙ	not 3N(b)
ГУ́ЛЬДЕН	3J2(b)
ГУММИ-	not 3N(b)
ГУММИ́РОВАННЫЙ	not 3N(b)
ГУММО́ЗНЫЙ	not 3N(b)

Д

ДАМА́ССКИЙ	not 3N(d)
ДВАДЦАТ-	3V3
ДВО́ЕЧНИК	3H4
ДЕА́ЭРА́ЦИЯ	3J2(b)
ДЕБАРКАДЕ́Р	3J2(b)
ДЕ́БЕТ	3J2(b)
ДЕБИ́Т	3J2(b)
ДЕБЛОКИ́РОВАН- НЫЙ	3J2(b)
ДЕВАЛЬВА́ЦИЯ	3J2(b)
ДЕВИА́ЦИЯ	3J2(b)
ДЕВИ́ЧНИК	3H4
ДЕВО́Н	3J2(b)
ДЕВЯТЬСО́Т	3Z

ДЕГАЗА́ЦИЯ	3J2(b)	ДЕМАСКИРО́ВКА	3J2(b)
ДЕГЕНЕРА́ЦИЯ	3J2(b)	ДЕМИЛИТАРИЗА́-ЦИЯ	3J2(b)
ДЕГРАДА́ЦИЯ	3J2(b)		
ДЕГУСТА́ЦИЯ	3J2(b)	ДЕМИУ́РГ	3J2(b)
ДЕДУ́НКЦИЯ	3J2(b)	ДЕМОГРА́ФИЯ	3J2(b)
ДЕДУЦИ́РОВАТЬ	3J2(b)	ДЕМОНЕТИЗА́ЦИЯ	3J2(b)
ДЕЗАБИЛЬЕ́	3J2(b)	ДЕМОНТА́Ж	3J2(b)
ДЕЗАВУИ́РОВАТЬ	3J2(b)	ДЕМОРАЛИЗА́ЦИЯ	3J2(b)
ДЕЗИДЕРА́ТЫ	3J2(b)	ДЕ́МОС	3J2(b)
ДЕЗИНСЕКЦИО́Н-НЫЙ	3J2(b)	ДЕ́МПИНГ	3J2(b)
		ДЕ́МПФЕР	3J2(b)
ДЀЗИНСТРУ́КТОР	3J2(b)	ДЀМУНИЦИПАЛИ-ЗА́ЦИЯ	3J2(b)
ДЕЗИНТЕГРА́ЦИЯ	3J2(b)		
ДЕЗИНФОРМА́ЦИЯ	3J2(b)	ДЀНАТУРАЛИЗА́ЦИЯ	3J2(b)
ДЕЗОДОРА́ТОР	3J2(b)	ДЀНАЦИОНАЛИ-ЗА́ЦИЯ	3J2(b)
ДЕЗОРИЕНТА́ЦИЯ	3J2(b)		
ДЕЙ́ЗМ	3J2(b)	ДЀНАЦИФИКА́ЦИЯ	3J2(b)
ДЕ́КА	3J2(b)	ДЕ́НДИ	3J2(b)
ДЕКАБРИ́СТСКИЙ	3B1(b)	ДЕНДР-	3J2(b)
ДЕКАДА́НС	3J2(b)	ДЕНОМИНАТИ́ВНЫЙ	3J2(b)
ДЕКА-́	3J2(b)	ДЕНОНСА́ЦИЯ	3J2(b)
ДЕКАЛЬКИ́РОВАТЬ	3J2(b)	ДЕНТИ́Н	3J2(b)
ДЕКАЛЬКОМА́НИЯ	3J2(b)	ДЕПОЛЯРИЗА́ЦИЯ	3J2(b)
ДЀКАРТЕЛИЗА́ЦИЯ	3J2(b)	ДЕПОНЕ́НТ	3J2(b)
ДЕКА́ЭДР	3J2(b)	ДЕПРЕ́ССИЯ	3J2(b) 3N(a)
ДЕКВАЛИФИКА́ЦИЯ	3J2(b)		
ДЕНО́КТ	3J2(b)	ДЕРАТИЗА́ЦИЯ	3J2(b)
ДЕНОЛЬТЕ́	3J2(b)	ДЕ́РБИ	3J2(b)
ДЕНО́РУМ	3J2(b)	ДЕРИВА́Т	3J2(b)
ДЕЛИБА́Ш	3J2(b)	ДЕРМАТОЛО́ГИЯ	3J2(b)
ДЕ́ЛЬТА	3J2(b)	ДЕРМОГРАФИ́ЗМ	3J2(b)
ДЕЛЮВИА́ЛЬНЫЙ	3J2(b)	ДЕ́РРИК	3J2(b) 3N(a)
ДЕМАРНА́ЦИЯ	3J2(b)		
ДЕМА́РШ	3J2(b)	ДЕТЕКТИ́В	3J2(b)
		ДЕТЕ́КТОР	3J2(b)

ДЕТЕРМИНИ́ЗМ	3J2(b)	ДОРМЕ́З	3J2(b)
ДЕ-ФА́КТО	3J2(b)		not 3U
	not 3U	ДОСЬЕ́	not 3U
ДЕФЕ́КТ	3J2(b)†	ДОСЮ́РА	not 3U
ДЕФЕНЗИ́ВА	3J2(b)	ДРОМАДЕ́Р	3J2(b)
ДЕФИЛЕ́	3J2(b)		not 3U
ДЕФИНИ́ЦИЯ	3J2(b)	ДУ́ЧЕ	not 3W2
ДЕФОРМА́ЦИЯ	3J2(b)	Е	
ДЕЦЕНТРАЛИ-ЗА́ЦИЯ	3J2(b)	ЕЙ-БО́ГУ	3C2†
		Ё́ЛОЧНЫЙ	3H4†
ДЕЦИ-	3J2(b)	Ж	
ДЕЦИМА́ЛЬНЫЙ	3J2(b)	ЖАВЕ́ЛЬ	3V3
ДЕШИФРО́ВАННЫЙ	3J2(b)	ЖАКЕ́Т	3V3
ДЕ́ЭТИМОЛОГИ-ЗА́ЦИЯ	3J2(b)	ЖАЛЕ́ЙКА	3V3
		ЖАЛЕ́ТЬ	3V3
ДЕ-Ю́РЕ	3J2(b)	ЖАСМИ́Н	3V3
ДЖЕ́МПЕР	3J2(b)	ЖИ́РО	not 3U
ДЖЕНТЛЬМЕ́Н	3J2(b)	ЖУРНАЛИ́СТСКИЙ	3B1(b)
ДЗЕ́КАНЬЕ	3Z	ЖЮРИ́	3Z
ДИАБЕ́Т	3J2(b)	З	
ДИАДЕ́МА	3J2(b)	ЗДРА́ВСТВ-	3B3
ДИЕ́З	3Y1(b)	ЗЕРО́	3J2(b)
ДИЕ́ТА	3Y1(b)	ЗО́ОЛОГ	not 3U
ДИЕТЕ́ТИКА	3J2(b)	ЗУЛУ́ССКИЙ	not 3N(d)
	3Y1(b)	ЗУ́ММЕР	3J2(b)
ДИ́НГО	not 3U†	И	
ДИСКУ́ССИЯ	3N(a)	ИДЕНТИ́ЧНЫЙ	3J2(b)
ДИСПАНСЕ́Р	3J2(b)	ИДЕФИ́КС	3J2(b)
ДИССИДЕ́НТ	not 3N(b)	ИДИ́ЛЛИЯ	3N(a)
ДИССИМИЛЯТИ́В-НЫЙ	not 3N(b)	ИЕЗУЙ́Т	3Z
		ИЗОГЛО́ССА	3N(a)
ДИССОНА́НС	not 3N(b)	ИЗОЛЯЦИОНИ́СТ-СКИЙ	3B1(b)
ДЛИННО-	not 3N(b)		
ДОКЛА́ССОВЫЙ	3N(a)		
ДОЛЬМЕ́Н	3J2(b)		

ИЗОТЕ́РА	3J2(b)	ИРРЕГУЛЯ́РНЫЙ	not 3N(b)
ИЗОТЕ́РМА	3J2(b)	ИРРИГАЦИО́ННЫЙ	not 3N(b)
ИЛЛЮЗИОНИ́СТ- СКИЙ	3B1(b)	ИСЛА́НДСКИЙ	3B1(b)
		ИТЕЛЬМЕ́НКА	3J2(b)
ИММАНЕ́НТНЫЙ	not 3N(b)	ИТЕРАТИ́ВНЫЙ	3J2(b)
ИММАТЕРИА́ЛЬНЫЙ	not 3N(b)	Й	
ИММИГРА́НТ	not 3N(b)	ЙОТА́ЦИЯ	not 3U
ИММОРТЕ́ЛЬ	3J2(b) not 3N(b)	К	
ИММУНИТЕ́Т	not 3N(b)	КАБАРЕ́	3J2(b)
ИМПЕРИАЛИ́СТ- СКИЙ	3B1(b)	КАДЕ́НЦИЯ	3J2(b)
		КА́ЙЗЕР	3J2(b)
ИМПРЕСА́РИО	not 3W2	КАНАВЕ́ЛЛА	3J2(b)
ИНВЕ́СТОР	3J2(b)	КАКА́О	not 3U†
ИНГРЕДИЕ́НТ	not 3W2 3Y1(b)	КАЛА́ЧНИК	3H4†
И́НДЕКС	3J2(b)	КАМЕ́Я	3J2(b)
ИНДЕТЕРМИНИ́ЗМ	3J2(b)	КАНАПЕ́	3J2(b)
ИНДИВИДУАЛИ́СТ- СКИЙ	3B1(b)	КАНАРЕ́ЕЧНИК	3H4†
		КА́НТЕЛЕ	3J2(b)
ИНКАССА́ТОР	not 3N(b)	КА́НТЕЛЕ	not 3W2
ИННЕРВА́ЦИЯ	3J2(b) not 3N(b)	КАПЕ́ЛЛА	3J2(b)
ИНТЕГРА́Л	3J2(b)	КАПРИ́ЧЧИО	not 3U†
ИНТЕНСИ́ВНО	3J2(b)	КАРАВЕ́ЛЛА	3J2(b)
ИНТЕРВА́Л	3J2(b)†	КАРЕ́	3J2(b)
ИНТЕРВЬЮЕ́Р	3J2(b) 3Y1(b)	КАРМАНЬО́ЛА	3Y2
		КАРТВЕ́ЛЫ	3J2(b)
ИНТЕРЛЮ́ДИЯ	3J2(b)	КАРТЕ́ЛЬ	3J2(b)
ИНТЕРМЕ́ЦЦО	3J2(b)	КАРЬЕРИ́СТСКИЙ	3B1(b)
ИНТЕРНИ́РОВАТЬ	3J2(b)	КАССИ́Р	not 3N(b)
ИНТЕРПРЕТИ́РО- ВАТЬ	3J2(b)	КАССИ́РОВАТЬ	not 3N(b)†
		КАТЕ́РНА	3J2(b)
ИНТЕРФЕРЕ́НЦИЯ	3J2(b)	КАТЕ́ТЕР	3J2(b)
ИРЛА́НДСКИЙ	3B1(b)	КАФЕ́	3J2(b)
ИРРЕА́ЛЬНЫЙ	not 3N(b)	КАФЕТЕ́РИЙ	3J2(b)

КАШНЕ́	3J2(b)	КОММУНИ́ЗМ	not 3N(b)†
КВАДРИЛЬО́Н	3Y2	КОММУНИКА́ЦИЯ	not 3N(b)†
КВЕ́СТОР	3J2(b)	КОММУТА́ЦИЯ	not 3N(b)†
КВИЕТИ́ЗМ	not 3W2 3Y1(b)	КОММЮНИКЕ́	not 3N(b)
КВИНТИЛЬО́Н	3Y2	КОМПАНЬО́Н	3Y2
КИБЕРНЕ́ТИКА	3J2(b) not 3W2	КОМПАРАТИВИ́СТ-СКИЙ	3B1(b)
КИЛОГРА́ММ	not 3N(d)	КОМПА́РТИЯ	not 3U
КИЛЬВА́ТЕР	3J2(b)	КОМПРЕ́ССОР	3N(a)
КИНЕМА́ТИКА	3J2(b)†	КОМПРОМИ́СС	not 3N(d)
КИНЕСКО́П	3J2(b)	КОНГРЕССМЕ́Н	3J2(b)
КИНОАТЕЛЬЕ́	3J2(b)	КОНГРЕССМЕ́Н	not 3W2
КИРГИ́ЗСКИЙ	not 3N(d)	КОНДЕНСА́ТОР	3J2(b)
КИРИ́ЛЛИЦА	3N(a)	КОНЕ́ЧНО	3H4
КИ́РШВА́ССЕР	3J2(b)	КОННЕТА́БЛЬ	3J2(b) not 3N(b)
КЛА́ССИК	3N(a)		
КЛА́ССОВЫЙ	3N(a)†	КОНСЕКВА́НС	3J2(b)
КЛИЕ́НТ	3Y1(b)	КОНСОМЕ́	3J2(b) not 3U†
КНИ́КСЕН	3J2(b)		
КОДЕ́ЙН	3J2(b)	КОНСО́РЦИУМ	not 3U
КО́ДЕКС	3J2(b)	КОНСТЕ́БЛЬ	3J2(b)
КОЙНЕ́	3J2(b)	КОНСТРУКТИ́-ВИСТСКИЙ	3B1(b)
КОКТЕ́ЙЛЬ	3J2(b) not 3U†	КОНТЕ́ЙНЕР	3J2(b)
КОЛЛЕКТИВИ́СТ-СКИЙ	3B1(b)	КОНТРАБАНДИ́СТ-СКИЙ	3B1(b)
КОЛЛИ́ЗИЯ	not 3N(b)	КОНФЕДЕРА́ЦИЯ	3J2(b)†
КОЛОНИ́СТСКИЙ	3B1(b)	КОНЦЕРТИ́НО	not 3U†
КОЛО́ННА	3N(a)†	КОНЦЕ́ССИЯ	3N(a)
КОЛЬЕ́	not 3U	КОПЕ́ЕЧНЫЙ	3H4†
КОМИЛЬФО́	not 3U	КОРА́ЛЛОВЫЙ	3N(a)
КОМИ́ССИЯ	3N(a)	КОРВЕ́Т	3J2(b)
КО́ММИВОЯЖЁР	3N(a)	КОРДЕБАЛЕ́Т	3J2(b)
КОММУ́НА	not 3N(b)†	КОРДЕГА́РДИЯ	3J2(b)
		КОРИ́ЧНЕВЫЙ	3H4†

КОРТЕ́Ж	3J2(b)	ЛЕГГО́РН	not 3N(b)
КОРТЕ́СЫ	3J2(b)		not 3W2
КОСТЛЯ́-	not 3B1(e)	ЛЕГИТИМИ́СТСКИЙ	3B1(b)
КОТИЛЬО́Н	3Y2	ЛЕЙБОРИ́СТСКИЙ	3B1(b)
КОТТЕ́ДЖ	3J2(b)	ЛЕ́ЙДЕНСКИЙ	3J2(b)
КОЭФФИЦИЕ́НТ	3Y1(b)	ЛЕКСЕ́МА	3J2(b)
КРЕВЕ́ТКА	3J2(b)	ЛЁССОВЫЙ	3N(a)
КРЕ́ДО	3J2(b)	ЛИБРЕ́ТТО	3N(a)
	not 3U†	ЛИМФАДЕНИ́Т	3J2(b)
КРЕ́ЙЦЕР	3J2(b)	ЛО́ДОЧНИК	3H4†
КРЕПДЕШИ́Н	3J2(b)	ЛОНГШЕ́З	not 3U
КРИСТА́ЛЛИН	3N(a)	ЛО́РД-МЭ́Р	3J2(b)
КРО́НВЕРК	3J2(b)	ЛОТО́ЧНИК	3H4†
КРОНГЛА́С	not 3U	ЛОША́Д-	3V3
КРО́НШНЕП	3J2(b)		
КРОНШТЕ́ЙН	3J2(b)	**М**	
	not 3U	МАДЕМУАЗЕ́ЛЬ	3J2(b)
КУЗЕ́Н	3J2(b)		3Z
КУПЕ́	3J2(b)	МАЖОРДО́М	not 3U
КУРА́РЕ	3J2(b)	МАЙОНЕ́З	3Z
КЮРЕ́	3J2(b)	МАЙОРА́Т	3Z
		МАКСИМАЛИ́СТ-СКИЙ	3B1(b)
Л		МА́НГО	not 3U
ЛА́ВОЧНИК	3H4†	МАНЬЧЖУ́Р-	3Z
ЛАМАЙ́СТСКИЙ	3B1(b)	МАРАБУ́	3Z
ЛАНДВЕ́Р	3J2(b)	МАРЕ́НГО	not 3U†
ЛАНДТА́Г	not 3N(c)	МАРКСИ́СТСКИЙ	3B1(b)
ЛАНДША́ФТ	3Z	МАРКШЕ́ЙДЕР	3J2(b)
ЛАРЁЧНИК	3H4†	МАРТЕ́Н	3J2(b)
ЛАССО́	not 3N(b)	МАССИ́В	not 3N(b)
ЛАТЕ́НТНЫЙ	3J2(b)	МАССОВИ́К	not 3N(b)
ЛАТЕРА́ЛЬНЫЙ	3J2(b)	МАТИНЕ́	3J2(b)
ЛЕГА́Т	not 3W2		3Z
ЛЕГА́ТО	not 3W2†	МАТРО́ССКИЙ	not 3N(d)

МЕДАЛЬО́Н	3Y2	МОДЕ́ЛЬ	3J2(b)
МЕДИЕВИ́СТИКА	not 3W2		not 3U†
	3Y1(b)	МОДЕРА́ТОР	3J2(b)
МЕДРЕСЕ́	3J2(b)		not 3U†
-МЕ́ЙСТЕР	3J2(b)	МОДЕ́РН	3J2(b)
МЕ́ЛОС	3J2(b)		not 3U†
МЕМЕ́НТО	3J2(b)	МОДЕРНИ́СТСКИЙ	3B1(b)
МЕНЕСТРЕ́ЛЬ	3J2(b)		3J2(b)
МЕ́НТОР	3J2(b)		not 3U†
МЕНЬШЕВИ́СТ-	3B1(b)	МО́ЛВСТВ-	3B3
СКИЙ		МОЛИБДЕ́Н	3J2(b)
-МЁ́РЗШ-	not 3N(c)	МОЛО́ЧНЫЙ	3H4†
МЕРКАНТИЛИ́СТ-	3B1(b)	МОНА́ДА	not 3U†
СКИЙ		МОНАРХИ́СТСКИЙ	3B1(b)
МЕ́ССА	3J2(b)	МОНОПОЛИ́СТСКИЙ	3B1(b)
МЕССИ́Я	not 3N(b)	МОНСЕНЬЁ́Р	3J2(b)
МЕТАТЕ́ЗА	3J2(b)	МОНТЕКРИ́СТО	3J2(b)
МЕТОДИ́СТСКИЙ	3B1(b)	МОРДЕ́НТ	3J2(b)
МЕ́ТР*	3J2(b)	МО́РЗЕ	3J2(b)
МЕТРДОТЕ́ЛЬ	3J2(b)	МОРФЕ́МА	3J2(b)
МЕТРЕ́ССА	3J2(b)	МУЛИНЕ́	3J2(b)
МЕТРОПОЛИТЕ́Н	3J2(b)	МУЛЛА́	not 3N(b)
МЕ́ЦЦО-	3J2(b)	МУНДШТУ́К	3Z
МИЛИТАРИ́СТ-	3B1(b)	МУССИ́РОВАННЫЙ	not 3N(b)†
СКИЙ			
МИЛЛИАРДЕ́Р	3J2(b)	Н	
МИЛЛИОНЕ́Р	3Z	НАРО́ЧНО	3H4
МИННЕЗИ́НГЕР	3J2(b)	НАЦИОНАЛИ́СТ-	3B1(b)
	not 3N(b)	СКИЙ	
МИ́ССИЯ	3N(a)	НАЦИ́СТСКИЙ	3B1(b)
МИ́СТЕР	3J2(b)	НЕЙРОХИРУ́РГИЯ	3J2(b)
МИ́ТЕНКИ	3J2(b)	НЀО-	3J2(b)
МИ́ТТЕЛЬШПИ́ЛЬ	3J2(b)	НЕСЕССЕ́Р	3J2(b)
		НЕ́ТТО	3J2(b)

*Note that 3J2(b) applies to МЕ́ТР only in the mean-
ing "master, teacher". When МЕ́ТР means "metre",
3J2(b) does not apply.

НИГИЛИ́СТСКИЙ	3B1(b)	ПА-ДЕ-ТРУА́	3J2(b)
НИ́ППЕЛ	3N(a)	ПАЛИМПСЕ́СТ	3J2(b)
НОВЕ́ЛЛА	3J2(b)† not 3U†	ПАНДЕ́КТЫ	3J2(b)
		ПАНДЕМИ́Я	3J2(b)
НОКТЮ́РН	not 3U†	ПАННО́	not 3N(b)
НО́НСЕНС	3J2(b)	ПАНТЕО́Н	3J2(b)
НОРДВЕ́СТ	3J2(b)	ПАПИЛЬО́ТКА	3Y2
НОРМА́ННЫЙ	3N(a)	ПАПУА́ССКИЙ	not 3N(d)
НО́ТАБЕ́НЕ	3J2(b)	ПАРВЕНЮ́	3J2(b)
О		ПАРЕ́З	3J2(b)
ОА́ЗИС	not 3U†	ПАРЛА́МЕНТСКИЙ	3B1(b)
ОБСКУРАНТИ́СТ-СКИЙ	3B1(b)	ПАРМЕЗА́Н	3J2(b)
		ПАРТЕНОГЕНЕ́З	3J2(b)
ОБЪЕКТИВИ́СТ-СКИЙ	3B1(b)	ПАРТЕ́Р	3J2(b)
		ПАРЦЕ́ЛЛА	3N(a)†
ОГО́	3C2	ПАССА́Т	not 3N(b)
О́-ГО́-ГО́	3C2	ПАССЕЙ́ЗМ	3J2(b) not 3N(b)
ОДЕО́Н	3J2(b)		
ОДИ́ННАДЦАТЬ	3N(a)	ПАССИ́В	not 3N(b)
ОКТЯБРИ́СТСКИЙ	3B1(b)	ПА́ССИЯ	3N(a)†
О́НТОГЕНЕ́З	3J2(b)	ПАСТЕ́ЛЬ	3J2(b)
ОПЕРЕ́ТТА	3N(a)	ПАСТЕРИЗА́ЦИЯ	3J2(b)
ОППОРТУНИ́СТ-СКИЙ	3B1(b)	ПА́ТЕР	3J2(b)
		ПАТЕ́ТИКА	3J2(b)
ОРХИДЕ́Я	3J2(b)	ПАТРОНЕ́ССА	3N(a)†
ОСТЕО́ЛОГ	3J2(b)	ПАЦИЕ́НТ	3Y1(b)
ОТЕ́ЛЬ	3J2(b) not 3U	ПАЦИФИ́СТСКИЙ	3B1(b)
		ПЕ́ДЕЛЬ	3J2(b)
ОТЗОВИ́СТСКИЙ	3B1(b)	ПЕДЕРА́СТИЯ	3J2(b)
ОЧЕРКИ́СТСКИЙ	3B1(b)	ПЕ́ЛЕНГ	3J2(b)
ОЧЕ́ЧНИК	3H4	ПЕНИТЕНЦИА́РНЫЙ	3J2(b)
П		ПЕ́НС	3J2(b)
ПАВИЛЬО́Н	3Y2	ПЕНСНЕ́	3J2(b)
ПА-ДЕ-ДЕ́	3J2(b)	ПЕНТА́МЕТР	3J2(b)
ПАДЕКА́ТР	3J2(b)		

ПЕНТА́ЭДР	3J2(b)	ПОЛУНО́ЧНИК	3H4
ПЕ́РЕЧНИЦА	3H4†	ПОМА́ЗАННИК	not 3N(b)†
ПЕ́РИ	3J2(b)	ПОРТВЕ́ЙН	3J2(b)
ПЕРПЕ́ТУУМ-МО́БИЛЕ	3J2(b)	ПОРТМОНЕ́	3J2(b)
ПЕРФЕ́КТ	3J2(b)	ПОРТШЕ́З	not 3U
ПЕРЦЕ́ПЦИЯ	3J2(b)	ПОРТЬЕ́	not 3U
ПЕССИМИ́ЗМ	not 3N(b)	ПОРЯ́ДОЧНЫЙ	3H4†
ПЕТЕРБУ́РГСКИЙ	3B2	ПОСЕ́ССИБНЫЙ	3J2(b) not 3N(b)
ПИЕЛИ́Т	not 3W2 3Y1(b)	ПОТЕНЦИА́Л	3J2(b)
ПИЕТИ́ЗМ	not 3W2 3Y1(b)	ПОЧТА́МТСКИЙ	3B1(b)
ПИККОЛО	3N(a)	ПОЧТАЛЬО́Н	3Y2
ПИ́РРОВ	3N(a)	ПОЭ́ЗИЯ	not 3U†
ПИТЕКА́НТРОП	3J2(b)	ПОЭ́МА	not 3U†
ПЛЕРЕ́ЗЫ	3J2(b)	ПОЭ́Т	not 3U†
ПЛИССЕ́	3J2(b)	ПОЭТЕ́ССА	3J2(b) 3N(a) not 3U†
ПОДЕ́СТА	3J2(b)		
ПОДСВЕ́ЧНИК	3H4†	ПРА́ЧЕЧНАЯ	3H4
ПОДСО́ЛНЕЧНИК	3H4†	ПРЕ́ССА	3N(a)†
ПОДШТА́ННИКИ	3N(a)	ПРЕТЕНЦИО́ЗНЫЙ	3J2(b)
ПОЗИТИВИ́СТСКИЙ	3B1(b)	ПРИЙТИ́	3Z
ПОЖА́ЛУЙСТА	3Z	ПРИНЦЕ́ССА	3N(a)
ПО́ЙНТЕР	3Z	ПРОВИДЕНЦИАЛИ́ЗМ	3J2(b)
ПОЛЕ́ННИЦА	3N(a)	ПРОГРЕ́ССИЯ	3N(a)
-ПОЛЗШ-	not 3N(c)	ПРОЕ́КТ	3Y1(b)
ПОЛИОМИЕЛИ́Т	not 3W2 3Y1(b)	ПРОПАГАНДИ́СТСКИЙ	3B1(b)
ПОЛИСИНТЕТИ́ЧЕСКИЙ	3J2(b)	ПРОПЕДЕ́ВТИКА	3J2(b)
ПОЛИСМЕ́Н	3J2(b)	ПРОПЕ́ЛЛЕР	3J2(b)
ПОЛИЦЕЙМЕ́ЙСТЕР	3J2(b) 3Z	ПРОСПЕ́РИТИ	3J2(b)
ПО́ЛО	not 3U	ПРОСЦЕ́НИУМ	not 3U
ПОЛОНЕ́З	3J2(b)	ПРОТЕЖЕ́	3J2(b)
		ПРОТЕ́З	3J2(b)
		ПРОТЕ́ИН	3J2(b)

ПРОТЕКЦИОНИ́СТ-СКИЙ	3B1(b)	РЕ́ДЕ́ЧНЫЙ	3H4†
ПРОТОИЕРЕ́Й	3Z	РЕЕ́СТР	3J2(b)
ПРОФЕ́ССОР	3N(a)	РЕЗЮМЕ́	3J2(b)
ПРОЦЕ́ССИЯ	3N(a)	РЕ́ЙДЕ́Р	3J2(b)
ПРУ́ССКИЙ	not 3N(d)	РЕЙНВЕ́ЙН	3J2(b)
ПРУ́ССЫ	3N(a)	РЕ́ЙС-	3J2(b)
-ПРЯ́Г-	3Z	РЕ́ЙХСВЕ́Р	3J2(b)
ПРЯ́НИЧНИК	3H4†	РЕ́КВИЕМ	3J2(b) 3Y1(b)
-ПРЯ́Ч-	3Z		
ПСИХОСТЕ́НИК	3J2(b)	РЕКОРДСМЕ́Н	3J2(b)
ПТЕРОДА́КТИЛЬ	3J2(b)	РЕКОРДИ́СТСКИЙ	3B1(b)
ПУРИ́СТСКИЙ	3B1(b)	РЕЛЕ́	3J2(b)
ПУСТЯ́ЧНЫЙ	3H4	РЕЛЯТИВИ́СТСКИЙ	3B1(b)
ПУТЧИ́СТСКИЙ	3B1(b)	РЕНЕССА́НС	3J2(b)
ПФЕ́ННИГ	3N(a)	РЕНКЛО́Д	not 3W2
ПШЮ́Т	3Z	РЕНОМЕ́	3J2(b)
ПЮРЕ́	3J2(b)	РЕПРЕ́ССИЯ	3N(a)
ПЯТЁРОЧНИК	3H4†	РЕФОРМИ́СТСКИЙ	3B1(b)
ПЯТЬСО́Т	3Z	РЖАНО́Й	3V3†
Р		РИТУРНЕ́ЛЬ	3J2(b)
РАДАМЕ́	3J2(b)	РО́ББЕР	3N(a)
РА́ДИО	not 3U†	РОДОДЕ́НДРОН	3J2(b)
РА́ДИОРЕЛЕ́Й-НЫЙ	3J2(b) not 3U†	РОКОКО́	not 3U
		РОССИЯ́НИН	not 3N(b)†
РАНДЕВУ́	3J2(b)	РОЯЛИ́СТСКИЙ	3B1(b)
РАСИ́СТСКИЙ	3B1(b)	РУСИ́СТСКИЙ	3B1(b)
РЕВАНШИ́СТСКИЙ	3B1(b)	РУТЕ́НИЙ	3J2(b)
РЕ́ВЕ́РС	3J2(b)	С	
РЕВИЗИОНИ́СТ-СКИЙ	3B1(b)	САДИ́СТСКИЙ	3B1(b)
		СА́ЛЬТО-МОРТА́ЛЕ	not 3U not 3W2
РЕВЮ́	not 3W2	САНДРИЛЬО́НА	3Y2
РЕ́ГБИ	3J2(b)	СВЯ́ТОЧНЫЙ	3H4†
РЕ́ДУПЛИКА́ЦИЯ	3J2(b)	СЕ́КАНС	3J2(b)

СЕКРЕТЕ́Р	3J2(b)
СЕКРЕТЕ́Р	not 3W2
СЕКСАГОНА́ЛЬ-НЫЙ	3J2(b)
СЕ́КСТА	3J2(b)
СЕКСТАЛЬО́Н	3J2(b) 3Y2
СЕКСТЕ́Т	3J2(b)
СЕЛЁДОЧНИЦА	3H4†
СЕМИКОПЕ́ЕЧНЫЙ	3H4†
СЕМЬСО́Т	3C3
СЕНБЕРНА́Р	3J2(b)
СЕНЕША́ЛЬ	3J2(b)
СЕНСО́РНЫЙ	3J2(b)
СЕНСУАЛИ́ЗМ	3J2(b)
СЕ́НТЕ́НЦИЯ	3J2(b)
СЕНТИМЕНТА-ЛИ́ЗМ	3J2(b)
СЕНЬО́Р	3J2(b) 3Y2
СЕПАРАТИ́СТ-СКИЙ	3B1(b)
СЕ́ПИЯ	3J2(b)
СЕ́ПСИС	3J2(b)
СЕПТАККО́РД	3J2(b)
СЕПТЕ́Т	3J2(b)
СЕ́ПТИМА	3J2(b)
СЕРВА́НТ	3J2(b)†
СЕ́РВИС	3J2(b)
СЕРВИТУ́Т	3J2(b)
СЕРДЕ́ЧНЫЙ	3H4†
СЕ́ТТЕР	3J2(b) 3N(a)
СЕ́ТТЛЬМЕНТ	3J2(b)
СЕ́ТТЛЬМЕНТ	not 3W2
СИЛЛАБИ́ЧЕСКИЙ	not 3N(b)†
СИЛЛОГИ́ЗМ	not 3N(b)†
СИМВОЛИ́СТСКИЙ	3B1(b)
СИНДИКАЛИ́СТ-СКИЙ	3B1(b)
СИНТЕ́ТИКА	3J2(b)
СИНЬО́Р	3Y2
СИОНИ́СТСКИЙ	3B1(b)
СИРО́ККО	3N(a)†
СКВОРЕ́ЧНИК	3H4
СКЛЕРОДЕ́РМА	3J2(b)
СКО́РБЬ	3R(c)
СКУ́ТЕР	3J2(b)
СКУ́ЧНЫЙ	3H4
СЛАВИ́СТСКИЙ	3B1(b)
СЛИВО́ЧНЫЙ	3H4†
СОБА́ЧНИК	3H4†
СОЖАЛЕ́НИЕ	3V3
СОЛИТЕ́Р	3J2(b) not 3U
СО́ЛНЦЕ	3Z
СОМБРЕ́РО	3J2(b) not 3U
СОНЕ́Т	3J2(b)† not 3U†
СПАРДЕ́К	3J2(b)
СПЕ́РМА	3J2(b)
СПИ́ННИНГ	3N(a)
СПИ́ЧЕЧНИЦА	3H4†
СПОНДЕ́Й	3J2(b)
СПОРТСМЕ́Н	3J2(b)†
СПРА́ВОЧНИК	3H4†
СТА́ТОЧНЫЙ	3H4
СТЕ́К	3J2(b)
СТЕ́НД	3J2(b)
СТЕНО́З	3J2(b)

СТЕНОКАРДИЯ	3J2(b)†	ТЕННИС	3J2(b) 3N(a)
СТЕТОСКОП	3J2(b)	ТЕНТ	3J2(b)
СТЛА-	not 3B1(e)	ТЕО-	3J2(b)
СТОГРАММОВЫЙ	3N(a)	ТЕРАПИЯ	3J2(b)
СТРЕЛОЧНИК	3H4†	ТЕРАТОЛОГИ-ЧЕСКИЙ	3J2(b)
СТЮАРДЕССА	3J2(b)		
СУБЪЕКТИВИСТ-СКИЙ	3B1(b)	ТЕРМО-	3J2(b)†
		ТЕРМОС	3J2(b)
СУММАРНЫЙ	not 3N(b)	ТЕРМЫ	3J2(b)
СУММИРОВАТЬ	not 3N(b)	ТЕРРАКОТА	3J2(b)
СУППОРТ	3N(a)	ТЕРРАРИЙ	3J2(b)
СУТОЧНЫЙ	3H4	ТЕРРИТОРИАЛЬ-НЫЙ	3J2(b)
СУФФИКС	3N(a)		
СЮЗАНЕ	3J2(b)	ТЕРРОР	3J2(b)†
СЮЗЕРЕН	3J2(b)	ТЕРРОРИСТСКИЙ	3B1(b) 3J2(b)†
СЮРРЕАЛИЗМ	not 3N(b)		
		ТЕРЦИЯ	3J2(b)
Т		ТЕРЦЕТ	3J2(b)
ТАБАЧНИК	3H4†	ТЕРЬЕР	3J2(b)
ТАВЕРНА	3J2(b)	ТЕССИТУРА	3J2(b)
ТАИЛАНДСКИЙ	3B1(b)	ТЕТ-А-ТЕТ	3J2(b)
ТАЛМУДИСТСКИЙ	3B1(b)	ТЕТРАГОНАЛЬ-НЫЙ	3J2(b)
ТАМПЛИЕР	3Y1(b)		
ТАНКИСТСКИЙ	3B1(b)	ТИРЕ	3J2(b)
ТАРАНТЕЛЛА	3J2(b)	ТОННЕЛЬ	3J2(b) not 3N(b) not 3U†
ТЕЗА	3J2(b)		
ТЕЗИС	3J2(b)		
ТЕЙЗМ	3J2(b)	ТОТЕМ	3J2(b)
ТЕЙН	3J2(b)	ТРАССА	3N(a)†
ТЕМБР	3J2(b)	ТРЕД-ЮНИОН	3J2(b)
ТЕМП	3J2(b)	ТРЕК	3J2(b)
ТЕМПЕРА	3J2(b)	ТРЕМБИТА	3J2(b)
ТЕНДЕНЦИЯ	3J2(b)	ТРЕМОЛО	3J2(b)
ТЕНДЕР	3J2(b)	ТРЕН	3J2(b)

ТРИДЦАТ́	3V3
ТРИ́О	not 3U†
ТРИ́ППЕР	3N(a)
ТРО́ЕЧНИК	3H4†
ТРОКАД́ЕРО	3J2(b)
ТРУВ́ЕР	3J2(b)
ТР́УППА	3N(a)†
ТРЯПИ́ЧНИК	3H4†
ТРЯ́ПОЧНЫЙ	3H4†
Т́УБДИСПАНС́ЕР	3J2(b)
ТУНН́ЕЛЬ	3J2(b)
	not 3N(b)
ТУРИ́СТСКИЙ	3B1(b)
ТУРН́Е	3J2(b)
ТУРН́ЕПС	3J2(b)
Т́ЮБИНГЩИК	3Z
ТЯЃЧАЙШИЙ	3Z

У

УКЛОНИ́СТСКИЙ	3B1(b)
УР́ЕТРА	3J2(b)
УТИЛИТАРИ́СТ-СКИЙ	3B1(b)

Ф

ФАБЛ́О	3Y2
ФАЙДЕШИ́Н	3J2(b)
ФАКСИ́МИЛЕ	not 3W2
ФАЛАНСТ́ЕР	3J2(b)
ФАРВ́АТЕР	3J2(b)
ФАШИ́СТСКИЙ	3B1(b)
ФЕДЕРАЛИ́СТ-СКИЙ	3B1(b)
	3J2(b)†
ФЕ́ЕРИЯ	3Y1(b)
ФЕЙЕРВ́ЕРК	3J2(b)

ФЕЛЛ́АХ	3J2(b)
	not 3N(b)
ФЕЛЬДМ́АРШАЛ	3J2(b)
Ф́ЕЛЬДШЕР	3Z
ФЕНОМЕНАЛИ́СТ-СКИЙ	3B1(b)
ФЕ́БД	3J2(b)
ФЕРМ́ЕНТ	3J2(b)
ФЕРМУ́АР	3J2(b)
ФЕ́РРОСПЛ́АВ	3N(a)†
ФЕШЕН́ЕБЕЛЬНЫЙ	3J2(b)
ФИД́ЕИЗМ	3J2(b)
Ф́ИДЕР	3J2(b)
ФИЛАТЕЛИ́СТ-СКИЙ	3B1(b)
	3J2(b)
ФИЛОГЕН́ЕЗ	not 3W2
ФИЛОГЕН́ЕЗ	3J2(b)
ФИЛОД́ЕНДРОН	3J2(b)
ФИЛЬДЕЌОС	3J2(b)
ФИЛЬДЕП́ЕРС	3J2(b)
ФИНЛ́ЯНДСКИЙ	3B1(b)
Ф́ИННЫ	3N(a)†
ФЛАМ́АНДСКИЙ	3B1(b)
ФОБ́ИЯ	not 3U
ФОКСТЕРЬ́ЕР	3J2(b)
	not 3U
ФОН́АЦИЯ	not 3U†
ФОН́ЕМА	3J2(b)†
	not 3U†
ФОН́ЕТИКА	3J2(b)†
	not 3U†
ФОНБЛА	not 3U
ФОРМАЛИ́СТСКИЙ	3B1(b)
ФОРП́ОСТ	not 3U†
Ф́ОРТЕ	3J2(b)

ФОРТИ́ССИМО	not 3U
ФОРШТЕ́ВЕНЬ	3J2(b)
ФОСФОРЕСЦЕ́НЦИЯ	not 3U
ФРЕ́ЙЛЕЙН	3J2(b)
ФРЕ́КЕН	3J2(b)
ФРИКАДЕ́ЛЬКА	3J2(b)
ФРИКАСЕ́	3J2(b)
ФРОНТИСПИ́С	not 3U†
ФУ́ТЕР	3J2(b)
ФЬО́РД	3Y2

Х

ХАНА́ССКИЙ	not 3N(d)
ХА́ОС	not 3U
ХАРАНЕ́РА	3J2(b)
ХВАСТЛИ́В-	3B1(e)†
ХВОСТИ́СТСКИЙ	3B1(b)
ХЕ́ДЕР	3J2(b)
ХЕ́ТТЫ	3N(a)
ХРИЗАНТЕ́МА	3J2(b)

Ц

ЦАРИ́СТСКИЙ	3B1(b)
ЦЕЙХГА́УЗ	3Z
ЦЕ́РБЕР	3J2(b)
ЦЕ́РКОВЬ	3R(c)
ЦИКЛАМЕ́Н	3J2(b)
ЦИНЕРА́РИЯ	3J2(b)
ЦИ́ННИЯ	3N(a)
ЦИТАДЕ́ЛЬ	3J2(b)

Ч

ЧАХО́ТОЧНЫЙ	3H4†
ЧЕКИ́СТСКИЙ	3B1(b)
ЧЕЛЕ́СТА	not 3W2
ЧЕРКЕ́ССКИЙ	not 3N(d)

ЧЕТВЁРОЧНИК	3H4†
ЧИЧЕРО́НЕ	3J2(b)
ЧИЧЕРО́НЕ	not 3W2
ЧУ́ВСТВ-	3B3
ЧУ́ТОЧНЫЙ	3H4†

Ш

ШАМПИНЬО́Н	3Y2
ШАПОКЛЯ́К	not 3U
ША́ПОЧНЫЙ	3H4†
ШАССИ́	not 3N(b)
ШАТЕ́Н	3J2(b)
ШЕДЕ́ВР	3J2(b)
ШЕМИЗЕ́ТКА	3J2(b)
ШЕСТЬСО́Т	3Z
ШИ́ЛЛИНГ	3N(a)
ШИМПАНЗЕ́	3J2(b)
ШИНЬО́Н	3Y2
ШНЕ́К	3J2(b)
ШОССЕ́	3J2(b) not 3N(b) not 3U†
ШОТЛА́НДСКИЙ	3B1(b)
ШПА́ТЕЛЬ	3J2(b)
ШПИ́НДЕЛЬ	3J2(b)
ШПИЦРУ́ТЕНЫ	3J2(b)
ШТЕ́ВЕНЬ	3J2(b)
ШТЕ́ЙГЕР	3J2(b)
ШТЕ́МПЕЛЬ	3J2(b)
ШТЕ́ПСЕЛЬ	3J2(b)
ШУ́ТОЧНЫЙ	3H4†

Э

ЭБЕ́НОВЫЙ	3J2(b)
ЭВОЛЮЦИОНИ́СТ- СКИЙ	3B1(b)

ЭВФЕМИ́ЗМ	not 3N(b)	ЭНЕ́РГИЯ	3J2(b)†
ЭВФО́НИЯ	not 3N(b)	ЭНТЕРИ́Т	3J2(b)
ЭГЕ́	3C2	ЭОЗО́ЙСКИЙ	not 3U
Э́-ГЀ-ГЕ́	3C2	ЭОЛИ́Т	not 3U
ЭДЕЛЬВЕ́ЙС	3J2(b)	ЭПИДЕ́РМА	3J2(b)
ЭДЕ́М	3J2(b)	ЭПИЗОО́ТИ́ЧЕСКИЙ	not 3U
ЭНЗЕ́МА	3J2(b)	ЭПИТЕЛИА́ЛЬНЫЙ	3J2(b)
ЭНЗЕМПЛЯ́Р	3J2(b)	ЭСДЕ́К	3J2(b)
ЭНЗЕ́РСИС	3J2(b)	ЭСЕ́Р	3J2(b)
ЭКОСЕ́З	3J2(b) not 3U†	ЭСКИМО́ССКИЙ	not 3N(d)
		ЭСПАНЬО́ЛКА	3Y2
ЭКСПАНСИОНИ́СТ-СКИЙ	3B1(b)	ЭСТЕ́Т	3J2(b)
		ЭТЕ́РИЯ	3J2(b)
ЭКСПОЗЕ́	not 3U	ЭТНОГЕНЕ́З	3J2(b)
ЭКСПРЕ́ССИЯ	3N(a)	ЭФЕМЕ́РНЫЙ	3J2(b)
ЭКСТЕНСИ́ВНЫЙ	3J2(b)		
ЭКСТЕ́РН	3J2(b)	Ю	
ЭКСТЕРЬЕ́Р	3J2(b)	Ю́БОЧНИК	3H4†
ЭЛЛИНИ́ЗМ	not 3N(b)	Я	
Э́ЛЛИПС	3N(a)	Я́БЛОЧНЫЙ	3H4†
ЭЛОКВЕ́НЦИЯ	3J2(b)	ЯГДТА́Ш	3Z
ЭЛЬЗА́ССКИЙ	not 3N(d)	ЯИ́ЧНИЦА	3H4
ЭМИ́ССИЯ	3N(a)	Я̀ХТСМЕ́Н	3J2(b)
ЭМФИЗЕ́МА	3J2(b)	Я́ЧНЕВЫЙ	3H4†

EXERCISES

Listed below are a number of words, phrases and sentences which are recommended for written exercises. Students are urged to do as many of these as possible. The materials have been selected to exemplify all the major rules and most of the minor ones. They are arranged so that each of these rules is practised not only immediately after it has been met, but also at a later stage; in this way all the important rules will be constantly reviewed.

To save space, the words, phrases and sentences are listed separately, and are identified for each exercise by, respectively, arabic numerals, alphabet letters, and roman numerals. There are 15 words, 4 phrases, and one or two sentences in each exercise.

Material for Exercises

1. АББА́ТСТВ
2. АЛЛИЛУ́ЙЯ
3. БЕЗЗВЁЗДНОЕ
4. БЕЗНРА́В-СТВЕННО
5. БЕСЧИ́СЛЕННЫЕ
6. ВОЛШБА́
7. ВИВЕ́РРЕ
8. ВЪЕЗЖА́ТЬ
9. ГРУ́СТНЕЕ
10. ГРЫ́ЗСЯ
11. ГРЯЗЕВОДО-ЛЕЧЕ́БНИЦЕ
12. ДА́ЛЬШЕ
13. ДЛИННОШЕ́ЕЕ
14. ДРЕСВУ́
15. ЁЖЬСЯ
16. Е́ЗДИЛИ
17. ЖАСМИ́Н
18. ЖЕ́НЩИНА

19. ЖИГУЛЁВСКАЯ
20. ИНГРЕДИЕ́НТ
21. ИЗЪЕДА́ТЬ
22. И́СКРЕННЕГО
23. ИСКУ́ССТВЕННО
24. КОМПРОМИ́СС
25. КО́ШЕЧЬИ
26. КРУ́ЖЕВЦЕ
27. ЛЁГКИЕ
28. ЛЕ́ЗТЬ
29. ЛЮ́БЯЩИЙ
30. МАСШТА́Б
31. МЁРЗНЕШЬ
32. МУЗЕ́Й
33. МУ́ССОРГСКИЙ
34. НАВЕЩЁННУЮ
35. НАЕ́СТЬСЯ
36. НИ́МФЕ
37. НО́ГТИ

38. НОРВЕ́ЖЦЫ
39. О́БЩЕСТВО
40. ОБЪЕДИНЁННЫЕ
41. ОБЪЯВЛЯ́Ю
42. ОСТРИ́ГШИСЬ
43. ОТСЧИ́ТЫВАТЬ
44. ОТЩЕПИ́ЛА
45. ОТЪЕ́ЗД
46. ОФИЦИА́НТКА
47. ПАССАЖИ́РСКОГО
48. ПЛАСТМА́СС
49. ПОДДЁВКЕ
50. ПОДСЧЁТ
51. ПОДТЯ́ЖКИ
52. ПО́ЗЖЕ
53. ПОЛУОЯГНИ́В-ШИМСЯ
54. ПОЛУСМЕ́РТЬ
55. ПРА́ЧЕЧНАЯ

56. ПРИНАДЛЕЖА́ТЬ	72. СЪЯ́ЗВИТЬ	88. ЯГДТА́Ш
57. РАСПО́ЛЗСЯ	73. ТРЕЛЬЯ́Ж	89. ЯЗВЛЮ́
58. РАСТЕ́ШИТЬСЯ	74. ТРЕ́ТЬЕ	90. ЯРЦЕВЧА́НКЕ
59. РЕВМЯ́	75. ТРЯПЬЁ	91. Я́ЩЕРИЦА
60. РУЧЬЯ́	76. ТУМА́ННЫЙ	92. ГЛА́ВКО́М
61. СЖЕ́ЧЬ	77. ТЯГЧА́ЙШИЙ	93. ГО́СПЕ́ДИЗДА́Т
62. СМЯГЧИ́ТЬ	78. ХРУ́СТЧЕ	94. КО́ЖИМИ́Т
63. СОЧУ́ВСТВИЕ	79. ФА́ЛЬШЬ	95. ПЕ́ДИНСТИТУ́Т
64. СПЕЦЕЕ́ДСТВ	80. ФРАНЦУ́ЗСКИЙ	96. СВЕ́РХ-ГИГА́НТСКИЙ
65. ССЕ́СТЬ	81. ЦЕНИ́ТЕЛЬ	97. ШТА́БРО́ТМИ́СТР
66. СТРЕ́ЖЕНЬ	82. ЦИМЛЯ́НЕЦ	98. Ю́БОЧНИК
67. СТРУЁЙ	83. ШЕСТЬДЕСЯ́Т	99. Ю́ЖУРА́ЛМА́ШЗАВО́Д
68. СЧАСТЛИ́ВЩИК	84. ШЕСТНА́ДЦАТЬ	100. Ю́РИС-КО́НСУЛЬСТВЕ
69. СШИБИ́ТЬСЯ	85. ШИПЯ́ЩИЙ	
70. СЫЗДЕ́ТСТВА	86. ШУ́ШЕНЦЕВ	
71. СЪЁМКИ	87. ЮРКНЁШЬ	

A. В МА́ССЕ	F. К ГОРЕ́	L. ЧЕРЕЗ Я́МУ
B. В СВЯЗИ́	G. К ГО́СТЬЮ	M. ЧЕ́РЕЗ Я́МУ
C. БЕЗ НЕГО́	H. ОБ ПОЛ	N. ЧЕ́РЕЗ ИЛЛЮ́ЗИЮ
D. БЕЗ СЕМЬИ́	J. С ЗНО́ЕМ	P. НАПРО́ТИВ Я́СТРЕБА
E. ИЗ-ПО́Д ВО́ЗА	K. С ШЕ́РСТЬЮ	

I. ЛЮБО́ВЬ АНДРЕ́ЕВНА И ОЛЕ́Г ЛЬВО́ВИЧ ВДВОЁМ НЕ СДА́ЛИ ЭКЗА́МЕНОВ В ШКО́ЛЕ.

II. АРИСТА́РХ ГЛЕ́БОВИЧ РЕ́ПИН И Ю́ДИФЬ ЗИНО́ВЬЕВНА ШАЛЯ́ПИНА ВЫ́ДВИНУЛИ ОФИЦЕ́РОВ ВПЕРЁД.

III. ПОЧТАЛЬО́НЫ СТИРА́ЮТ ГРЯ́ЗНОЕ БЕЛЬЁ И ИЗЪЕ́ДАННЫЕ МО́ЛЬЮ ШУ́БЫ ПО́МОЩЬЮ МАЙО́РШАМИ, ЗАТЕ́М ГУЛЯ́ЮТ НА МАЁВКУ.

IV. ВЕДЬ СО́РОК ИЗ ТЕ́Х ЖЕ́НЩИН ЗНА́ЮТ ГЛА́ВТО́РГ ВПЛО́ТЬ ДО МЕЛЬЧА́ЙШИХ ПОДРО́БНОСТЕЙ.

Schedule of Exercises

Exercise	Words	Phrases	Sentence
1 (after 2B)	2, 13, 15, 21, 27, 34, 41, 45, 60, 64, 67, 71, 75, 89, 100	B, D, E, N	I
2 (after 3A)	8, 19, 22, 25, 29, 31, 35, 40, 42, 43, 56, 62, 70, 72, 87	A, H, L, M	II
3 (after 3C)	3, 4, 5, 9, 22, 33, 47, 63, 68, 76, 78, 79, 84, 95, 98	C, G, K, P	III
4 (after 3F)	6, 38, 39, 49, 51, 57, 61, 73, 80, 84, 90, 94, 96, 97, 99	B, F, J, M	IV
5 (after 3I)	1, 8, 23, 30, 37, 50, 52, 55, 62, 65, 70, 75, 77, 79, 92	A, E, K, N	I
6 (after 3K)	11, 12, 18, 28, 59, 61, 66, 69, 74, 81, 82, 85, 91, 94, 97	C, D, H, P	II
7 (after 3N)	1, 2, 10, 15, 23, 34, 35, 40, 48, 53, 57, 58, 76, 80, 83	F, G, J, L	III
8 (after 3R)	7, 8, 14, 16, 17, 28, 36, 44, 45, 54, 71, 72, 88, 93, 100	A, C, K, N	IV
9 (after 3S)	19, 30, 32, 37, 48, 53, 60, 65, 67, 69, 85, 87, 95, 96, 99	B, D, G, L	I
10 (after 3V)	3, 6, 11, 12, 17, 25, 26, 33, 38, 42, 43, 46, 52, 66, 86	E, F, H, N	II

Exercise	Words	Phrases	Sentence
11 (after 3X)	4, 7, 9, 11, 20, 21, 39, 49, 55, 63, 74, 77, 78, 83, 90	A, E, M, P	III
12 (after 3Z)	5, 10, 13, 18, 20, 27, 29, 40, 51, 59, 64, 73, 81, 92, 98	B, F, J, M	IV
13 (rewrite in *PT* with all relevant steps)	23, 24, 31, 34, 36, 41, 47, 56, 58, 62, 68, 82, 84, 88, 91	C, G, K, N	I, III
14 (rewrite in *PT*; *SO*, *RO*, *PO*, *PT* only)	2, 4, 14, 16, 22, 26, 44, 46, 50, 54, 75, 86, 89, 93, 100	D, H, L, P	II, IV

NOTES TO CHAPTER I

[1]Needless to say, the rules which are provided here to achieve this pragmatic end are *pedagogical* rules only and make no claim whatever to "psychological reality," or even to formal simplicity (although pains have been taken to make them as simple and general as possible without sacrificing clarity or utility for the uninitiated student). For a useful discussion of different kinds of grammars for various aims and purposes, see Gleason (1961:195-221).

[2]As indicated below, one qualification needs to be made here with regard to the denoting of Russian stress and the dieresis, neither of which are normally marked in the "standard orthography" of Russian, any more than in English, though both are marked in dictionaries and in most pedagogical texts. Since the position of unstressed vowels and the Ë must be known for many of our rules to operate, the student who uses this book may sometimes have to refer to a dictionary for this information.

[3]The format of this Indiana paper was essentially the same as that developed in Gvozdev (1947:10-13) for Russian and Wijk (1966) for English. Another common approach has been to present lists of this kind to illustrate grapheme-phoneme (rather than grapheme-phone) correspondences, as in Hall (1961) and Conlin (1961:273-80). A systematic set of reading rules was, however, developed by Lotz (1969) for Hungarian, and for Polish by Fischer (1976). The study by Zlatoustova et al. (1970) was not available to the authors of the present work. See also Haas (1970).

[4]For contrast, and a discussion of some of the principles involved and their relation to Russian language pedagogy, see Daniels (1975).

[5]One other, more serious shortcoming of this book is that it has absolutely nothing to say about intonation or voice contours, but is concerned only with the segmental phonology and phonetics of the language. For information on Russian intonational patterns, the reader is referred particularly to Bryzgunova (1963, 1969).

[6]On the term *register*, and a discussion of the dimensions along which language may vary, see Gregory (1967) and Ward (1971). For the relationship of *CSR* to other styles of Russian, see Avanesov (1972:8-24)

[*RLP*], Filin (1973), and the references in Chapter V, note 9.

[7]Variation in tempo is of a different order than the variations along the axes of time, space and style; strictly speaking, therefore, it should be discussed separately. See 5.2. and the references there; also Bailey (1973).

[8]On mixtures of styles in modern Soviet usage, and their harmfulness, see Utexina (1961).

[9]The sources for all supplementary information are cited in the notes, except for Avanesov (*RLP*), and Avanesov & Ožegov (1960) [*RLPU*], to which references are made in the text, and the following works, which discuss most of the variations concerned and may generally be recommended for further study; Vinokur (1948), Ward (1965), Panov (1967:301-33), Kunert (1968), Jones & Ward (1969), Gorbačevič (1971), Romportl (1973), and especially Shapiro (1968).

NOTES TO CHAPTER II

[1]See Avanesov (1955), Kiparsky (1962), Bryzgunova (1963), Forsyth (1963), Ward (1965:45-68), Stankiewicz (1968), Nicholson (1970), Red'kin (1971), Avanesov (1974:79-118), Coats (1976).

[2]As an example of an exception to this type of generalization, note that the word БОБР 'beaver' is spelled with a final "consonant letter" Р, but is ordinarily pronounced either with a final syllabic (i.e., vocalic) *sound* [r̃], or with the vowel+consonant sequence [ər̃] (cf. Rule-Block 4F on p. 145). Our terminology is borrowed from Lunt (1958).

[3]Again, of course, there are some exceptions to these statements. In the *OM* (Old Moscow) dialect, for example, the geminate ЖЖ in words like ВОЖЖИ is pronounced "soft" (more like the sound in the English word *azure* than like the typical, retroflexed Russian counterpart as in ЖУРНАЛ); and the letter Ч is often pronounced "hard" in the word ЛУЧШЕ (cf. pp.141-42 for discussion). The classification of Russian consonants into "soft" and "hard" categories is traditional in classic descriptive and pedagogical accounts. The use of these terms as labels for different classes of sounds goes back at least to the time of Marius Victorinus (Fónagy 1963:24).

[4]The phonemic status of the high central vowels [ɨ] and [ɨ] has been hotly contested; see for example

Boyanus (1947), Zinder (1957), and Panov (1967:58-61).
But whether it is five or six vowel phonemes that
these ten letters represent, the situation in Russian
is practically the opposite of the one that obtains
in English, where a meager system of five orthographic "vowel-letters" is employed to represent at least
a dozen vowel phonemes.

[5]Note that the first consonant of СЪЕЛ is pronounced "soft", while that of ОБЪЁМ is pronounced
"hard", despite the use of the so-called "hard sign"
in the standard spelling of both words. Though this
information is fortuitously supplied even in the *RO*
for these particular words, such phonetic details, in
general, will not be supplied until much later in the
derivational sequence (cf. 3Q). See, e.g., Karcevskij (1937) and Jakobson (1963) for a discussion of
such inconsistencies in the Russian *SO*, and also
Vinogradov (1965:21-51, 87-101, 140-41).

[6]This is well illustrated by Townsend (1975:
7ff.).

[7]Indeed, if certain promoters of orthographic
reform for Russian had had their way, we would be
able to dispense with most or all of this chapter.
In particular, Juraj Križanić, in his *Grammatičeskoe
upravlenie* (Tobol'sk, 1666) suggested a use of the
letter *j* which would have made rule 2A superfluous
(Kuznecov 1958:37, Jakobson 1963:562-63). See also
Vinogradov (1965:67-72, 102-16).

NOTES TO CHAPTER III

[1]The letter Г has been proposed for the *SO* of
Russian; see Vinogradov (1965:403-405).

[2]This letter has been suggested for the Russian
SO, too, to represent the sound [w] in borrowed words
(cf. p. 142) (Vinogradov 1965:405). This letter is
indeed used to represent [w] in the *SO* of Belorussian.

[3]See Vinogradov (1965:73-75) for proposals to
introduce single new letters into the Russian *SO* with
the function of our дж and жж.

[4]For a discussion of "hard" versus "soft" жж,
see Barinova (1966), Panov (1968:81-84, 91-102), and
Krysin (1974:84-94).

[5]Cf. Halle (1959:48-50), where five different
boundary symbols are used, and also Panov (1961,
1967:169-91), Shapiro (1967).

[6]E.g., rule 3V1(b) reads: "э → a / H ─ $\begin{Bmatrix} \# \\ \#\# \end{Bmatrix}$
only in n/a sg. neut. nouns." We could avoid this
wordiness by setting up a special boundary, say //,
for this grammatical category (cf. Halle 1959:50),
the rule would then *look* much simpler, viz.: "э → a
/ H // ─ $\begin{Bmatrix} \# \\ \#\# \end{Bmatrix}$." The rule would not however *be* any
simpler in fact, and we would be setting up a special
symbol for this one rule only.

[7]This is similar to, but not identical with, the
"Phonemic Phrase Boundary" in Halle (1959:48-49).
Note that the symbol ## is often used in linguistic
analyses to represent a sentence-boundary.

[8]Clearly, no actual or "potential" pauses occur
at hyphens. If other punctuation marks (e.g., parentheses, quotation marks) occur separately from the
marks listed here, they will normally indicate "potential" pauses.

[9]See Paufošima & Agaronov (1971) and the references therein. On sentence-stress, see Daneš (1967),
Isačenko (1967), Jones & Ward (1969:208-10),
Zlatoustova (1962), and the works by Bryzgunova (e.g.
1963, 1969, 1971).

[10]On the problem of "in-between" words (those
which may be fully stressed, partly stressed, or unstressed, e.g., the personal pronouns), see Ivanova-
Luk'janova (1971).

[11]See Halle (1959:50, 63-65), Grebnev (1959),
Alekseev (1963a, 1963b, 1965) and Shapiro (1968:35-
36). On "stump-compounds" in general, see Ward
(1965:156-63) and Molinsky (1973).

[12]Note that the wording of the rule-block is simplified because the rules are *ordered*. If they were
not, 3A3(a) could not be phrased ". . . in all other
spaces."

[13]Cf. in English the apparent lack of distinctive
meaning of -*ceive* in *perceive*, *receive* (see Bloomfield 1933:242); or of -*mote* in *promote*, *demote* (see
Hockett 1958:173); or (the most well-known example) of
cran- in *cranberry* (see Gleason 1961:76-77). On the
isolatability of morphemes, see especially Nida
(1949:58-61). On Russian word-formation, see Švedova
(1970:30-301), Čurganova (1973) and Townsend (1975).
Note also that if an *IW* has more than one prefix,
more than one / symbol must be inserted, e.g.: ПЕРЕ/
ВЫ/ПОЛНЯТЬ, НЕ/ПРЕД/НА/МЕРЕННЫЙ.

[14]Similarly, it might surprise many English-speakers to learn that the element *stan* in the word *distance* has something in common etymologically with similar-sounding elements in the words *stand* and *stanchion*.

[15]Most of these letters, it can be argued, should nonetheless be kept in the Russian *SO* for grammatical (morphophonological) reasons. Thus the Д in the word СЕ́РДЦЕ occurs in the pronunciation of the grammatically related word СЕРДЕ́ЧНЫЙ; and the Т in the word ХВОСТЦА́ occurs in the pronunciation of the N.Sg., ХВОСТЕ́Ц. Note, however, that this reasoning will not always apply; there is no grammatical justification for the Т in ЛЕ́СТНИЦА, nor for the first В in ЧУ́ВСТВО. On this subject, see Vinogradov (1965:53, 195-96).

[16]This cluster is not mentioned in *RLP*; we have, however, found no counterexamples to this rule.

[17]These clusters are not mentioned in *RLP*. *RLPU*, however, explicitly states that the Н and Г are to be deleted in specified words.

[18]Panov (1967:328); the roots are ГРУ́СТН-, СО́-ВЕСТН-, ПО́ЗДН-, ПРА́ЗДН-.

[19]Namely: for 3B1(b), *RLPU* shows no deletion in the stems ГИГА́НТСН- and ПАРЛА́МЕНТСН-; and for 3B3, *RLPU* lists the stem НРА́ВСТВ- also as having deletion of the first В. For 3B1(f), where *RLP* has 3 exceptions, *RLPU* has *36*.

[20]Note that Shapiro (1968:31) states that Т is deleted "especially in the feminine form of words" in -ИСТ. See also Shapiro (1972).

[21]See Ganiev (1966), Terexova (1966), Panov (1967:328-29, 1968:79), Glovinskaja, Il'ina, Kuz'mina & Panov (1971:25).

[22]The *SO* spelling with Г here is a historical accident. See Vinogradov (1965:277-80).

[23]See Superanskaja (1959), Ward (1959, 1965:36), Panov (1967:332-33), Jones & Ward (1969:144). On the historical origin of this pronunciation, see, e.g., Vinokur (1971:70, 103).

[24]The inclusion in *RLP* of these three words may be ascribed to the fact that they are *numerals* and hence pronounced "carelessly" more often than other word-categories (cf. 3Z, where the pronunciation of other numerals is given, and 5.1., where numerals in *RR* are discussed). Note that depalatalization of

labials in prepausal and preconsonantal positions is
characteristic of many Russian dialects and
nearly all the Slavic languages. See also Drage
(1968:370).

[25]See Vinogradov (1965:202-205) for suggestions
made that the results of voicing assimilations be incorporated into the Russian *SO*; and Vinogradov (1965:
230-40) for the bureaucratic reasons for the decision
that some prefixes (e.g., РАЗ/РАС) should follow
these rules, while others (e.g., ОТ) should not.

[26]For the phonetic facts, see Boyanus (1965:8),
Fant (1960:216), Bryzgunova (1963:58-59), Bondarko &
Zinder (1966), Jones & Ward (1969:119). For the
history of [v] in Slavic, and its development from
*w, see e.g., Shevelov (1964:282-84).

[27]See Orlova (1950), Jakobson (1956, 1968:728-33),
Halle (1959:31, 61-65), Ševoroskin (1963:175, 1971),
Shapiro (1966:33-36), Panov (1967:87), Baranovskaja
(1968, 1969), Andersen (1969b), Es'kova (1971), Coats
& Harshenin (1971), Lightner (1972:72-75).

[28]Assimilation is said to be *regressive* if some
characteristic feature of one sound or letter is in-
fluenced by a following sound or letter; and *progressive*, if the influence moves in the other direction.
Cf. the word *observer* which shows regressive voicing
assimilation in French (with the phonetic cluster
[-ps-]), but progressive voicing assimilation in
English (with [-bz-]). The vast majority of assimilations in Russian are regressive; cf. note 56.

[29]Cf. note 9; on логическое ударение, see
Bryzgunova (1963:175-82, 290-94) and Raspopov (1966).

[30]Cf. Halle (1959:73-74), Shapiro (1968:34-35),
Drage (1968:361).

[31]This does not necessarily mean that there is no
difference between the two phonetic "natures" of В;
see the authorities cited in note 26 for the phonetic
facts.

[32]See also Panov (1967:36), Jones & Ward (1969:
189-90), Baranovskaja (1969), and Ševoroskin (1971).

[33]See Coats & Harshenin (1971:471-72):

[34]On boundaries as obstruents, see, e.g., Lass
(1971), Lightner (1972:331-34), and Anwar (1974).

[35]This chart is adapted from the one by Paufošima
& Agaronov (1971).

[36]Avanesov discusses the pronunciation of ТЩ and ТЦ as they occur within roots only. We assume, in the absence of any discussion about these clusters at preposition- and prefix-boundaries, that in these environments their pronunciation follows the *SO*.

[37]*RLP* 81-82, 146; see Černyšev (1915/1970:78), Košutić (1919:67), Aksenov (1954:70, 72), Panov (1967: 327-28, 1968:79-80), and Drage (1968:370-72).

[38]Shapiro (1968:31); see also Panov (1967:327-28).

[39]See also Panov (1967:90).

[40]Panov (1967:35), however, reports *hard* Ч in ЛУЧШЕ; cf. pp. 141-42.

[41]*RLPU* lists over 300 words with this pronunciation, e.g., ГОТСКИЙ [ЦᶜК]. Most of these words are adjectives formed from loanwords, and may therefore be pronounced a little more carefully than native words. Cf. Panov (1967:90).

[42]Proposals have been made to change the *SO* in this way (Vinogradov 1965:76-86).

[43]See Borunova (1966), Barinova (1966), Panov (1967:329-31, 1968:81-91), Drage (1968:377-79), Jones & Ward (1969:140), Shapiro (1972), Avanesov (1974: 170-79), Krysin (1974:95-104), and Isačenko (1975). For further discussion of the phonological status of the realizations of Щ, see Isačenko (1971), Thelin (1974), and the references therein.

[44]See Shapiro (1968:30-31) and, e.g., Superanskaja (1959), Bulaxovskij (1954:20-22).

[45]E.g., Shapiro (1968:29).

[46]Paufošima (1971).

[47]Avanesov (1956:190), Drage (1968:379-80).

[48]For proposals that the *SO* should be revised in this way, see Vinogradov (1965:133-40).

[49]Note the results of a questionnaire (Superanskaja 1959), which showed a very small minority of speakers with a consistent *OM* pronunciation; e.g., 10 speakers out of 299 for the word НАТЯГИВАТЬ, and 19 out of 233 for the word ЗВОНКИЙ. In earlier editions of *RLP* (see Avanesov 1958:125-26) the *OM* style was prescribed.

[50]For suggested revisions to the *SO* along these lines, see Vinogradov (1965:141).

[51]Note that if E is to be rewritten Э *in final position*, as in the word ШОССЕ, this means that the vowel is part of the stem; and, hence, it may be assumed that the word is indeclinable.

[52]Cf. Panov (1967:328, 1968:38-39, 78-79), Glovinskaja (1971), Drage (1968:375-77).

[53]Glovinskaja (1971:76-86).

[54]See Vinogradov (1965:208-11) for proposals to revise the *SO* in this way.

[55]Panov (1967:320-22, 1968:103-107). In the study reported by Superanskaja (1959), all but 16 of the 220 respondents pronounced the word БОЮСЬ with a "soft" сь; compare the prescription by Aksenov (1954: 70) for theatrical pronunciation with "hard" с! For a contrary view to Panov's, and further references, see Drage (1968:373-75).

[56]Cf. note 28 above. Stages II and III exemplify *progressive* assimilation in that the palatalization of the сь is determined by the frontness of the preceding vowel (Stage II) and the palatalization of the preceding consonant (Stage III). Other examples of progressive assimilation in Russian are rare; see 3.11. on the influence of preceding vowels on palatalization assimilation in consonants, and rule 4F2(b) for the qualitative effects of palatalized consonants on following vowels. See also 5.8. on reported examples of progressive assimilation in *RR*.

[57]Note that *RLPU* shows all native words with НН as having *no* degemination.

[58]Bylinskij (1960:641), Shapiro (1968:33). The latter suggests that the stressed quality of not only the preceding, but also of the following vowel is involved. See also Shapiro (1972).

[59]Panov (1967:88) disagrees, and states that *all* final geminate consonants are degeminated.

[60]Nonetheless, *RLPU* indicates that the words ИРРЕА́ЛЬНЫЙ and ИРРЕГУЛЯ́РНО *are* to be pronounced with geminate рр.

[61]Glovinskaja (1971:69-74).

[62]For the phonetic equivalence of тц and цц see Panov (1967:90) and 4.3. below. Note that we could have incorporated the rule тц → цц in rule-block 3G; in this way, ДВА́ДЦАТЬ → два́тцать (by 3E1(с)) and then → два́ццать; since the цц occurs after a stressed vowel, 3N(b) would not apply. However, in the

oblique cases, where the stress shifts to the ending,
3N(b) would apply, e.g., ДВАДЦАТИ́ → два́тцати́ →
два́ццати́ → два́цатьи́. (The same remarks would hold
good for ТРИ́ДЦА̄ТЬ and, e.g., ТРИДЦАТИ́.) Since
Avanesov does not recommend pronunciation of ДВАДЦАТ⁼
and ТРИДЦАТ⁼ with single ц (*RLP* 142), we would therefore have had to list these oblique case-forms as
exceptions to 3N(b). For this reason, 3G above does
not include the rule indicated.

[63]Normally, palatalization of the non-final mem-
bers of consonant clusters is not shown in the *RO*.
The chief exception to this statement concerns ЛЬ,
which is regularly written thus; this follows from
the fact that Л is never palatalized by regressive
assimilation (except when geminate), cf. 3P restriction 4 and see Panov (1967:91-92). For suggestions
that other "soft" consonants be spelled with the soft
sign when they occur in clusters, see Vinogradov
(1965:206-207).

[64]See Drage (1967a) and Panov (1967:93-94).

[65]Cf. note 60.

[66]The string x/йа (*SO* ХЪЯ) is seldom mentioned in
the literature. Panov (1967:99) gives a table which
suggests that x is always palatalized before й; on
the other hand, clusters of velars before soft dentals or soft palatals have only rarely been noted
with regressive palatalization assimilation, even in
the *OM* style (see Drage 1967b).

[67]When educated speakers of *CSR* perceive a
"transparent" boundary (cf. pp. 35-36) -- if, for
example, they understand the meaning of the Latin
prefixes involved -- then, presumably, there may be
less palatalization here.

[68]For example -- cf. our 3P3 and 3P restriction 1
-- Avanesov prescribes (among a number of other delicate points) that С and З are to be palatalized before soft labials, with the stipulation that this
applies across *prefix*- boundaries *unless* the prefix
is ВОЗ-, ЧРЕЗ-, НИЗ-, РАЗ- or БЕЗ- and, at the same
time, the word is "bookish"; and that it applies
across *preposition*- boundaries *only if* the preposition is С and not e.g., if it is ИЗ or БЕЗ.

[69]See Ward (1958, 1965:39-40), Boyanus (1965:31-
32), Panov (1967:324-27, 1968:54-79), Ganiev (1971),
Vasil'eva (1971), Žukovskaja & Každan (1971), Jones
& Ward (1969:200-201), Krysin (1974:41-83),
Siekierzycki (1974), and in particular Drage (1967a,

1967b, 1968:362-70).

[70]For *consonants*, cf. our subdivisions between labials, dentals and velars, and between stops and fricatives. Reports suggest that in general fricatives are more likely to be palatalized than stops, that voiced consonants are more likely to be palatalized than voiceless ones, and that palatalization is more likely before fricatives than before stops (e.g., Žukovskaja & Každan 1971). For the influence of different *vowels*, see Drage (1967b:127-28); on the effects of different *tempos*, see Drage (1967b:39).

[71]The first of these factors may be exemplified as follows: the word БЙТВЕ is less likely (all other factors being equal) to be pronounced with a palatalized ТЬ than the word ДВЕРЬ, since the Russian words for *battle* include many with a "hard" т (e.g., БЙТВА, БЙТВ, etc.), while the Russian words for *door* all have "soft" вь. This factor is emphasized by Avanesov and other Soviet Russian authorities. On the importance of the presence or absence of grammatical boundaries, see Panov (1968:67-68) and Drage (1967b: 130-36).

[72]Panov (1968:67). Note that *loanwords* frequently show little or no regressive palatalization assimilation in consonant clusters.

[73]Generally speaking, Soviet Russian phonologists prefer to emphasize the stylistic, grammatical and lexical factors. Drage (1967b) ranks the factors, according to their relative importance, as follows: (1) the phonetic nature of the consonants concerned; (2) the presence of, and the nature of, the boundaries; (3) the presence of a *preceding* stressed vowel (N.B.: this is a case of *progressive* assimilation, cf. note 62); (4) the influence of related grammatical forms; (5) the speed of speech. Drage states that the other factors are insignificant.

[74]Glovinskaja (1971:76-96).

[75]Avanesov discusses these cases at some length (*RLP* 120-22), but fails to give any examples corresponding to the spelling эр in our rules. We include э in 3R(a) quite arbitrarily. See Bulaxovskij (1954: 22-23).

[76]Panov (1967:95, 1968:57-58).

[77]On *neutralization*, see Trubetzkoy (1969:78-83 and passim), Martinet (1973).

[78]On neutralization in Russian, see e.g., Ďurovič

(1963), Gvozdev (1963:98-106), Avanesov (1956:28-40, 213-36). Suggestions that vowel-reduction be explicit in the Russian *SO* belong with general proposals that the *SO* abandon its morphophonemic character; see 2.2., and Vinogradov (1965:21-30), for some practical suggestions that have indeed been made. See also Panov (1967:276-82).

[79] In theory, an *absolute* scale of degrees of stress could be devised, with some reference to physical facts such as amplitude or muscular energy, or to the psychological or physiological factors involved in perception. See Oliverius (1974:54-59), Thelin (1971:56-58), and Ward (1975:101-02) on the theoretical and historical background to scales of degrees of stress, and (for English) see Ladefoged (1975:99-103), Chomsky & Halle (1968).

[80] Namely, by Halle (1959:74-75: "five degrees of prominence . . . this is probably more than are usually met with in actual speech.") Jones & Ward (1969:207) also give an example of a five-point scale, but state that "It is generally sufficient to distinguish two degrees of stress . . ." Thelin (1971:134) distinguishes only three degrees.

[81] Inevitably, some distinctions will be glossed over in this simplified approach. In particular, the problem of "partially-stressed" words (cf. note 10) is by-passed.

[82] A final degree of vowel-reduction might be described to specify totally unstressed vowels, i.e., vowels which are elided (omitted) altogether. *CSR*, as prescribed by Avanesov, includes no examples of *obligatory* vowel-elision, but a few *optional* instances are allowed. Vowel-elision is a phenomenon characteristic of conversational Russian (*RR*), and with allied features of this style is discussed in chapter V (see the foot of p. 163 for Avanesov's list of words with "optional" elision in *CSR*). Rather than include an optional rule specifying vowel-elision in a short list of words, we postpone the whole topic so that it is dealt with *en bloc* in chapter V.

[83] On this notation, see Chomsky & Halle (1968:17, 344).

[84] On vowel-clusters in Russian, see Halle (1959: 30, 56-59), Vetvickij (1966:42-46), Panov (1967:62-65), Shapiro (1968:24-25), Ward (1975).

[85]Toporov (1966) has a valuable listing of the different clusters of consonant-letters and of vowel-letters which occur in Russian.

[86]See 4.3. for the phonetic transcription for these symbols. Note that, e.g., Broch (1911:257) transcribes Я И ТЫ phonetically as [я̄йты̄]; and that in Standard Ukrainian both У and И are pronounced as glides when occurring after a vowel and before a consonant.

[87]One possible factor might be the pronunciation of the word in the language of its origin (to the extent that this is a familiar language to Russian-speakers). If the language of origin has a glide (as in, e.g., English *clown*), perhaps Russian is more likely to have a glide also (КЛОУН → клоўн).

[88]This seems to be true only of the *SO* sequence *consonant + И + stressed vowel*, which may be spelled in two ways and pronounced in three, corresponding to C̲ь̲и̲V̌, C̲ь̲и̲V or C̲ь̲й̲V̌; for example, БРИЛЛИАНТ → бр̌ьильйа̂нт *or* бр̌ьильйа̂нт, with the alternative spelling БРИЛЬЯНТ → бр̌ьильйа̂нт. (Note that *RLPU* only allows the last of these three pronunciations.) See also Vinogradov (1965:262-67) on the vacillations in spelling and pronunciation involved in neuter nouns ending in ИЕ or ЬЕ.

[89]For example, for the one spelling МИЛЛИОН, which would give мьильйо̂н by the normal application of 3S, *RLPU* allows two pronunciations: мьильйо̂н and мьильйо̂н. The same holds true, but with minor variations, for the words БИЛЛИОН and ТРИЛЛИОН also.

[90]For proposals that this rule be incorporated into the *SO*, see Vinogradov (1965:258-60).

[91]For suggestions that the *SO* be changed to mirror the more modern pronunciation, see Vinogradov (1965:267-72). On the history of the ending -ЫЙ, which was established in the *SO* of Russian during the 15th-17th centuries, see, e.g., Efimov (1971:62). See also note 49 above.

[92]See Kasatkin (1971) and cf. Panov (1967:272, 1968:22-31), Kodzasov (1973:113-114).

[93]A number of proposals have been made that A be spelled in the *SO*, instead of O, *either* in all unstressed positions (the 'phonemic principle'), *or* at least in those words where so-called 'hyperphonemes' occur (Vinogradov 1965:198-201). Conversely, it has also been proposed that unstressed A should, in

certain cases and on morphophonemic grounds, be written Ɵ (Vinogradov 1965:218-28). For some of the theoretical problems involved in akan'e, see Thelin (1971:66-67) and the references therein.

[94]See also Jones & Ward (1969:61-62), Glovinskaja (1971).

[95]Cf. note 6 above.

[96]See Isačenko (1947:184-85) and Thelin (1971:134).

[97]Glovinskaja (1971:89).

[98]For example, Panov (1967:308-15, 1968:32-41), Krysin (1974:105-109); see also Superanskaja (1959) and Jones & Ward (1969:51-52).

[99]What might be called "step-zero vowel-reduction" (VR-0), i.e., the style with *all four* unstressed vowels distinguished after C_s, is typical of many Russian dialects, and of Standard Belorussian. In many dialects reduction does occur, but under very limited conditions: see, e.g., Kuznecov (1973:35-76) on the different types of *jakan'e*.

[100]For general discussions, see Ward (1965:30-31), Jones & Ward (1969:44-46), and cf. note 105 below.

[101]It is not just a theoretical possibility, but is typical of certain Russian dialects, that VR-1 occurs with a resulting vowel which is not close to é, but is more like á. In cases like this, the *phonological* system may be identical to that of *CSR*, while the *phonetic* details differ. See Kuznecov (1973:51), for example, on "strong jakan'e".

[102]Thus in one place (*RLP* 19) he states that the choice between VR-1 and VR-2 depends on the stylistic marking of the lexical item concerned; in another (*RLP* 63) he prescribes VR-1, but admits that VR-2 is widely known in the literary language; while in a third place (*RLP* 187) he admits that VR-2 is becoming more and more common at the expense of VR-1. In his examples of transcribed text (*RLP* 355-94) and his tables "От буквы к звуку" (*RLP* 213-88) and "От звука к букве" (*RLP* 291-354), however, he still prefers to use VR-1.

[103]For example, linguists within and outside the Soviet Union (Panov (1967, 1968), Axmanova (1971), Jakobson (1929, 1948, etc.), Halle (1959), Bidwell (1969), Ward (1965)); and pedagogical authorities such as Bryzgunova (1963), Ward (1966), Davydov (1970),

and Jones & Ward (1969). See, however, Thelin (1971), Ward (1975).

[104]For proposals involving the reflection of VR-2 (and/or VR-1) in the *SO*, see Vinogradov (1965:228-30, 240-61, 294). Jones & Ward (1969:37) point out that 3W1 does not apply in some loanwords after "soft" consonants, e.g., чарлстóн, чартúзм. This is not mentioned in *RLP*.

[105]For a review of the historical and cultural background to the stylistic variation between VR-1 and VR-2, see Panov (1967:301-305) and Thelin (1971: 68-81).

[106]See, e.g., Panov (1967:271), Kasatkin (1971), Panov & Čečin (1971), Kodzasov (1973:113-114).

[107]A number of grammatical endings might be spelled with greater linguistic consistency in the Russian *SO*; see Vinogradov (1965:280-94) for proposals that have been made.

[108]Note that this style of pronunciation involves a distinction between the -ЕМ declensional ending and the -ЕМ conjugational ending; thus, e.g., МЫ ЕДЕМ МЕДВЕДЕМ will be pronounced as ##мы#йéдьим#мьйдьвьé-дьам## and МЫ ПОЛЕМ ЗА ПОЛЕМ as ##мы#пóльим#зá/пó-льам##.

[109]Kuz'mina (1966), Panov (1967:315-19, 1968:54-55), Thelin (1971:93-104), Krysin (1974:111-16).

[110]See Jones & Ward (1969:72-73). The fact that 3Y applies to Й before И which is derived, by vowel-reduction rules, from other vowel-letters, means that 3Y must necessarily be ordered after 3W and 3X. Further: it would have been economical to postpone 3I to the present stage for incorporation with 3Y; but 3I must precede 3J1(b). For these reasons, the elision of Й appears in two separate rules.

[111]In other words: for the sake of consistency, these loanwords should be spelled with Э rather than Е in the *SO* (see Vinogradov 1965:409-17).

[112]*RLPU* lists this stem, with this pronunciation, with the eight prefixes В-, ЗА-, ОТ-, ПЕРЕ-, ПРИ-, ПОД-, РАС- and НА- (for the last of which, this pronunciation is optional). *RLP* only gives this stem with this pronunciation with the two prefixes ЗА- and ОТ-. Note that other forms, e.g., the Fem. Past tense forms, have stress on the *final* vowel, and 3Z will therefore not apply; e.g., ВПРЯГЛА → ф/прьаглá and N/C under 3Z. Shapiro (1968:12-13) mentions that

-ТРЯ́С- also shows this pronunciation (i.e., as if it were spelled -ТРЕ́С-) in "colloquial or obsolete styles." Shapiro (1968:13) also mentions the non-standard pronunciation of stressed А́ as О́ in some styles (e.g., пло́тят for *SO* ПЛА́ТЯТ). See also Bulaxovskij (1954:18).

[113]For example, by Černyšev (1914) and Košutić (1919). See Shapiro (1968:3-6, 80-81) for a concise summary.

[114]Note that *some* of these verbal forms may be pronounced in this way in *CSR* also, as optional vari-ants to the normal pronunciation with -a-; see *RLP* 158-61. One such form even gained a foothold in *RLPU*: сто́йущий for *SO* СТО́ЯЩИЙ. Cf. Panov (1967:319-20), Shapiro (1968:18-19).

[115]See Shapiro (1968:19) for some of these "dis-tortions". Two pronunciations given in *RLP* as be-longing to "vulgar speech" are нь͡изьа́ for *SO* НЕЛЬЗЯ́ and о́чин for *SO* О́ЧЕНЬ.

[116]This is true as far as our rules are concerned, which are *generalizations* based on Avanesov's pre-scriptions. Specifically, a few loanwords may, especially in "elevated" *CSR*, be pronounced with less than normal regressive palatalization assimilation (cf. note 72 above), as Avanesov himself points out (*RLP* 108).

[117]See, e.g., Krysin (1968), Vinogradov (1938), and Bloomfield (1933:444-95).

[118]The chief exceptions are the studies made by Glovinskaja (Panov 1968:117-31, Glovinskaja 1971).

[119]See, however, Holden (1976).

[120]See Halle (1959:73-74).

[121]For additional minor items, see Shapiro (1968:44-45) and Pirogova (1971).

[122]This trend was artificially accelerated by the spelling-reform of 1917-1918 (for details of which, see Vinogradov 1965:52-68).

[123]See note 38.

[124]There is *some* evidence: (1) the tendency to-wards the more extreme degrees of vowel-reduction (cf. pp. 95 - 96, 107); (2) the tendency towards pro-nouncing Ч as ш (p. 57); (3) the tendency towards 'dzekan'e', i.e., pronouncing ТЬ and ДЬ (as they appear in the *PO*) as цЬ and дзЬ, respectively

(Dobrodomov 1971, Kuznecova 1971).

[125]Shapiro (1968:45), for instance, would allow "spelling influence" only if, concomitantly, " a suspension of phonological neutralization is involved." On spelling pronunciation in general, see Ward (1965: 42-43), St. Clair-Sobell (1956), and Panov (1968:15-17, 32-35, 72-73, 94, 106).

[126]Shapiro (1968:33) and Drage (1968:355-61), however, report the non-application of the voicing assimilation rules under certain conditions.

NOTES TO CHAPTER IV

[1]Durnovo & Ušakov (1926), Halle (1959:72), Shapiro (1968:13-14).

[2]See Trubetzkoy (1939:61), Chomsky (1964:84).

[3]The sound [ž:] may, since it is a fricative, be equally well considered as a combination of two successive [ž] sounds. The other two digraphs, however, normally represent short affricate sounds; for this reason the single symbols [ʒ] and [ǯ] may be preferred to the digraphic symbols [dz] and [dž] (see 4.8.).

[4]See also notes 4 and 36 to chapter III.

[5]We use [j] for the fricative sound, and [y] for the glide (or approximate). See Isačenko (1959), Jones & Ward (1969:71-73), Avanesov (1974:200-205), and Ladefoged (1975:54-56) for details.

[6]We use [r̃] for the rolled or trilled 'r', and [ř] for the flapped 'r'; see Jones & Ward (1969:175-88) and Ladefoged (1975:147-50) for details.

[7]See Jones & Ward (1969:81-83).

[8]*RLP* 140-42, 147.

[9]Note that "soft" [č':] is equivalent to [t':š'] and "hard" [čš] is equivalent to [tš:]. Cf. note 34 in chapter III.

[10]Panov (1967:34-35).

[11]See the authorities cited in note 43 to chapter III.

[12]See note 79 to chapter III.

[13]Note that in *OM*, our first alternative rule applied also in the environment C_{vd} ___#; and further, that any C_{vd} was devoiced (as if by 3E1(c)):

РУ́БЛЬ → ·ру́бль → [rúp] or even [rúp]

ЙГР → ѝгр → [íkɾ̥] or even [ík]

ЖИ́ЗНЬ → жы́зьнь → [žís'n̥'] or even [žís't']

See Bulaxovskij (1954:12-14), Panov (1967:269-71),
Ševoroškin (1971), and Ljubimova (1975). Note also
that in the extremely rare instances when liquids
occur between consonants, and when the preceding consonant is voiced, this consonant may in turn (like
those in the *OM* pronunciation just described) be devoiced; thus,

МУ́ДРСТВОВАТЬ   ИЗ ЛХА́СЫ

му́дрставать   из/лха́сы

mút̥ɾ̥stəvət'   is̥lx̥ásI

Under these unusual circumstances, the voiceless
liquid may be fricativized, giving the two phones [ɾ̥]
(similar to the Czech "ř") and [ɬ] (similar to the
Welsh "ll").

[14]Oliverius (1974:124-25) has a useful table con-
trasting different transcriptions.

NOTES TO CHAPTER V

[1]There are not much more than passing remarks
in, e.g., Černyšev (1914), Šaxmatov (1941), Panov
(1963), Ward (1965) and Avanesov (*RLP*). Panov (1967:
264) has an extensive bibliography of works which include similar brief remarks, and (on pp. 265, 272,
275) gives some literary quotations which exemplify
RR; see also Bulaxovskij (1954:8-11). Exceptionally,
Bogorodickij (1880) and Isačenko (1947, 1959, 1975)
devote more attention to the subject, but do not
treat it comprehensively. Recent years have seen
more deliberate studies: in the West, Shapiro (1968)
and, for one aspect, Thelin (1971); in the Soviet
Union, Panov (1967:264-75), Barinova (1970, 1971a,
1971b), Kodzasov (1973), and Zemskaja (1973:40-150)--
this section of the book was written by Barinova.
Zemskaja's book is the first easily-available study
to be devoted entirely to "Colloquial Russian" (the
earlier study--Sirotinina, Barannikova and Serdobincev (1970)--being difficult to obtain). Note that,
coincidentally, разговорная речь (the usual name for
the perhaps preferable разговорный язык) is also ab-
breviated PP.

[2]The definition in Barinova (1970) and Zemskaja
(1973)--непринужденная речь носителей литературного

языка--is thus very close to ours. These scholars restrict *RR* to speakers who (1) have Russian as their native language, (2) were born and raised in a city, (3) have a certain standard of education, and (4) show no "dialect" features. We agree with the first two of these restrictions, but query the third and (as mentioned) are not happy with the fourth. One difference between Leningrad *RR* and Moscow *RR* has been cited as follows: for *CSR* [xərʌšó], the Leningrad [xʌršó] corresponds to the Muscovite [xrʌšó] (Žirmunskij 1925; see Zemskaja 1973:46).

[3]On this problem, see Zwicky (1972b:608) and Panov (1967:276).

[4]Panov (1967:268, 271).

[5]See Zemskaja (1973:9-25) and the references there.

[6]See, e.g., Panov (1967:275), Barinova (in Zemskaja 1973:72-75), and Bondarko et al. (1974). Shapiro (1968), for example, expressly derives his "elliptic" (*RR*) forms from his "explicit" (*CSR*) ones; most other writers cite the *SO* without further comment on the problem. Exceptionally, Thelin (1971: 127) does speak of "alternative phonological reduction rules" in this context; but he also (p. 126) states that "it is obvious that we get a more economic and natural description if we derive the more 'normal' pronunciation [i.e., *RR*] from an underlying representation that is nearer to the explicit [i.e., *CSR*] pronunciation." See also the valuable Kučera (1973) on these problems as they apply to Czech.

[7]Thus Axmanova (1971) describes *RR* as "an indistinct, careless pronunciation of sounds . . . that leads to their reduction (shortening)."

[8]Thelin (1971:127). See Ščerba (1915/1957:21) who, for *SO* ГОВОРИТ, gives the six variants [gʌvʌr'ít], [gəvʌr'ít], [gəʌr'ít], [gər'ít], [gr'ít] and [gr'ɪ́t], and adds that these "by no means exhaust the occurrent variants"; and Panov (1963:5, 1968:110) who gives five of the possibilities for *SO* ЗДРАВСТВУЙТЕ.

[9]For discussion of *RR* as one of many styles, see Avanesov (1961, *RLP*), Shapiro (1968:7-10), Panov (1967:264, 345-47, 1968:108-12), Zemskaja (1970, 1973:5-27) and the references therein.

[10]All the examples in this chapter are from Panov (1967), Barinova (1971a, 1971b), Zemskaja (1973) or

Kodzasov (1973).

[11]For numerals, see Shapiro (1968:26), and cf. our remarks in chapter III (pp. 42, 75, 115-16); for personal names, see Avanesov (*RLP*:176-82).

[12]The correlation between textual frequency and susceptibility to indistinct pronunciation must be assumed to exclude certain very frequently-occurring words, such as prepositions, pronouns, conjunctions, etc., which are so short already that any elision would eliminate them and tend to make the sentences in which they occur unintelligible. Indeed, many frequently-occurring nouns, verbs, adjectives and so on are unusually short (see, e.g., Mańczak (1968) for arguments for a causal connection between frequency of occurrence and brevity). For word-frequency counts for Russian, see Josselson (1953), Štejnfeldt (n.d.), Vakar (1968), Turko (1968) and El'kina & Judina (1970). On the use of some high-frequency verbs in *RR*, see Baxmutova (1970). Panov (1967:274) suggests that high-frequency words should, for the purposes of a study of the pronunciation of *RR*, be analyzed as a separate sub-system. See also Kodzasov (1973:130) for derivational categories in which suffixes of high frequency are often subject to elision in *RR*.

[13]See, e.g., Zwicky (1972b:610-13).

[14]See Zemskaja (1973:11), Kodzasov (1973:110-13, 131) and also Zwicky (1972b:608).

[15]Of the variations in approach to the problem of defining the relationship between language-variety and language-context, we may mention: (1) the traditional Soviet approach, exemplified by Avanesov (1961, *RLP*), in which "style" is defined in terms of the forms used *and* of their usual contexts. Avanesov thus defines his "neutral *CSR*", for example, by reference both to "distinct pronunciation" and to the situations in which it is used; and, since these situations allow for the indistinct pronunciation of the categories of words we have described, he is forced to describe them also; (2) the approach of, e.g., Shapiro (1968), following Jakobson (1960), who define "codes" (in Shapiro's case, the *elliptic* and the *explicit* codes) and thus use the *forms alone* as their starting-point; (3) the other extreme approach --starting with the contexts, and relating formal varieties to each context--is proposed, but not elaborated, by Thelin (1971). Our own approach, by default, and that of Zemskaja (1973; see, e.g., p. 42),

comes very close to the second of these.

[16] It may be suggested that, given the factors cited in 5.1., and in particular the factor of reduced time-span, perhaps the general effect is the *overlap* of syllables in time. Cf. Čistovič et al. (1965:95), cited by Kodzasov (1973:114), and also Fromkin (1971).

[17] Cf. the phonological changes between Late Latin and Early Old French (e.g., CABALLUS [kaḇáːʊs] > cheval [šəv̱ál]; or, in Slavic territory, the change from [g] to [ɦ] in, e.g., Old Czech and in Old Ukrainian (see Andersen (1969a) on this and other cases of historical lenition in Slavic).

[18] One or two other *RR* phenomena may also involve lenition. The first is exemplified particularly by a number of frequently-occurring verbs, where the sequence [d'ɪ] of *CSR* is replaced by [ɪ] in *RR*. At first glance this might seem to involve simple elision of the [d']. Another possibility, though, is that there is an (attested) first stage with elision of the [ɪ], and this is followed by lenition of the [d'] to [y]; since the [d'] is syllabic, the [y] is also syllabic, i.e., is realized as [ɪ]. For example, *SO* ХОДИТ, *CSR* [xód'ɪt]; *either* with syncope of [d'] → [xóɪt]; *or* with elision of [ɪ] → [xód't] and then lenition of [d'] → [xóɪt]. So also *SO'* ПРИ-ХОДИТЬСЯ, ВИДИТЕ, БУДЕШЬ, and *RR* [pr'ɪxóḭcə], [v'íṟt'ɪ], [búṟš]. For discussion see Isačenko (1959:123) and Barinova (1971b:121-27); to their arguments we add the suggestion that investigation of Bulgarian ([dváysɛt] < [dvaḏɛsě̌tɪ̆]) and of Czech (Standard Czech [buḏte], Colloquial Czech [búyte]) may throw further light on this problem; see Broch (1911:254). The second case does not properly come under this heading, but is of interest and may be mentioned here. ВИДИТЕ ЛИ has been noted in *RR* as [v'iṉ't'ɪl'ɪ] and ОТКУДА ТЫ as [ʌtkúṉtɪ]. Here, the combination *voiced stop + reduced vowel* is replaced by a *voiced nasal*, which is syllabic, before a voiceless stop. See Zemskaja (1973:59-60) for details and further discussion.

[19] See Kodzasov (1973:113-14) and notes 92 and 106 in chapter III. Our conclusion, that complete neutralization is not widespread, is based on the examples of *RR* cited in the literature, which show many instances of oppositions among unstressed vowels.

[20] The first example is from Shapiro (1968); see

also Avanesov (*RLP*:76-77). The paucity of examples may be merely a gap in the available data; more likely, this "weakening" stage may be restricted to certain limited environments--thus, in particular, to pretonic vowels occurring before liquids, and to vowel-clusters.

[21]Panov (1967:265) calls this *kompensirovanie*; Barinova (in Zemskaja 1973:52-54) discusses this in terms of information retention. See also Avanesov (1974:205).

[22]Panov (1967:63) considers these pronunciations as acceptable in *CSR*.

[23]Note also *SO* ПРÁВИЛЬНО, *CSR* [práv'ɪl'nə], *RR* [prá̝ɛl'nə]; here a [v'] is lost, and the following vowel is *lowered*. It is difficult to find a connection between the loss of [v'] and the vowel-lowering; perhaps the preceding low [a] is exerting a progressive assimilatory influence.

[24]Syllabicity is a phenomenon which is difficult to define, to describe, and to discriminate aurally; on this problem, and for a survey of syllabic consonants in a number of languages, see Bell (1970). Two factors seem generally relevant with regard to which consonant--the preceding or the following--will be syllabicized: (1) the total syllabic structure of the word, and (2) the types of consonant concerned. In the first and third examples cited, the syllabification of [d'] and of the two [v]'s can be explained in terms of the syllabic structure of the words concerned (in their *CSR* forms): thus, [v'í|d'ɪ|mə] → [v'í|d'|mə] and [s'ɪ'í|və|və|və] → [s'ɪ'í|v̩|v̩|ə]. This kind of explanation will however not work for the second example: applying the same process, we get [ʌ|b'ɛ́|də|lə] → *[ʌ|b'ɛ́|d̩|lə]. For this particular example, one might adduce a factor of consonantal type: the liquid [l] is presumably more easily syllabicized than the stop [d], hence [ʌb'ɛ́d̩lə]; but this explanation will not work for the first example, since this criterion would surely specify that [m] is more easily syllabicized than [d']. We propose a hierarchy of ease of syllabicization applicable to Russian, as follows: (1) stops/affricates--(2) fricatives--(3) nasals--(4) liquids, where the higher the number of the consonant type, the more likely it is to be syllabicized. On this problem, see Panov (1967:265-68) and Zemskaja (1973: 52-55).

[25]This is a relatively rare phenomenon (Zemskaja 1973:56).

[26]This is based on Barinova (1971b). Barinova omits any reference to voiceless fricatives, and we place them, arbitrarily and ambiguously, in group (2); although they may well be more or less liable to elision than voiced stops, it is reasonable to assume that they are less susceptible than voiced fricatives, and more susceptible than voiceless stops. See Zwicky (1972a, 1972b:610), Vennemann (1972), Hankamer & Aissen (1974), and Hooper (1976:195-206). Compare also the hierarchy of susceptibility to syllabicization given in note 24 above.

[27]A possible parallel may be found in the stress-assignment rule 3S(c), which states that vowels are half-stressed when preceding о, а, э but fully unstressed when preceding и, у; here again, we have a distinction between high and non-high vowels, with an effect on the "strength" of adjacent segments in this particular case. See note 30 below for possible counterevidence.

[28]Barinova (1971a:100-104), Zemskaja (1973:43-48). Note that the factor of grammatical information, carried by most vowels in absolute final position, must also be taken into account.

[29]See note 24 above. Note that the sequences [ərə] and [ələ] may "go either way", namely to [ər] *or* [rə] and to [əl] *or* [lə]; for example, *SO* ВОРОТ-НИЧОК, *CSR* [vərət'n'ɪčók], *RR* [vərt'n'ɪčók] ~ [vrət'n'ɪčók]. This phenomenon is not fully understood; see Barinova (1973:52), *RLP* 72-76, Shapiro (1968:22).

[30]See Avanesov (*RLP*:76-80) and Shapiro (1968:24-25). The few data available prompt the following tentative suggestion: when two vowels are reduced to one, it is usually the *less central* (or the *higher*) of the two that remains; thus, [ɪʌ]→[ɪ], [ʌʊ]→[ʊ] and [ʊʌ]→[ʊ].

[31]In particular, CTC → [s:] and ЗДЗ → [z:] (Kodzasov 1973:127).

[32]Panov (1967:273), Zemskaja (1973:77-86), Kodzasov (1973:129).

[33]Two opposing factors may be involved here. In the first place, it can be suggested that the greater force with which stressed vowels are pronounced would tend to result in a resistance to elision in adjacent

consonants. On the other hand, there is the factor
of information-loss: with the elision of unstressed
vowels, the information conveyed by the syllable as a
whole is thrown onto the remaining consonants; with
the *non*-elision of stressed vowels, there is less
burden on the adjacent consonants, which may therefore be elided without so much information-loss.

[34]This discussion of rule-ordering relates only
to a very specialized situation, namely, a pedagogical exposition of *RR* which takes *CSR* as the starting
point. Needless to say, conclusions drawn do not
necessarily extend to any other possible situation.

[35]Kodzasov (1973:131) has examples of derivations
with intermediate stages, but does not allow for alternative routes between the explicit and the elliptic forms. Barinova (in Zemskaja 1973:121-22) has
examples with intermediate stages *and* alternative
routes, together with some discussion of the problem.

[36]But for the anecdotal evidence cited here of
the non-application of the devoicing rule, which may
also hold for other rules of Russian, it would have
been reasonable to suggest that rules such as the
ones listed here should be regarded as general "output conditions" (Derwing 1975) or "surface accept-
ability" constraints (Zwicky 1972b:609) operating on
all styles of Russian. See also Barinova (in Zemskaja 1973:57-61).

[37]Note the alternation between [s'] and [s] in
CSR, as in, e.g., *SO* ОСЛА ~ ОСЁЛ, *CSR* [ʌsˈla]~[ʌsˈól]
and *SO* СОСНА́ ~ СО́СЕН, *CSR* [sʌsná]~[sós'ɪn]. These
examples suggest that the depalatalization of [s']
before [n] may be a valid rule for the phonology of
CSR in any case, given an abstract representation of
these stems with a "soft s". Cf. the historical
change from Old Russian ВЪНОУСЬНЫИ (pronounced approximately [vəkús'ɪnɨy]) to a form with the sequence
[s'n] after the "fall of the jers", and thence to *CSR*
[fkúsnɨy].

[38]Cf. our remarks in note 56 to chapter III on
other forms of progressive assimilation in Russian.

[39]Cf. our remarks on the ("non-standard") reduction of Э in loanwords on pp. 100-01. See also
Kodzasov (1973:129), Panov (1967:273), *RLP* 68, 92.

[40]See note 6 above. The suggestion we make here
may be considered as a tentative addendum to Thelin's
criticism (1971:55-56) of the way in which Chomsky &

Halle (1968:110-11) avoid this whole problem by reference to "performance-factors" which are left
undescribed. Another solution to the problem would
be to treat *RR* and *CSR* as separate languages, and not
to attempt any hypotheses concerning their interre-
lationship. We suggest that such a solution should
only be considered as a last resort.

BIBLIOGRAPHY

ABBREVIATIONS:

IJSLP = *International Journal of Slavic Linguistics and Poetics*
JL = *Journal of Linguistics*
Lg = *Language*
MPh = *Le maître phonétique*
RJaš = *Russkij jazyk v škole*
RL = *Russian Linguistics*
SEEJ = *Slavic and East European Journal*
VJa = *Voprosy jazykoznanija*
VKR = *Voprosy kul'tury reči*
ZPSK = *Zeitschrift für Phonetik, Sprachwissenschaft und Kommunikationsforschung*

Aksenov, V.N. 1954. *Iskusstvo xudožestvennogo slova.* Moscow: Iskusstvo.

Alekseev, D.I. 1963a. "Grafičeskie sokraščenija i slova-abbreviatury," 145-60 in *Ožegov & Panov* 1963.

———. 1963b. "Proiznošenie složnosokraščennyx slov i bukvennyx abbreviatur," *VKR* 4:22-37.

———. 1965. "Sokraščenija blagozvučnye i neblagozvučnye," *VKR* 6:33-43.

Andersen, Henning. 1969a. "Lenition in Common Slavic," *Lg* 45:553-74.

———. 1969b. "The phonological status of the Russian 'labial fricatives'," *JL* 5:121-26.

Anwar, M.S. 1974. "Consonant devoicing at word boundary as assimilation," *Language Sciences* 32:6-12.

Avanesov, R.I. 1955. *Udarenie v sovremennom russkom literaturnom jazyke.* Moscow: Učpedgiz.

———. 1956. *Fonetika sovremennogo russkogo literaturnogo jazyka.* Moscow: Izd. moskovsk. universiteta. Reprint, Ann Arbor, Mich., 1967.

———. 1958. *Russkoe literaturnoe proiznošenie.* 3rd. ed., Moscow: Učpedgiz.

Avanesov, R.I. 1961. "O normax russkogo literaturnogo proiznošenija," *RJaŠ* 6:7-12.

——————. 1972. *Russkoe literaturnoe proiznošenie*.
5th. ed., Moscow: Prosveščenie.

——————. 1974. *Russkaja literaturnaja i dialektnaja
fonetika*. Moscow: Prosveščenie.

—————— & S.I. Ožegov. 1960. *Russkoe literaturnoe
proiznošenie i udarenie. Slovar'-spravoč-
nik*. 3rd. ed., Moscow: Gos. izd. inno-
strannyx i nacional'nyx slovarej.

Axmanova, O.S. 1971. *Phonology, Morphophonology,
Morphology*. The Hague: Mouton.

Bailey, C-J.N. 1973. *Variation and Linguistic
Theory*. Arlington, Va.: Center for Applied
Linguistics.

Baranovskaja, S.A. 1968. "Pozicionnye vlijanija na
var'irovanie soglasnyx po gluxosti-zvonkosti
v sovremennom russkom literaturnom jazyke,"
Trudy universiteta družby narodov 29:24-38.

——————. 1969. "Pozicionnoe oglušenie sonornyx
soglasnyx v sovremennom russkom literaturnom
jazyke," 3-8 in D.E. Mixal'či, ed., *Problemy
lingvističeskogo analiza*. Moscow: Universitet družby narodov.

Barinova, G.A. 1966. "O proiznošenii [$\bar{\check{z}}$'] i [$\bar{\check{s}}$'],"
25-54 in *Vysotskij & al. 1966*.

——————. 1970. "Nabljudenija nad vokalizmom razgovornoj reči," 26-32 in *Sirotinina & al.
1970*.

——————. 1971a. "Redukcija glasnyx v razgovornoj
reči," 97-116 in *Vysotskij & al. 1971*.

——————. 1971b. "Redukcija i vypadenie intervokal'-
nyx soglasnyx v razgovornoj reči," 117-27 in
Vysotskij & al. 1971.

Baxmutova, N.I. 1970. "Upotreblenie nekotoryx
naibolee častotnyx glagolov v razgovornoj
reči," 89-97 in *Sirotinina & al. 1970*.

Bell, Alan. 1970. "Syllabic consonants," *Working
Papers on Language Universals (Stanford
University)* 4.B1-B49.

Bidwell, C.E. 1969. *The Structure of Russian in
Outline*. Pittsburgh: Univ. of Pittsburgh
Press.

Bloomfield, L. 1933. *Language*. New York: Holt.

Bogorodickij, V.A. 1880. "Glasnye bez udarenija v obščerusskom jazyke," *Russkij filologičeskij vestnik* 4:87-102.

Bondarko, L.V., & L.R. Zinder. 1966. "O nekotoryx differencial'nyx priznakax russkix soglasnyx fonem," *VJa* 1966/1:10-14.

-------, L.A. Verbickaja, & *alii*. 1974. "Stili proiznošenija i tipy proiznesenija," *VJa* 1974/2:64-70.

Borunova, S.N. 1966. "Sočetanija [šč] i [š:] na granicax morfem," 55-72 in *Vysotskij & al. 1966*.

Boyanus, S.C. 1947. "The Russian i-ɨ phoneme," Supplement to *MPh*.

-------. 1965. *Russian Pronunciation*. London: Lund Humphries.

Broch, Olaf. 1911. *Slavische Phonetik*. Heidelberg: Winter.

Bryzgunova, E.A. 1963. *Praktičeskaja fonetika i intonacija russkogo jazyka*. Moscow: Izd. moskovsk. universiteta.

-------. 1969. *Zvuki i intonacija russkoj reči*. Moscow.

-------. 1971. "O smyslorazličitel'nyx vozmožnostjax russkoj intonacii," *VJa* 1971/4:42-52.

Bulaxovskij, L.A. 1954. *Russkij literaturnyj jazyk pervoj poloviny XIX veka. Fonetika. Morfologija. Udarenie. Sintaksis*. 2nd. ed., Moscow: Učpedgiz.

Bylinskij, K.I. 1960. *Slovar' udarenija dlja rabotnikov radio i televidenija*. Moscow: Sovetskaja ènciklopedija.

Chomsky, Noam. 1964. *Current Issues in Linguistic Theory*. The Hague: Mouton.

------- & M. Halle. 1968. *The Sound Pattern of English*. New York: Harper & Row.

Coats, Herbert S. 1974. *Stress Assignment in Russian: Inflection*. Edmonton: Linguistic Research Inc.

------- & Alex P. Harshenin. 1971. "On the phonological status of Russian *v*," *SEEJ* 15:466-78.

Conlin, David A. 1961. *Grammar for Written English*. Boston: Houghton Mifflin.

Černyšev, V.I. 1914. *Pravil'nost' i čistota russkoj reči. I. Fonetika*. St. Petersburg. (Reprinted, *Izbrannye trudy*, Moscow: Prosveščenie, 1960.)

———. 1915. *Zakony i pravila russkogo proizno-šenija*. 3rd. ed., St. Petersburg. (Reprinted, *Izbrannye trudy*, Moscow: Prosveščenie, 1960.)

Čistovič, L.A., & alii. 1965. *Reč'. Artikulacija i vosprijatie*. Moscow.

Čurganova, V.G. 1973. *Očerk russkoj morfonologii*. Moscow: Nauka.

Daneš, F. 1967. "Order of elements and sentence intonation," 499-512 in *To Honor Roman Jakobson*. The Hague: Mouton.

Daniels, W.J. 1975. "Natural phonology and the teaching of pronunciation," *SEEJ* 19:66-84.

Davydov, M.V. 1970. *Russkaja reč'*. Leningrad: Izd. leningradsk. universiteta.

Derwing, Bruce L. 1975. "Linguistic rules and language acquisition," *Cahiers linguistique d'Ottawa* 4:13-41.

Dobrodomov, I.G. 1971. "Dzetsi v Moskve," 242-43 in *Vysotskij & al. 1971*.

Drage, Charles K.L. 1967a. "Factors in the regressive palatalization of consonants in Russian," *ZPSK* 20:119-42.

———. 1967b. "Changes in the regressive palatalization of consonants in Russian," *ZPSK* 20:181-206.

———. 1968. "Some data on Modern Moscow pronunciation," *Slavonic and East European Review* 16:353-82.

Durnovo, N.N., & D.I. Ušakov. 1926. "Opyt foneti-českoj transkripcii russkogo literaturnogo proiznošenija," *Slavia* 5/2:342-47.

Ďurovič, L. 1963. "Fonematičeskaja interpretacija russkogo bezudarnogo vokalizma," *Česko-slovenská rusistika* 1963/4:188-93.

Efimov, A.I. 1971. *Istorija russkogo literaturnogo jazyka*. 3rd. ed., Moscow: Vysšaja škola.

El'kina, V.A. & L.S. Judina. 1964. "Statistika slogov v russkoj reči," *Vyčislitel'nye sistemy* (Novosibirsk) 1964/10:58-78.

Es'kova, N.A. 1971. "K voprosu o svojstvax sonornyx soglasnyx v russkom jazyke," 243-47 in *Vysotskij & al. 1971.*

Fant, Gunnar. 1960. *Acoustic Theory of Speech Production.* The Hague: Mouton.

Filin, F.P. 1973. "O strukture sovremennogo russkogo literaturnogo jazyka," *VJa* 1973/1:3-12.

Fischer, Gero. 1976. "Automatische Transkription polnischer orthographischer Texte," 145-58 in H.D. Pohl, ed., *Opuscula Slavica et Linguistica. Festschrift für Alexander Issatschenko.* Klagenfurt: Heyn.

Fónagy, Ivan. 1963. *Die Metaphern in der Phonetik.* The Hague: Mouton.

Forsyth, James. 1963. *A Practical Guide to Russian Stress.* Edinburgh: Oliver & Boyd.

Fromkin, Victoria. 1971. "The non-anomalous nature of anomalous utterances," *Lg* 47:27-52.

Ganiev, Z.V. 1966. "O proiznošenii sočetanij <stk>, <zdk>, <ntk>, <ndk>," 85-95 in *Vysotskij & al. 1966.*

--------. 1971. "O proiznošenii rabočix-urožencev g. Moskvy," 33-53 in *Vysotskij & al. 1971.*

Gleason, H.A.L. 1961. *An Introduction to Descriptive Linguistics.* New York: Holt, Rinehart & Winston.

Glovinskaja, M.JA. 1971. "Ob odnoj fonologičeskoj podsisteme v sovremennom russkom literaturnom jazyke," 54-96 in *Vysotskij & al. 1971.*

--------, M.E. Il'ina, S.M. Kuz'mina & M.V. Panov. 1971. "O grammatičeskix faktorax razvitii fonetičeskoj sistemy sovremennogo russkogo jazyka," 20-32 in *Vysotskij & al. 1971.*

Gorbačevič, K.S. 1971. *Izmenenie norm russkogo literaturnogo jazyka.* Leningrad: Prosveščenie.

Grebnev, A.A. 1959. "Fonetičeskoe i morfologičeskoe oformlenie abbreviatur v russkom jazyke," *Bulletin vysoké školy ruského jazyka a literatury* 3:5-22.

Gregory, Michael. 1967. "Aspects of varieties differentiation," *JL* 3:177-98.

Gvozdev, A.N. 1947. *Osnovy russkoj orfografii.* Moscow-Leningrad: Akad. pedagog. nauk RSFSR.

———. 1963. *Izbrannye raboty po orfografii i fonetike.* Moscow: Akad. pedagog. nauk RSFSR.

Haas, W. 1970. *Phono-Graphic Translation.* Manchester: Manchester University Press.

Hall, Robert A. 1961. *Sound and Spelling in English.* Philadelphia: Center for Curriculum Development.

Halle, Morris. 1959. *The Sound-Pattern of Russian.* The Hague: Mouton.

Hankamer, J., & J. Aissen. 1974. "The sonority hierarchy," 131-45 in *Papers from the Parasession on Natural Phonology.* Chicago: Chicago Linguistic Society.

Hockett, C.F. 1958. *A Course in Modern Linguistics.* New York: Macmillan.

Holden, Kyril T. 1976. "Assimilation rates of borrowing and phonological productivity," *Lg* 52:131-47.

Hooper, Joan B. 1976. *An Introduction to Natural Generative Phonology.* New York: Academic Press.

Isačenko, Aleksandr V. 1947. *Fonetika spisovnej ruštiny.* Bratislava: Slov. akad. vied.

———. 1959. "Der Schwund des intervokalischen /j/ im Russischen," *Zeitschrift für Phonetik* 12:116-24.

———. 1967. "Frazovoe udarenie i porjadok slov," 967-76 in *To Honor Roman Jakobson.* The Hague: Mouton.

———. 1971. "Morfonologičeskaja interpretacija dolgix mjagkix soglasnyx [š:], [ž:] v russkom jazyke," *IJSLP* 14:32-52.

———. 1975. "O parallelizme sinxronnyx i istoričeskix zvukovyx processov v russkom jazyke," *IJSLP* 20:13-22.

Ivanova-Luk'janova, G.N. 1971. "Ob udarnosti

dinamičeski neustojčivyx slov," 170-88 in *Vysotskij & al. 1971*.

Jakobson, Roman. 1929. *Remarques sur l'évolution phonétique du russe*. Prague: Jednota československých matematiků a fysiků.

--------. 1948. "Russian conjugation," *Word* 4:155-67.

--------. 1956. "Die Verteilung der stimmhaften und stimmlosen Geräuschlaute im Russischen," 199-202 in M. Woltner, ed., *Festschrift für Max Vasmer*. Wiesbaden: Harrassowitz.

--------. 1960. "Closing statement: linguistics and poetics," 350-77 in T. Sebeok, ed., *Style in Language*. Cambridge, Mass.: MIT Press.

--------. 1963. "Izbytočnye bukvy v russkom jazyke," 173-78 in M. Hraste & al., eds., *Zbornik u čast Stjepana Ivšića*. Zagreb: Hrvatsko filološko društvo.

--------. 1968. "K voprosu o gluxosti i zvonkosti russkix ščelinnyx soglasnyx," 728-33 in R. Jakobson, *Selected Writings II*, 2nd. ed., The Hague: Mouton.

Jones, Daniel, & Dennis Ward. 1969. *The Phonetics of Russian*. Cambridge: CUP.

Josselson, Harry H. 1953. *The Russian Word Count*. Detroit: Wayne University Press.

Karcevskij, Serge. 1937. "Sur la rationalisation de l'orthographe russe," 31-38 in *Zbornik lingvističkih i filoloških rasprava A. Beliću*. Belgrade: Mlada Srbija.

Kasatkin, L.L. 1971. "Novaja stupen' v razvitii sistemy glasnyx russkogo jazyka," 255-57 in *Vysotskij & al. 1971*.

Kiparsky, Valentin. 1962. *Der Wortakzent der russischen Schriftsprache*. Heidelberg: Winter.

Kodzasov, S.V. 1973. "Fonetičeskij èllipsis v russkoj razgovornoj reči," 109-33 in V.A. Zvegincev & al., eds., *Teoretičeskie i èksperimental'nye issledovanija v oblasti strukturnoj lingvistiki*. Moscow: Prosveščenie.

Košutić, R. 1919. *Gramatika ruskog jezika. I.*

Glasovi. A. Opšti deo (kniǰiževni izgovor).
Petrograd: Russkaja akad. nauk.

Krysin, L.P. 1968. *Inojazyčnye slova v sovremennom
russkom jazyke*. Moscow: Nauka.

———————. 1974. (ed.) *Russkij jazyk po dannym mas-
sovogo obsledovanija. Opyt social'no-
lingvističeskogo izučenija*. Moscow: Nauka.

Kučera, Henry. 1973. "Language variability, rule
interdependency, and the grammar of Czech,"
Linguistic Inquiry 4:499-522.

Kunert, Ilse. 1968. *Veränderungsprozesse und
Entwicklungstendenzen im heutigen Russisch*.
Wiesbaden: Harrassowitz.

Kuz'mina, S.M. 1966. "O fonetike zaudarnyx fleksij,"
5-24 in *Vysotskij & al. 1966*.

Kuznecov, P.S. 1958. *U istokov russkoj grammati-
českoj mysli*. Moscow: Akad. nauk.

———————. 1973. (ed.) *Russkaja dialektologija*.
Moscow: Prosveščenie.

Kuznecova, A.M. 1971. "O dzekan'e v russkom jazyke," 257-59 in *Vysotskij & al. 1971*.

Ladefoged, Peter. 1975. *A Course in Phonetics*.
New York: Harcourt, Brace & Jovanovich.

Lass, Roger. 1971. "Boundaries as obstruents: Old
English voicing assimilation and universal
strength hierarchies," *JL* 7:15-30.

Lightner, Theodore M. 1972. *Problems in the Theory
of Phonology. I. Russian Phonology and
Turkish Phonology*. Edmonton: Linguistic
Research, Inc.

Ljubimova, N.A. 1975. "Zavisimost' kačestva sonan-
tov ot fonetičeskogo položenija v slove,"
112-24 in A.A. Leont'ev & N.I. Samuilova,
eds., *Voprosy fonetiki i obučenija proizno-
šeniju*. Moscow: Izd. moskovsk. universiteta.

Lunt, Horace G. 1958. *Fundamentals of Russian*.
New York: Norton.

Lotz, John. 1969. "The conversion of script to
speech as exemplified by Hungarian," *Linguistic Reporter* 1969 (October) [Supple-
ment] 17-30.

Lyons, John. 1968. *Introduction to Theoretical Linguistics*. Cambridge: CUP.

Mańczak, Witold. 1968. "Le développement phonétique
    irrégulier dû à la fréquence en russe,"
    Lingua 21:287:93.

Martinet, André. 1973. "Neutralization" [transl. E.
    Fudge], 74-80 in Erik Fudge, ed., *Phonology*.
    Selected Readings. Harmondsworth: Penguin.

Molinsky, Steven J. 1973. *Patterns of Ellipsis in
    Russian Compound-Noun Formations*. The
    Hague: Mouton.

Nicholson, John G. 1970. *Russian Normative Stress
    Notation*. Montréal: McGill University
    Press.

Nida, E.A. 1949. *Morphology. The Descriptive Anal-
    ysis of Words*. Ann Arbor, Mich.: Univer-
    sity of Michigan Press.

Oliverius, Zdeněk F. 1974. *Fonetika russkogo jazy-
    ka*. Prague: Státní pedagogické naklada-
    telství.

Orlova, V.G. 1950. "Gubnye spiranty v russkom ja-
    zyke," *Trudy instituta russkogo jazyka AN
    SSSR* 2:167-209.

Ožegov, S.I. 1963. *Slovar' russkogo jazyka*. 5th.
    ed., Moscow: Gos. izdat. inostrannyx i
    nacional'nyx slovarej.

-------, & M.V. Panov. 1963 (eds.) *Razvitie sov-
    remennogo russkogo jazyka*. Moscow: Nauka.

Panov, M.V. 1961. "O razgraničitel'nyx signalax,"
    VJa 1961/1:3-19.

-------. 1963. "Nekotorye tendencii v razvitii
    russkogo literaturnogo jazyka XX veka," *VJa*
    1963/3:1-17.

-------. 1967. *Russkaja fonetika*. Moscow: Pros-
    veščenie.

-------. 1968 (ed.) *Fonetika sovremennogo russkogo
    literaturnogo jazyka. Narodnye govory*.
    Moscow: Nauka.

-------, & O.I. Čečin. 1971. "Russkie glasnye
    skvoz' ispanskoe fonetičeskoe sito," 264-67
    in *Vysotskij & al. 1971*.

Paufošima, R.F. 1971. "O proiznošenii č v litera-
    turnom jazyke," 268-69 in *Vysotskij & al.
    1971*.

Paufošima, R.F., & D.A. Agaronov. 1971. "Ob uslovijax assimiljativnogo ozvončenija soglasnyx na styke fonetičeskix slov v russkom jazyke," 189-99 in *Vysotskij & al. 1971.*

Pirogova, N.K. 1970. *Russkoe literaturnoe proiznošenie.* Moscow: Prosveščenie.

Raspopov, I.P. 1966. "Logičeskoe udarenie kak osoboe sredstvo strukturnoj organizacii predloženija," *RJaš* 1966/4.

Red'kin, V.A. 1971. *Akcentologija sovremennogo russkogo literaturnogo jazyka.* Moscow: Prosveščenie.

Romportl, Milan. 1973. "Trends in the development of Standard Russian pronunciation," 118-27 in M. Romportl, *Studies in Phonetics.* The Hague: Mouton.

St. Clair-Sobell, J.O. 1956. "Notes on spelling pronunciation with special reference to Modern Standard Russian," *Canadian Slavonic Papers* 1:66-75.

Shapiro, Michael. 1966. "On non-distinctive voicing in Russian," *JL* 2:189-94.

-------. 1967. "Remarks on phonological boundaries in Russian," *SEEJ* 11:433-41.

-------. 1968. *Russian Phonetic Variants and Phonostylistics.* Berkeley-Los Angeles: University of California Press.

-------. 1972. "Consonant syncope in Russian," 404-23 in D.S. Worth, ed., *The Slavic Word.* The Hague: Mouton.

Shevelov, George Y. 1965. *A Prehistory of Slavic.* New York: Columbia University Press.

Siekierzycki, E. 1974. *Assimiljativnaja mjagkost' soglasnyx v sovremennom russkom jazyke.* Poznań: Uniwersytet im. A. Mickiewicza.

Sirotinina, O.B., L.I. Barannikova & N.Ja. Serdobincev. 1970. (eds.) *Russkaja razgovornaja reč'. Sbornik naučnyx trudov.* Saratov: Izd. saratovsk. universiteta.

Smirnitskij, A.I. 1959. *Russko-anglijskij slovar'.* Moscow: Gos. izdat. inostrannyx i nacional'nyx slovarej.

Stankiewicz, Edward. 1968. *Declension and Gradation*

*of Russian Substantives in Contemporary
Standard Russian.* The Hague: Mouton.

Superanskaja, A.V. 1959. "O proiznošenii sovremen-
noj studenčeskoj molodeži," *VKR* 2:157-62.

Swan, Oscar. 1975. "The morphographemic description
of Russian," *Russian Language Journal* 29:
6-12.

Šaxmatov, A.A. 1941. *Očerk sovremennogo russkogo
literaturnogo jazyka.* 4th. ed., Moscow:
Gos. izd. Narkomprosa RSFSR.

Ščerba, L.V. 1915. "O raznyx stiljax proiznošenija
i ob ideal'nom fonetičeskom sostave slov,"
in *Zapiski neofilologičeskogo obščestva,
Petrogradski universitet*, 8, and 21-25 in
L.V. Ščerba, *Izbrannye raboty po russkomu
jazyku.* Moscow: Učpedgiz, 1957.

Ševoroškin, V.V. 1963. "O strukture zvukovyx
cepej," in S.K. Šaumjan, ed., *Problemy
strukturnoj lingvistiki.* Moscow.

‒‒‒‒‒‒‒. 1971. "O dvux [v] v russkom jazyke," 279-
86 in *Vysotskij & al. 1971.*

Šteinfeldt, E. no date. *Russian Word Count.* Moscow:
Progress.

Švedova, N.Ju. 1970. (ed.) *Grammatika sovremennogo
russkogo literaturnogo jazyka.* Moscow:
Nauka.

Terexova, T.G. 1966. "Proiznošenie sočetanij trex
soglasnyx v sovremennom russkom literaturnom jazyke," 72-84 in *Vysotskij & al. 1971.*

Thelin, Nils B. 1971. *On Stress Assignment and
Vowel Reduction in Contemporary Standard
Russian.* Uppsala: Skriv Service AB.

‒‒‒‒‒‒‒. 1974. "On the phonological status of the
Russian geminate palatals," *RL* 1:163-76.

Toporov, V.N. 1966. "Materialy dlja distribucii
grafem v pis'mennoj forme russkogo jazyka,"
65-143 in V.V. Ivanov, eds., *Strukturnaja
tipologija jazykov.* Moscow: Nauka.

Townsend, Charles E. 1975. *Russian Word-Formation.*
Corrected reprint, Cambridge, Mass.:
Slavica, of original edition, New York:
McGraw Hill, 1968.

Trubetzkoy, N.S. 1969. *Principles of Phonology*
    [transl. C.A.M. Baltaxe]. Berkeley-Los
    Angeles: University of California Press.

Turko, L.A. 1968. "Častotnyj slovar' russkoj raz-
    govornoj reči," 191-99 in P.M. Alekseev &
    al., eds., *Statistika reči*. Leningrad:
    Nauka.

Ušakov, D.N. 1934/40. *Tolkovyj slovar' russkogo
    jazyka I-IV*. Moscow: Sovetskaja ènciklo-
    pedija.

Utexina, N.P. 1961. "K voprosu ob orfoèpičeskix
    normax v jazyke sovremennoj poèzii," 52-63
    in K.I. Bylinskij, ed., *Očerki po stilistike
    russkogo jazyka*. Moscow: Izd. moskovsk.
    universiteta.

Vakar, N.P. 1966. *A Word Count of Spoken Russian:
    the Soviet Usage*. Columbus, Ohio: Ohio
    State Univ. Press.

Vasil'eva, N.V. 1971. "Fonetičeskie 'otcy' i
    'deti'," 229-35 in *Vysotskij & al. 1971*.

Vennemann, T. 1972. "On the theory of syllabic
    phonology," *Linguistische Berichte* 18.1-18.

Vetvickij, V.G. 1966. *Zanimatel'noe jazykoznanie
    (Fonetika, imja suščestvitel'noe)*. Moscow:
    Prosveščenie.

Vinogradov, V.V. 1938. *Očerki po istorii russkogo
    literaturnogo jazyka XVII-XIX vv.* Moscow.
    Reprint, Leiden: Brill, 1949.

--------. 1965. (ed.) *Obzor predloženij po usover-
    šenstvovanija russkoj orfografii (XVIII-
    XX vv.)*. Moscow: Nauka.

Vinokur, G.O. 1948. *Russkoe sceničeskoe proizno-
    šenie*. Moscow: Vserossijskoe teatral'noe
    obščestvo.

--------. 1971. *The Russian Language: A Brief
    History* [transl. M.A. Forsyth]. Cambridge:
    CUP.

Vysotskij, S.S., M.V. Panov, & V.N. Sidorov. 1966.
    (eds.) *Razvitie fonetiki sovremennogo
    russkogo jazyka*. Moscow: Nauka.

--------, M.V. Panov, A.A. Reformatskij, & V.N.
    Sidorov. 1971. (eds.) *Razvitie fonetiki
    sovremennogo russkogo literaturnogo jazyka.
    Fonologičeskie podsistemy*. Moscow: Nauka.

Ward, Dennis. 1958. *Russian Pronunciation*. Edinburgh: Oliver & Boyd.

———. 1959. "Is there a phoneme [ɣ] in Russian?" *MPh* 12:29-31.

———. 1965. *The Russian Language Today: System and Anomaly*. London: Hutchinson.

———. 1966. *Russian Pronunciation Illustrated*. Cambridge: CUP.

———. 1971. "Diachrony and register. Aspects of the study of contemporary language," *Forum for Modern Language Study* (St. Andrews) 7: 170-82.

———. 1975. "Unaccented vowels in Russian," *RL* 2:91-104.

Wheeler, Marcus. 1972. *The Oxford Russian-English Dictionary*. Oxford: Clarendon Press.

Wijk, Axel. 1966. *Rules of Pronunciation for the English Language. An Account of the Relationship between English Spelling and Pronunciation*. London: CUP.

Zemskaja, E.A. 1970. "O ponjatii 'razgovornaja reč''," 3-10 in *Sirotinina & al. 1970*.

———. 1973. (ed.) *Russkaja razgovornaja reč'*. Moscow: Nauka.

Zinder, L.R. 1957. "O zvukovyx izmenenijax," *VJa* 1957/1:69-77.

Zlatoustova, L.V. 1962. *Fonetičeskaja struktura slova v potoke reči*. Kazan'.

———, S.V. Kodzasov, O.F. Krivnova & I.G. Frolova. 1970. *Algoritmy preobrazovanija orfografičeskix tekstov v fonetičeskuju zapis'*. Moscow: Izd. MGU.

Zwicky, Arnold M. 1972a. "Note on a phonological hierarchy in English," 275-301 in R.P. Stockwell & R.K.S. Macaulay, eds., *Linguistic Change and Generative Theory*. Bloomington, Ind.: Indiana Univ. Press.

———. 1972b. "On casual speech," 607-15 in *Papers from the Eighth Regional Meeting*, Chicago Linguistic Society.

Žirmunskij, V. 1925. *Vvedenie v metriku*. Leningrad: Akademia.

Žukovskaja, T.N., & A.G. Každan.   1971.   "Mjagkost'
    zubnyx pered gubnymi," 247-48 in *Vysotskij
    & al. 1971.*

(2A1) $\begin{bmatrix} я \\ ё \\ ю \end{bmatrix} \rightarrow \left\{ \begin{array}{l} \begin{bmatrix} ьа \\ ьо \\ ьу \end{bmatrix} \ / \ C \ \text{—} \\[2em] \begin{bmatrix} йа \\ йо \\ йу \end{bmatrix} \ / \ \text{elsewhere} \end{array} \right\}$

(2A2) $\begin{bmatrix} е \\ и \end{bmatrix} \rightarrow \begin{bmatrix} йе \\ йи \end{bmatrix}$

restriction

$\begin{bmatrix} е \\ и \end{bmatrix} \ -\!/\!\rightarrow \ \begin{bmatrix} йе \\ йи \end{bmatrix} \ / \ C \ \text{—}$

(2B1) $ь \rightarrow \emptyset$

(2B2) $ь \rightarrow \emptyset \ / \ \begin{Bmatrix} H \\ S \end{Bmatrix} \text{—}$

Delete Punctuation Marks and Insert Only One Boundary-Symbol in Each Space, According to the Following *Ordered* Rules:

(3A)

    1.   Insert ## before and after every *PP*.

Next,

    2.   Insert # $\begin{cases} \text{(a) between all } IW's \\ \text{(b) between all } CW's \end{cases}$

Finally,

    3.   Insert / $\begin{cases} \text{(a) in all other spaces} \\ \text{(b) after all prefixes} \end{cases}$

241

N.B. These Rules do not Apply Across the / Boundary

$$\text{3B} \quad 1. \begin{Bmatrix} т \\ д \end{Bmatrix} \rightarrow \emptyset \ / \ \begin{cases} \text{(a)} \quad \text{C} \ — \ \begin{Bmatrix} ч \\ ц \\ щ \end{Bmatrix} \\ \text{(b)} \ \begin{Bmatrix} с \\ н \\ м \end{Bmatrix} — \ \text{ск} \quad \text{(list)} \\ \text{(c)} \quad \text{н} \ — \ \text{к} \quad \text{(list)} \\ \text{(d)} \quad \text{с} \ — \ (\text{ь}) \ \text{б} \\ \text{(e)} \quad \text{с} \ — \ \text{л} \quad \text{(exc. list)} \\ \text{(f)} \ \begin{Bmatrix} с \\ з \end{Bmatrix} — \ \text{н} \quad \text{(exc. list)} \end{cases}$$

$$2. \begin{Bmatrix} к \\ г \end{Bmatrix} \rightarrow \emptyset \ / \qquad \text{C} \ — \ \text{ск} \quad \text{(list)}$$

$$3. \ \text{в} \ \rightarrow \emptyset \ / \qquad — \ \text{ств} \quad \text{(list)}$$

3C
1. го → во / in genitive singulars and their derivatives
2. г → ѓ / list
3. мь → м / in compound numerals containing СЕМЬ (list)

3D в → y̆ / — $\begin{Bmatrix} V \\ R \end{Bmatrix}$ (iterative)

3E1 $C_{vd} \rightarrow C_{vl}$ / $\begin{bmatrix} \text{(a)} \ — \ \#\# \\ \text{(b)} \ — \ \# \begin{Bmatrix} V \\ R \end{Bmatrix} \\ \text{(c)} \ — \ (\#) \ C_{vl} \end{bmatrix}$ (iterative)

3E2 $C_{vl} \rightarrow C_{vd}$ / — (#) C_{vd} (iterative)

3F y̆ → в (iterative)

N.B. These Rules do not Operate Across the / Boundary

3G
1. к → х / — $\left\{\begin{matrix} к \\ ч \end{matrix}\right\}$
2. т → ч / — щ
3. тс → ц / exc. in reflexives

3H
1. сш → шш
2. $\left\{\begin{matrix} шч \\ сч \\ сщ \end{matrix}\right\}$ → щ
3. зж → жж
4. $\left\{\begin{matrix} щ \\ ч \end{matrix}\right\}$ → ш / — $\left\{\begin{matrix} н \\ т \end{matrix}\right\}$ (list)

3I й → ∅ / $\left\{\begin{matrix} \#\# \\ \# \\ / \end{matrix}\right\}$ — и

3J
1. и → ы / $\left\{\begin{matrix} \text{(a) H} \quad — \\ \text{(b) } C_h \left\{\begin{matrix} \# \\ / \end{matrix}\right\} — \end{matrix}\right\}$
2. е → э / $\left\{\begin{matrix} \text{(a) H} \quad — \\ \text{(b) } C_p \quad — \quad \text{within stems of loanwords} \\ \text{(list)} \end{matrix}\right\}$

3K C_p → C_pь / — $\left\{\begin{matrix} и \\ е \end{matrix}\right\}$

3L
in reflexives
т(ь)cьа → цца

3M
in reflexives
cьа → ca / C_h — except in participles

N.B. This Rule does not Apply to жж
N.B. This Rule does not Apply Across the / Boundary

$$\text{3N} \quad C_1 \ C_1 \rightarrow C_1 \ / \begin{cases} \text{(a)} \ \begin{Bmatrix} \acute{V} \\ \check{V} \end{Bmatrix} \ — \ V \ \text{(list)} \\[1em] \text{(b)} \ \check{V} \ — \ V \ \text{(exc. list)} \\[1em] \text{(c)} \ \begin{Bmatrix} C \\ \# \\ \#\# \end{Bmatrix} \ — \ \quad \text{(exc. list)} \\[1em] \text{(d)} \ — \begin{Bmatrix} C \\ \# \\ \#\# \end{Bmatrix} \ \text{(exc. (1) list (2) "by analogy")} \end{cases}$$

$$\begin{array}{llll} 1. & П \rightarrow Пь & / — & Пь \\ 2. & К \rightarrow Кь & / — & Кь \\ 3. & Т \rightarrow Ть & / — & C_s \end{array} \bigg\} \text{(iterative)}$$

restrictions

3P

$$1. \quad \begin{bmatrix} п \\ б \\ к \\ г \\ т \\ д \end{bmatrix} -\!/\!\!\rightarrow \begin{bmatrix} пь \\ бь \\ кь \\ гь \\ ть \\ дь \end{bmatrix} \ / — / \ C_s \quad \text{unless geminate}$$

$$2. \quad Т \ -\!/\!\!\rightarrow \ Ть \ / — \begin{Bmatrix} рь \\ Кь \end{Bmatrix}$$

$$3. \quad н \ -\!/\!\!\rightarrow \ нь \ / — \quad Рь$$

$$4. \quad \begin{bmatrix} л \\ р \end{bmatrix} -\!/\!\!\rightarrow \begin{bmatrix} ль \\ рь \end{bmatrix} \ / — \quad C_s \quad \text{unless geminate}$$

$$\text{3Q} \qquad в \rightarrow вь \ / — й$$

$$\text{3R} \quad р \rightarrow рь \ / \begin{cases} \text{(a)} \ \begin{Bmatrix} \acute{e} \\ \acute{э} \end{Bmatrix} \ — \ C_s \\[1em] \text{(b)} \ \begin{Bmatrix} и \\ e \end{Bmatrix} \ — \ C_s \ \begin{Bmatrix} и \\ e \end{Bmatrix} \\[1em] \text{(c)} \qquad\qquad\qquad \text{(list)} \end{cases}$$

$$\text{(3S)} \quad V \rightarrow \hat{V} / \begin{cases} \text{(a)} \begin{Bmatrix} \#\# \\ \# \end{Bmatrix} \; - \\ \text{(b)} \qquad - \; C_o \begin{Bmatrix} \acute{V} \\ \overset{\cdot}{V} \end{Bmatrix} \\ \text{(c)} \quad V \; - \\ \qquad\quad - \begin{Bmatrix} o \\ a \\ э \end{Bmatrix} \end{cases}$$

$$\text{(3T)} \quad ы \rightarrow a / \; - \; вa \quad \text{in verbal stems}$$

$$\text{(3U)} \quad o \rightarrow a / \begin{Bmatrix} \frown \\ \underline{\quad} \end{Bmatrix} \quad \text{(except list (loanwords))}$$

(3V)

1. $э \rightarrow a / \begin{cases} \text{(a)} \; H - C \\ \text{(b)} \; H - \begin{Bmatrix} \# \\ \#\# \end{Bmatrix} \text{ only in n/a. sg. neut. nouns} \end{cases}$

2. $э \rightarrow ы / \begin{cases} \text{(a)} \; H - \begin{Bmatrix} \# \\ \#\# \end{Bmatrix} \text{ exc. in n/a. sg. neut. nouns} \\ \text{(b)} \; H \overset{\frown}{\underline{\quad}} \end{cases}$

3. $a \rightarrow ы / \quad H \overset{\frown}{\underline{\quad}} \quad \text{list}$

N.B. This Rule-Block does *not* Apply to *Grammatical Endings*

(3W)

1. $a \rightarrow и / C_s \begin{Bmatrix} \frown \\ \underline{\quad} \end{Bmatrix} C$

2. $e \rightarrow и / C_s \begin{Bmatrix} \frown \\ \underline{\quad} \end{Bmatrix} \quad \text{(except list (loanwords))}$

N.B. This Rule-Block Applies to Grammatical Endings *Only*

(3X)

1. $e \rightarrow a / \quad C_s \quad - \begin{Bmatrix} \# \\ \#\# \end{Bmatrix} \text{ in n/a. sg. adjectives only}$

2. $e \rightarrow и / \begin{cases} \text{(a)} \; C_s \quad - \begin{Bmatrix} \# \\ \#\# \end{Bmatrix} \text{ except in n/a. sg. adjectives} \\ \text{(b)} \; C_s \quad - \quad C \end{cases}$

(3Y1) й → ∅ / $\left\{\begin{array}{l}\text{(a)} \ \text{V} \longrightarrow \text{и} \\ \text{(b)} \ \text{V} \longrightarrow \text{е} \ \ (\text{list (loanwords)})\end{array}\right\}$

(3Y2) ∅ → й / ь ⎯ о (list (loanwords))

(3Z) see pp. 114-16

(4A)

1. a → $\left\{\begin{array}{l}æ \ / \ C_s \ \underline{\ \acute{} \ \text{or} \ \grave{} \ } \cdot C_s \\ a \ / \ \text{other} \ \underline{\ \acute{} \ \text{or} \ \grave{} \ } \\ \wedge \ / \ \underline{\ \hat{} \ } \\ ə \ / \ \text{elsewhere}\end{array}\right\}$

2. o → $\left\{\begin{array}{l}ö \ / \ C_s \ \underline{\ \acute{} \ \text{or} \ \grave{} \ } \ C_s \\ o \ / \ \text{elsewhere}\end{array}\right\}$

3. y → $\left\{\begin{array}{l}ü \ / \ C_s \ \underline{\ \acute{} \ \text{or} \ \grave{} \ } \ C_s \\ u \ / \ \text{other} \ \underline{\ \acute{} \ \text{or} \ \grave{} \ } \\ \ddot{ʊ} \ / \ \text{other} \ C_s \ \underline{\qquad} \ C_s \\ ʊ \ / \ \text{elsewhere}\end{array}\right\}$

4. ы → $\left\{\begin{array}{l}ɨ \ / \ \underline{\ \acute{} \ \text{or} \ \grave{} \ } \\ ɪ̵ \ / \ \text{elsewhere}\end{array}\right\}$

5. и → $\left\{\begin{array}{l}i \ / \ \underline{\ \acute{} \ \text{or} \ \grave{} \ } \\ ɪ \ / \ \text{elsewhere}\end{array}\right\}$

6. $\left\{\begin{array}{l}\text{е} \\ \text{э}\end{array}\right\}$ → $\left\{\begin{array}{l}e \ / \ \underline{\qquad} \ C_s \\ ɛ \ / \ \text{elsewhere}\end{array}\right\}$

(4B)

1. жж → ž̌ :

2. $\begin{bmatrix} дз \\ дж \end{bmatrix} \rightarrow \begin{bmatrix} ʒ \\ ǯ \end{bmatrix}$

(4C)

1. п → p
2. б → b
3. т → t
4. д → d
5. к → k
6. г → g
7. ц → c
8. ф → f
9. в → v
10. с → s
11. з → z
12. х → x
13. г' → $\begin{cases} ɦ & / \text{ list} \\ ɣ & / \text{ elsewhere} \end{cases}$
14. ч → č
15. щ → š' :
16. ш → š
17. ж → ž
18. м → m
19. н → n
20. л → l
21. р → r
22. й → j
23. ь → '

(4D)

1. delete $\begin{cases} (1) \text{ all boundary symbols} \\ (2) \text{ the "half-stressed" symbol } ˆ \end{cases}$

2. enclose all strings in square brackets

Jan L. Perkowski: *Vampires of the Slavs* (a collection of readings), 294 p., 1976.

Lester A. Rice: *Hungarian Morphological Irregularities*, 80 p., 1970.

Midhat Ridjanovic: *A Synchronic Study of Verbal Aspect In English and Serbo-Croatian*, ix + 147 p., 1976.

David F. Robinson: *Lithuanian Reverse Dictionary*, ix + 209 p., 1976.

Don K. Rowney & G. Edward Orchard, eds.: *Russian and Slavic History*, viii + 311 p., 1977.

Ernest A. Scatton: *Bulgarian Phonology*, xii + 224 p., 1976.

William R. Schmalstieg: *Introduction to Old Church Slavic*, 290 p., 1976.

Michael Shapiro: *Aspects of Russian Morphology, A Semiotic Investigation*, 62 p., 1969.

Rudolph M. Susel, ed.: *Papers in Slovene Studies, 1977*, 127 p., 1978.

Charles E. Townsend: *Russian Word-Formation, corrected reprint*, xviii + 272 p., 1975(1980).

Charles E. Townsend: *The Memoirs of Princess Natal'ja Borisovna Dolgorukaja*, viii + 146 p., 1977.

Daniel C. Waugh: *The Great Turkes Defiance   On the History of the Apocryphal Correspondence of the Ottoman Sultan in its Muscovite and Russian Variants*, ix + 354 p., 1978.

Susan Wobst: *Russian Readings & Grammar Terminology*, 88 p., 1978.

Dean S. Worth: *A Bibliography of Russian Word-Formation*, xliv + 317 p., 1977.

Charles E. Gribble, ed.: *Studies Presented to Professor Roman Jakobson by His Students*, 333 p., 1968.

Pierre R. Hart: *G. R. Derzhavin: A Poet's Progress*, iv + 164 p., 1978.

Raina Katzarova-Kukudova & Kiril Djenev: *Bulgarian Folk Dances*, 174 p., 1976.

Andrej Kodjak: *Pushkin's I. P. Belkin*, 112 p., 1979.

Demetrius J. Koubourlis, ed.: *Topics in Slavic Phonology*, viii + 270 p., 1974.

Michael K. Launer: *Elementary Russian Syntax*, xi + 140 p., 1974.

Jules F. Levin & others: *Reading Modern Russian*, vi + 321 p., 1979.

Maurice I. Levin: *Russian Declension and Conjugation: a structural sketch with exercises*, x + 160 p., 1978.

Alexander Lipson: *A Russian Course*, xiv + 612 p., 1977.

Thomas F. Magner, ed.: *Slavic Linguistics and Language Teaching*, x + 309 p., 1976.

Mateja Matejic & Dragan Milivojevic: *An Anthology of Medieval Serbian Literature in English*, 205 p., 1978.

Vasa D. Mihailovich & Mateja Matejic: *Yugoslav Literature in English: A Bibliography of Translations and Criticism (1821-1975)*, ix + 328 p., 1976.

Kenneth E. Naylor, ed.: *Balkanistica: Occasional Papers in Southeast European Studies*, I(1974), 189 p., 1975; II(1975), 153 p., 1976; III(1976), 154 p., 1978.

Felix J. Oinas, ed.: *Folklore Nationalism & Politics*, 190 p., 1977.

Hongor Oulanoff: *The Prose Fiction of Veniamin A. Kaverin*, v + 203 p., 1976.

American Contributions to the Eighth International Congress of Slavists, Zagreb and Ljubljana, Sept. 3-9, 1978. Vol. 1: Linguistics and Poetics, ed. by Henrik Birnbaum, 818 p., 1978; *Vol. 2: Literature,* ed. by Victor Terras, 799 p., 1978.

Henrik Birnbaum: *Common Slavic Progress and Problems in Its Reconstruction,* xii + 436 p., 1975.

Malcom H. Brown, ed.: *Papers of the Yugoslav-American Seminar on Music,* 208 p., 1970.

Ellen B. Chances: *Conformity's Children: An Approach to the Superfluous Man in Russian Literature,* iv + 210 p., 1978.

Catherine V. Chvany: *On the Syntax of Be-Sentences in Russian,* viii + 311 p., 1975.

Frederick Columbus: *Introductory Workbook in Historical Phonology,* 39 p., 1974.

Dina B. Crockett: *Agreement in Contemporary Standard Russian,* iv + 456 p., 1976.

Paul Debreczeny and Thomas Eekman, eds.: *Chekhov's Art of Writing A Collection of Critical Essays,* 199 p., 1977.

Ralph Carter Elwood, ed.: *Reconsiderations on the Russian Revolution,* x + 278 p., 1976.

Folia Slavica, a journal of Slavic and East European Linguistics. Vol. 1: 1977-78; Vol. 2: 1978; Vol. 3: 1979; Vol. 4: 1980.

Richard Freeborn & others, eds.: *Russian and Slavic Literature,* xii + 466 p., 1976.

Victor A. Friedman: *The Grammatical Categories of the Macedonian Indicative,* 210 p., 1977.

Charles E. Gribble, ed.: *Medieval Slavic Texts, Vol. 1, Old and Middle Russian Texts,* 320 p., 1973.

Charles E. Gribble, *Russian Root List,* 56 p., 1973.

Charles E. Gribble, Словарик русского языка 18-го века/*A Short Dictionary of 18th-Century Russian,* 103 p., 1976.